THE ROAD TO
ANN ARBOR

Incredible Twists and Improbable Turns
Along the Michigan Recruiting Trail

Tom VanHaaren

TRIUMPH
B O O K S

To my wife and kids. You are my inspiration.

Library of Congress Cataloging-in-Publication Data

Names: VanHaaren, Tom, author.
Title: The road to Ann Arbor : incredible twists and improbable turns along
   the Michigan recruiting trail / Tom VanHaaren.
Description: Chicago, Illinois : Triumph Books LLC, [2018]
Identifiers: LCCN 2018015503 | ISBN 9781629375922
Subjects: LCSH: University of Michigan—Football—History. | Michigan Wolverines (Football team)—History. | Football players—Recruiting—Michigan. | College athletes—Recruiting—Michigan. | College sports—Scouting—Michigan.
Classification: LCC GV958.U5284 V36 2018 | DDC 796.334/630977435—dc23
LC record available at https://lccn.loc.gov/2018015503

This book is available in quantity at special discounts for your group or organization. For further information, contact:
   Triumph Books LLC
   814 North Franklin Street
   Chicago, Illinois 60610
   (312) 337-0747
   www.triumphbooks.com

Printed in U.S.A.
ISBN: 978-1-62937-592-2
Design by Patricia Frey

Football Questionnaires Courtesy of University of Michigan Library

Contents

Foreword

My decision to walk on the football team at the University of Michigan has been well-documented, but the story of why I chose to do so has not been told in full. The stories of many Michigan football players—and their time in Ann Arbor—are similarly well-documented, but the reasons they chose this great university have not been told either.

My time at Michigan is something I will always hold in high regard. It's a time in my life that taught me great lessons of persistence, hard work, and not giving up in times of adversity. Those lessons have carried forward to my adult life and are part of what shaped me into who I am today. As a walk-on, I had to earn everything and prove to everyone that I was capable of playing at the level that was established before me. Even when I earned a scholarship, playing time was at a premium and was something I continued to fight for my entire college career.

I wouldn't have had the same experience in college had it not been for Michigan and the choice I made as a high school senior in Miami, Florida, to try to earn a scholarship and a spot on the roster. Nothing was ever promised from coach Gary Moeller or Cam Cameron, but I knew that Michigan would provide me with the best combination of academics and athletics to help me in my future career.

I never had NFL aspirations in high school. So few schools were recruiting me that I figured that was out of reach. Because of that I focused a great deal of my attention on the academics at each school and what they could provide me in life after football. That is why Stanford and Michigan were two of the main schools I was considering. It was Michigan, though, that provided me the best opportunities in athletics and also afforded me the best experience for the years I spent on campus.

I always had confidence in my ability to play, so the opportunity as a walk-on didn't deter me from thinking that I could compete at Michigan. And despite my father's success at quarterback, I never felt entitled to anything on the football field. Instead I always wanted to put in the work and loved the competition of earning something on my own.

Throughout my recruitment I had the opportunity to hear from some great coaches, including Mack Brown at North Carolina, George Welsh at Virginia, Bill Walsh at Stanford, and many other luminaries. Those conversations throughout my recruitment and the journey I took that led me to Michigan are all told in this book—along with the stories of many other Michigan football players who walked the halls of Schembechler Hall.

Tom VanHaaren allows the stories to come back to life through the voices of the players, our families, and the coaches who recruited us. Starting from 1968 all the way to the present time, the stories and the road the players took to Ann Arbor are all different, but the relationships that were built and the reasons those players chose Michigan over many other great institutions endure through the test of time and changes in coaching staffs. This book adds those stories to Michigan football's great history and gives you a look at how it all began for so many outstanding men who have played such a large part of Michigan's story.

You are brought along on the journey and get a glimpse of how the decisions of many former players could have changed the entire landscape of Michigan football and its storied past. Commitments to other programs, late scholarship offers, and the decisions of other players all factored into the names who ultimately signed with the Wolverines. The endings to our stories have already been written. Now you get a chance to see how it all started and where it all began for so many great men who wore the winged helmet.

—Brian Griese

Introduction

Have you ever wondered why Desmond Howard chose to attend the University of Michigan? Why was Tom Brady recruited so late in the process? How did some of the Michigan greats get to Ann Arbor and what are their recruiting stories? Many of those stories haven't been told—mainly because of the lack of information available. Until now.

College football recruiting has exploded into a highly anticipated, heavily covered, and thoroughly patrolled industry. Blogs and websites have popped up across the Internet to cover high school football players and track their every move, and fans are eating it up at a rapid pace.

The advancements of the Internet and the growing appetite for content has created an industry where fans are aware of every detail that happens in a high school football player's recruiting process and sometimes everyday life. Social media has only contributed to that coverage, as the recruits themselves tweet or post the latest happenings in their recruitment.

Whether it's which schools have offered them a scholarship, what visits they will be taking, the list of programs they're considering, or what schools have been eliminated from consideration, it will be found somewhere on the Internet. Recruits, some of whom are only freshmen or sophomores in high school, are seeing thousands and thousands of fans follow them on social media. Their tweets, posts, and videos are monitored for any hint of what school they favor. In the pictures posted, the clothes they wear, the color of those clothes, and the school moniker on their hat or gloves are analyzed and scrutinized, as fans try to glean any meaning. From camps to combines to media days, the prospects are interviewed at every event they attend, and every question tries to find the inside scoop.

Some dedicated websites have upwards of five to six writers covering one university to track the happenings and feed their fans' appetites for information on which blue-chip player will join their favorite team's recruiting class. It's not irregular or abnormal now to see prospects receiving scholarship offers as freshmen and sophomores in high school. There have even been instances of scholarship offers going to eighth graders and seventh graders, so there is more time to find out every detail of that recruit.

The coverage wasn't always that in-depth and detailed, though, as it has really only expanded in the 21st century. Before the Internet there were a few services that provided newsletters, and preps coverage in newspapers gave some updates as well. It was nowhere near as in-depth as it is now, though. How coaches recruit has changed greatly in the past 10 years as well. Universities now have full recruiting departments with staffers dedicated to scouting and editing highlight films. Graphic designers are a staple in any athletic department to help market and advertise its various sports to fans and recruits. If a college isn't creating photoshopped pictures for recruits, then it is likely behind in the race, which is a drastic difference in how recruits used to be courted.

Just going back to the early 1990s, it wasn't abnormal for a highly sought-after prospect to receive some letters in the mail, some pamphlets, and a phone call from either an assistant coach or the head coach. That was it. The recruit would take a visit to the campus, a coach would come out to the recruit's house for an in-home visit, and the prospect would decide.

There was more communication than that, but in terms of the extra frills and technology and recruiting staffs, it was non-existent. In the '60s and '70s and even into the '80s, the assistant coaches often relied on help from alumni in the communities they were recruiting, former players involved with their local high schools, or sources who scouted the areas they recruited.

Recruit questionnaires were relied upon heavily to find prospects and figure out who should be recruited and who could be passed up. A questionnaire often was simply a form that college coaches would give to a high school coach or a plugged-in member of the community. Given to a high school coach, the form would ask for the names of any player on the coach's team or the teams the coach had faced previously that he thought could play at that university. It was highly unreliable, but it was the best they could do back then. There were countless times where a prospect nearly slipped through the cracks or didn't hear from his favorite team because they simply were unaware of him.

That is one of the largest differences from today's recruiting landscape. Now nearly every recruit has an outlet or medium to showcase his ability and put himself in front of a college coach. Another major difference prior to the 1980s is that the recruiting process didn't start for most prospects until their senior season and sometimes not until after their senior campaign. It wasn't unusual to receive most of your scholarship offers once your senior season started, and the official visit process would start after the season was over. That left little time to make the final decision, but it also helped prevent any uncertainty with coaching changes and prospects changing their mind and flipping a commitment. As a result of all of this, the fans really only learned about the players on the field as they began to star in college. And even then, how he got to Michigan and why he chose Michigan oftentimes wouldn't be revealed. At that stage it was about the team, and the past was in the past, so fans were left wondering which schools could have stolen that player away from the Wolverines.

The University of Michigan football program has won 11 national championships and 42 conference championships. It is home to the largest capacity football stadium in the country and the most wins of any college football program. The history and tradition is as long and rich as it gets, and the numbers of great football players who have stepped on the field for Michigan are countless. There have been a total of 132 players who have earned All-American honors, dating all the way back to the 1800s and through the 2000s. Some of the most iconic names in college football are associated with Michigan football, including Charles Woodson, Tom Harmon, Dan Dierdorf, Mark Messner, Reggie McKenzie, Steve Hutchinson, Howard, and Brady.

All of those players earned accolades on the field, made spectacular plays, and won hard-fought games that brought them into the hearts of Michigan fans across the country. Their play on the field made them household names and, eventually, legends in Michigan football history. The fans watched as their favorite players donned the winged helmet and went to battle with the Buckeyes and other opponents year in and year out.

Michigan fans typically have a few memorable plays that launched their fandom for a specific player, like when Howard sprawled out horizontally to catch a touchdown on fourth down against Notre Dame in 1991. Or when he struck the Heisman pose in the end zone after returning a punt for a touchdown against Ohio State in the same year. Quarterback John Wangler threw a touchdown to Anthony Carter to beat Indiana, and Carter danced in the back of the end zone. Tim Biakabutuka ran for 313 yards against Ohio State in 1995 in a 31–23 win. Chad Henne threw a touchdown to Mario Manningham in the back of the end zone on fourth down with no time left in the fourth quarter to beat Penn State 27–25.

No matter what your favorite play is, it helped cement that player as a legend and a part of Michigan history. The stories of how Michigan legends wound up at Michigan are as much a part of Michigan history as the stories written about their time at the university and on the field. Some of the best players to come through the Michigan program have never had their recruiting stories told. What schools nearly stole them away from the Wolverines, how close was it between Michigan and the opposing schools, and what really sold the players on the Wolverines?

There are plenty of good stories with twists and turns that just have not been told. It's time for those stories to be released and for fans to get even closer to the program they love so dearly. Why did Howard spurn Nick Saban to play in Ann Arbor? How did Michigan really find All-American offensive lineman McKenzie? What did Bo Schembechler do that surprised Messner and his family?

Head coaches Bump Elliott, Schembechler, Gary Moeller, Lloyd Carr, and Jim Harbaugh all had different styles of recruiting and coached in different times that required unique changes to how they recruited. Each recruited All-Americans who would go on to play for championships and eventually in the NFL.

If you have ever wondered how your favorite players got to Michigan and why they chose the Wolverines, the answers to your questions are within these pages. Although there were many high school football players who just loved the University of Michigan and wanted to be a Wolverine, not every recruiting story was that straightforward. Some players nearly went to other programs and were hours away from choosing another school. These are the stories of how many Michigan greats became just that and how their road to Ann Arbor began.

Author's Note

The University of Michigan Library provided football questionnaires for many of the athletes profiled in this book. Included at the end of several chapters, these forms were filled out by the respective players while visiting Michigan.

Mark Messner provided several of the recruiting letters he received in 1983 from coaches at several programs. These are presented chronologically to give a sense of the level of interest these sought-after, blue-chip recruits receive.

CHAPTER 1

Reggie McKenzie

Growing up in a blue-collar family in Highland Park, Michigan, lanky high schooler Reggie McKenzie never thought he would end up an All-American offensive lineman for the University of Michigan. The humble giant never imagined he would be drafted by the Buffalo Bills and eventually lead the offensive line group nicknamed the Electric Company that blocked for O.J. Simpson during his historic 2,000-yard rushing season.

McKenzie wasn't the only one who didn't think football was in his future either, as most big-name college programs didn't know anything about the 6'3", 190-pound football player and wrestler in high school. The Michigan coaching staff found him through a happenstance conversation, which led to a phone call that would forever change his life.

Born in 1950, McKenzie was one of eight children growing up near Detroit at a time of high racial tension. Police brutality sparked the Detroit riots of 1967, which were close to home and took place during McKenzie's junior year of high school at Highland Park High. He came from a hardworking family that instilled much of his toughness early in life. The oldest of 13 children, Reggie's father,

Henry, was born in Georgia and quit school during his youth to help his father raise the family on their family farm. His mother, Hazel, went to college to become a nurse and eventually gave birth to Reggie at 40 years old and then had twins at age 41.

It was a tough family with little money, and they stuck together to get by the best they could. McKenzie credits his mother and father's work ethic for his own and for setting the example of what toughness really looks like. Raising eight children with minimal resources and always keeping their faith, the family stood by one another. "I thank God for my momma and daddy because that's why I'm at where I'm at today," McKenzie said. "They laid the groundwork. They said, 'You want this? You go out and work for it.' That's just the way it was."

In high school McKenzie wasn't the ideal size for an offensive lineman and didn't show much in terms of proper technique. He was a powerful wrestler, though, and showed his athleticism on the mat in his wrestling meets. He showed enough progress throughout his football career that a few programs saw potential and he started to receive recruiting letters from various schools. In the 1960s, though, the actual recruiting process typically didn't begin until a player was a senior in high school. That's when McKenzie saw letters come in from Nebraska, Western Michigan, and Brown. "I was really a Michigan State fan because you have to remember in 1966 they won the national championship with Bubba Smith," McKenzie said.

He was a fan of the Spartans and had a Michigan State coach come by his high school to conduct a preliminary interview to find out more about him as a person and player. His high school head coach, Jim Bobbitt, was an All-American for the Spartans, so he had connections at the program and knew that McKenzie could play in East Lansing, Michigan.

McKenzie had not heard a word out of the University of Michigan, so he figured that the schools that were in contact—Western Michigan and Michigan State—would be his final options. Bob Wyman was the offensive line coach at Western Michigan, and Bill Doolittle was the head coach. The two were recruiting the Highland Park linemen heavily and got McKenzie to visit Kalamazoo, Michigan, during his senior year in early 1968. That recruiting trip swung the momentum in favor of the Broncos to the point that McKenzie thought that's where he would play football in college.

It was still winter in the beginning months of the year, but McKenzie was done with his high school football career and starting to look ahead to college. Kalamazoo would potentially be his new home, but Michigan State was still lurking. Then, his mother went for a routine checkup at her gynecologist, Dr. Bernard Levine, and everything changed. Levine was a Michigan graduate and football fan. During the checkup Levine asked about the young McKenzie and found out he was a football player. "My mom was telling him about me and that I had been recruited by Nebraska, Michigan State, and Western Michigan and got letters from Brown," McKenzie said. "He asked her if Michigan had called. She said she didn't think so, but she would have to ask me to make sure. So Dr. Levine made a phone call to the [Michigan] coaches. Levine was an alum and he said, 'If Michigan State is talking to him, how come Michigan isn't down there?'"

George Mans was a former Michigan player and had a brief stint in the NFL before coaching at the college level. He joined Michigan head coach Bump Elliott's staff in Ann Arbor in 1966 after spending time as an assistant at Michigan Tech and Eastern Michigan. In those days the coaches regularly had alumni across the country who helped identify prospective student-athletes for the coaches. Bob Royal was one such alum who was a school teacher in the Detroit area. Royal and Mans knew each other well, and Royal happened to also know Dr. Levine. "The doctor and Mr. Royal knew one another, and they thought here's a guy that's going to grow a little bit, and Michigan should take a look at him," Mans said. "So they called me, and in my wisdom, I said let me call around a little bit, and nobody seemed to remember much about Reggie. So I said, 'Well I better go down there and take a look at this young man.' I called Dr. Levine and Mr. Royal, and they said there's going to be a wrestling meet that Reggie will be in, and I should come down to Highland Park and watch."

Mans made plans to watch the heavyweight match that McKenzie was participating in at around 190 pounds. His size wasn't prototypical for what Michigan looked for in offensive linemen, but Mans and Elliott loved toughness and players who worked hard, so Mans went to the wrestling match. "A young man was wrestling at 250 pounds, and I thought, *Well, this will be over quickly,*" Mans said. "Before I knew it, Reggie had this guy on his back and was all over him. He had a great disposition to mix things up, and when I met him afterward, he was such a great young man, so we went and talked to his high school football coach."

Mans and McKenzie's high school coach, Bobbitt, had played against each other in the Michigan-Michigan State games, so there was some familiarity there. Michigan had not gotten a recommendation from Bobbitt on McKenzie prior to this meeting, so this was the first communication. After the meeting with McKenzie and his coach, Mans went back to Michigan to report back to Elliott on what he saw: a scrawny kid with potential to grow who fought his way through a wrestling match against someone bigger and stronger.

The Michigan coaches worked to find some football film on McKenzie, as they couldn't offer him a scholarship based on his wrestling technique. "On the film that we saw, the two things that stood out for us were the fact that he had such great quickness and speed for a lineman," Mans said. "He was built more like a sprinter. The technique wasn't very good. The whole thing in terms of individual technique, he was very raw in that regard, but you could see the potential. The one word I would use with Coach Elliott was I thought this young man had the 'potential' to grow."

Elliott gave Mans the go-ahead to offer McKenzie a scholarship based on that potential.

In the meantime, McKenzie hadn't heard much from Michigan State, which is why he had Western Michigan out front. The Spartans conducted the initial interview but then dropped contact after that. "A guy named Ed Rutherford [an assistant coach] at Michigan State said I couldn't play at Michigan State. Later he denied it," McKenzie said. "He had another guy he wanted to sign, who I knew. He said he wanted so-and-so, and we just don't have the numbers."

Meanwhile, Mans was still going on a hunch. But if Michigan was going to offer a scholarship, it would go after him 100 percent. So Mans made his way to Highland Park High, said hello to McKenzie, and told him the coaches wanted him at Michigan. As a 17-year-old kid who never dreamed the University of Michigan would want him to play football for them, McKenzie was naturally taken aback by the magnitude of the conversation. It was something he really had to process. "My high school coach took his right hand and stuck it up in the air and said, 'McKenzie, calling McKenzie. At Michigan you start here,' then he lowered it and said, 'at Western Michigan you start here,'" McKenzie said. "It's always easier to take a step back than it is to take a step up. He said, 'If I didn't think you could play at Michigan, I wouldn't have had him come here.'"

That lanky wrestler had doubts about how he could succeed at such a big program like Michigan, but Mans sold him almost immediately. Mans' passion for Michigan and confidence in how badly he wanted McKenzie in turn gave McKenzie some confidence in himself that he could have success in Ann Arbor. "One of the things that really sold me on Reggie is the kind of person he is. If you talk to him, you would know he's just a great guy," Mans said. "How could we go wrong in taking a young man like that? That was one thing that Coach Elliott was very concerned about and strict about. He wanted to make sure he took good people in the truest sense of the word, and Reggie fits that bill."

McKenzie didn't need much time to think about it. He knew Michigan was the place for him. He told Mans and Elliott that he would be a Wolverine, and in the spring of 1968, the undersized lineman, who grew up with little more than a loving family and a work ethic that kept them afloat, was about to join one of the most prestigious football programs in the country.

But just because he was headed to college, that didn't mean he could stop working. After his recruitment was over, McKenzie was sitting at the dining room table with his father in June of 1968. *The Detroit News* was sprawled open. His father was taking in each article and, without looking up at his son, he asked Reggie what he planned to do. Having already signed his tender to Michigan, a confused Reggie asked his father what he meant. "He said, 'I'm going to tell you like my daddy told me. It's time for you to start being a man,'"

McKenzie recalled. "He said, 'You're going to need some money and you know me and your mom don't have any money.' So I went out and got a job."

Awaiting his 18th birthday in July, McKenzie found a job at a local moving company located at Clairmount Avenue and Woodward Avenue. He sat in a room with older men and waited until a driver came to pick them up and then went to work moving furniture. He worked that job until it was time to enroll at Michigan and left his home and family for Ann Arbor to start his new journey.

McKenzie takes pride in the fact that despite such times of racial tension he was part of a recruiting class that included a large number of African American players, including Glen Doughty, Mike Taylor, Billy Taylor, Butch Carpenter, and Mike Odom. Those players faced adversity on campus because of their race, but the whole class faced adversity on the field as well. Little did they know that one more piece of history would be added to their recruiting class. They would be the last class coach Bump Elliott would sign at Michigan as he moved into the associate athletic director role at the school.

Elliott was the coach for McKenzie's freshman season, but then a big change came in the 1969 season, McKenzie's sophomore year. Bo Schembechler took over after Michigan amassed an 8–2 record in 1968. Schembechler wanted to come in and instill toughness to his new team, and McKenzie and his teammates found out quickly that there would be no easy days with Schembechler in charge. "Because Bump was a nice guy, he thought we were soft," McKenzie said. "When Bo came in, we started winter conditioning, and a lot of guys left because he was so tough."

McKenzie was not among those who left. He knew he wasn't soft. And because of how he was raised, he knew what toughness meant.

He eventually filled out to more than 250 pounds, played guard for Schembechler, and helped Michigan to an 11–1 record in 1971 during his senior season. He was named an All-American after that season.

McKenzie was then drafted in the first round by the Bills in the 1972 NFL Draft and helped anchor the offensive line widely known as the Electric Company, blocking for Simpson. The name came to be because they helped "turn on the Juice." He would go on to be named to the All-NFL team two seasons in a row and eventually finished his 13-year career with the Seattle Seahawks. Once his playing days were over, the Seahawks brought him on as a scout to find potential draft prospects and free agents. In the 1980s Michigan State had a tight end named Veno Belk that the Seahawks and McKenzie were interested in drafting.

In those days the scouts would make a trip to the university to talk with the head coach. George Perles had now taken over in East Lansing, but Rutherford, the man who said McKenzie couldn't play at Michigan State, was still there. McKenzie made the trip to see Perles and spoke with the coaches about Belk. As McKenzie was waiting in the lobby before meeting with the coaching staff, Rutherford walked out of his office and past the burly lineman sitting in a chair.

Rutherford eventually came back and asked if he was Reggie McKenzie. The Seahawks scout and former Wolverine was sitting in enemy territory with the man who said he couldn't be a Spartan. Rutherford asked if he could have a word with McKenzie after his meeting with Perles. McKenzie obliged and stuck his head in Rutherford's office once he was finished with his work. "He said, 'I wasn't the one who said no to you.' I said, 'Yes you were,'" McKenzie recalled. "He said, 'No, we wanted this other kid.' I said, 'Coach, listen, don't worry about it. Everything worked out all right.'"

McKenzie walked out with a smile on his face, knowing that everything may not have worked out the way he pictured it, but it worked out in his favor nonetheless.

Before legendary Michigan State head coach Duffy Daugherty passed away in 1987, McKenzie ran into Daugherty at a mutual event, and the two found themselves in the restroom at the same time. Daugherty, according to McKenzie, apologized to him for not recruiting him and letting him slip away to the Wolverines. Again, McKenzie smiled and said everything worked out all right.

Once his football and scouting careers were over, McKenzie went on to found Reggie McKenzie Industrial Materials as well as the Reggie McKenzie Foundation. The foundation organizes athletic and academic programs for the youth of Detroit. Many of the foundation's events take place on the same field in which he played during his early days of football. The only difference is that when McKenzie was their age, the field was known as Hackett Field. Now, after all the success he has seen and what he has given back to the community, it's aptly named McKenzie Field.

That young boy from Highland Park never could have imagined that one day he would play football for the University of Michigan, the Seahawks, and eventually have a football field named after himself. As McKenzie would say, everything worked out all right.

CHAPTER 2

Jim Harbaugh

When reports surfaced in 2014 that the Wolverines would target Jim Harbaugh as their next head coach, longtime head equipment manager Jon Falk chuckled to himself. Falk reminisced to a time when Harbaugh was in high school and had yet to hear from Michigan in his recruitment. Falk mentioned to then-head coach Bo Schembechler that the young Harbaugh was hearing from other programs. "I remember going into Bo's office one day and said, 'Bo, what is this I hear Jim Harbaugh is looking at Miami of Ohio?' Bo looked at me and said, 'Jim Harbaugh is coming to Michigan; he just does not know it yet,'" Falk said. "I laughed when Jim was being recruited to be the head coach at Michigan. I remembered Bo's words that 'Jim Harbaugh is coming to Michigan; he just does not know it yet.'"

His recruitment to become Michigan's head coach was much different than his high school recruitment, but the love for the university was formed at a very young age. Harbaugh's father, Jack, was hired by Schembechler as an assistant coach in 1973 when Jim was only nine years old. Falk and assistant coach Paul Schudel fondly remember the young Harbaugh meandering through the hallways

11

of the Michigan facilities as a youngster, playing with the other coaches' kids, and building the foundation for his love of Michigan. "When we came to Michigan in 1975, Jack was coaching there, and John, Jim's older brother, babysat for our kids maybe once or twice. My son still has—John carved up some building blocks we had and put his number on there and made a racing car out of it," Schudel said. "Our kids grew up with them and would go to all the bowl games until Jack left after the 1979 season and went to Stanford. He grew up in the office and he grew up around the football field and the buildings."

He grew up around Schembechler, around quarterback Rick Leach, whom Jim idolized as a child, but more importantly, he grew up around the game of football. As the son of a football coach, Jim gained knowledge and experience that would later be invaluable to his career on the field and in coaching.

As Jim grew older, his acumen for all sports grew along with his ability. A standout athlete in baseball, football, and basketball at Ann Arbor Pioneer High School, Jim took over as the starting quarterback on the varsity team during his sophomore season in 1979. He started the offseason as the backup quarterback to Al Smith on junior varsity but eventually won the starting role before the season started and never looked back. He was moved to varsity after the first three games of the season and started to show flashes of what he was fully capable of as a quarterback.

Although the season wasn't a big success, his high school coaches knew they were sitting on something special. He would take some time to develop, but Jim was different than any other quarterback they had at the school. If his father, Jack, was planning to stay as an assistant at Michigan, Pioneer would be set at quarterback for the next two years. The problem for the Pioneer coaches was that Jack accepted a defensive backs coaching position at Stanford in 1980.

The newfound quarterback was off to California and left the town and university he had grown so fond of. "When I came to Michigan in 1974 as the head equipment manager at the University of Michigan, I met a very young Jimmy Harbaugh. I was single at the time, and all of the coaches' wives would have me over for dinner, and Jim's mother, Jackie Harbaugh, would have me over at least two times a week," Falk said. "I was treated like part of the family with Jack, Jackie, John, Jim, and Joanie and I got to know the family very well. Jim would always be in the locker room after practice, trying to pick up gloves and wristbands from the players. I loved having Jimmy around the locker room, and the players did, too. So when Jack got the job at Stanford and left while Jimmy was in high school, I really missed Jimmy around the locker room."

Jim hadn't heard from any college programs yet, which was normal for the times. But the move wouldn't help his recruitment as he was traveling all the way across the country. Publicity in newspapers, attention in the area, and relationships with high school coaches were all important in the process, and the young Harbaugh was now starting from scratch. "His high school was somewhat disrupted because we moved across the country. We left at the end of his sophomore year and moved to Palo Alto, California, when I took the job at Stanford," Jack said. "In some ways it was good because in California they had the quarterback passing leagues in the summer time, and at the end of his sophomore year, he was able to be a part of that. Then his junior year, he had a good year at Palo Alto High School, and that was the first time I had a conversation with a coach about him."

Jack, a coach himself, had conversations about other prospects with their families but never had a coach approach him about Jim. Older brother (and future Baltimore Ravens head coach) John was playing at Miami of Ohio, but he wasn't highly recruited. So seeing it from this side was all new territory for the Harbaugh family.

The first college coach to have a conversation with Jack about his son Jim happened to be somewhat of a familiar face. With Jack Harbaugh now coaching at Stanford, John Elway was the quarterback for the Cardinal, and his father, Jack Elway, was coaching at nearby San Jose State.

The elder Harbaugh and Elway had crossed paths before, and once Jack Elway found out that Jim was a quarterback, he asked Jack Harbaugh to meet him at a Stanford baseball game. This was after Jim's junior season, so there was still no real recruiting attention that took place.

Elway asked Jack Harbaugh about his son, what he thought about Jim's abilities, which schools might be interested, and where Jim was interested in playing. "I had never experienced that as a dad, so I started to give him coach speak: 'He does this real well, but…He does this real well, but,' throwing the buts in," Jack Harbaugh said. "He admonished me and said, 'Hold on a second. Let's get one thing straight here. [Jim's] going to have a lot of coaches. He's got a coach now at Palo Alto, and my thinking is he'll play college football and he'll have a lot of coaches there. You're a dad. You talk to me about your feelings as a dad, and I'll get the coaching information from the coaches.'"

That was a life lesson for Jack Harbaugh, who took Elway's words to heart that he should be viewing this recruitment completely different than the other players he was recruiting himself.

After a Stanford camp before his junior year, Jack Harbaugh really got to see what his son could do and that they should start sending out his film. Jim competed intensely against the other quarterbacks in attendance, and they included Jim Karsatos, who would go on and play at Ohio State, as well as Jeff Van Raaphorst, who would play for Arizona State.

Because his son was so fiercely competitive, Jack Harbaugh decided they needed to put together some film to send to coaches. "My recruitment was more—I had to reach out to people. I had one film. It was on videotape on a spool. It wasn't a VCR. I had sent it out to different schools and got letters back that they weren't interested," Jim said. "And the ones that were interested, every single one of them had a connection with my dad. Michigan, my dad coached there and I grew up there. Wisconsin, my dad was fraternity brothers with Dave McClain, and my mom was sorority sisters with Judy McClain, and they recruited me. Larry Smith was at Arizona, and he was a grad assistant at Bowling Green when my dad was there. So, it was mainly people that knew me, and, I guess, when people looked at my tape, they didn't quite see enough on that."

Arizona and Wisconsin had offered, as well as Miami of Ohio. Michigan had not, and neither had Stanford despite Jack being a coach on the staff. Jim and his father sent his tape out to various schools, including Ohio State and Notre Dame. Both schools replied back that they weren't interested, as Ohio State had taken multiple quarterbacks in the previous class. Notre Dame replied to Harbaugh's film with a letter that addressed him as "Tom Harbaugh" and went on to say they were not interested in him after viewing his film.

Schembechler never made a visit to Harbaugh's house because the Wolverines still had not offered him, even though it was now Jim's senior season. He was friends with Jack and Jackie, though, so he had made it a point to see Jackie while he was out in California for other reasons. "We were having lunch somewhere with Bo and his wife, Millie, and he said, 'By the way, Harbaugh, do you have Jim's tape?' I said, 'No. I don't have his tape, Bo,'" Jackie said. "He asked where it was, and I said, 'Well, Ohio State has it right now, so I guess you're going to have to call Ohio State and get it.' He gave me one of those looks that he always gave, and Millie just started laughing." Jackie laughed as well but hoped that Schembechler was genuinely interested in Jim.

In January of 1982, Jack Harbaugh took the head coaching job at Western Michigan. Because Jim and Joani were still in school, the Harbaugh family decided to stay in Palo Alto while Jack left for Kalamazoo, Michigan.

Despite not having a scholarship offer extended, Jim decided to take an official visit to Stanford. He had obvious connections to the program through his father, but the Cardinal just didn't seem interested. Jack came back from Kalamazoo shortly after Jim's official visit to Stanford, and the two went out to breakfast with then-Stanford head coach Paul Wiggins and got the definitive word that Stanford wouldn't be offering him a scholarship. Wiggins hemmed and hawed when Jim asked if they were interested. He explained that they had taken two quarterbacks the year before. The competitive Jim rebutted that he had no problem competing with the two signal-callers and said as humbly as he could that he felt as though he was better than them. But that wouldn't be enough, especially because there was another quarterback the Stanford coaches had their eyes on. "There was another great quarterback on the peninsula—just a junior, John Paye. My whole high school career for a couple years out there, I was in the shadow of John Paye," Jim said. "He was a year younger than me. [Wiggins] said they had two quarterbacks last year and John Paye next year and he didn't say that in so many words, but you could read that."

North Carolina State had initially shown interest in Jim as well while Monte Kiffin was the head coach, and Pete Carroll was the defensive coordinator. Carroll was recruiting junior colleges on the West Coast for Kiffin and had mentioned that Jim was someone they should look at. The two coaches were out recruiting in the area, and Carroll suggested that Kiffin go to Palo Alto High School and check in on Jim. "I went and saw his tape and I really liked it," Kiffin said. "We hit it off really good, and he didn't have a Michigan offer yet, so we invited him out to N.C. State for a visit."

Jim says the visit at his school with Kiffin was so quick that Kiffin left his car running and door open in the school parking lot. It was an in-and-out visit, but it resulted in some interest and a visit invite. Because he wasn't very highly recruited, the invitation to visit N.C. State was welcomed, and Jim was excited for the opportunity to see a new school.

The visit was planned to take place so Jim would be on campus when North Carolina came to town to take on N.C. State in basketball. It was January 13, 1982, and both teams were ranked in the top 25. It was a highly anticipated game between two rival programs.

However, shortly before the trip was supposed to happen, Jim got a call from the staff at N.C. State describing a snowstorm that was set to sweep through campus. Since official visits are only allotted to take place over two days, it would coincide with when Jim was scheduled to leave campus. The snowstorm would prevent him from being able to fly back home, so the N.C. State coaches told him it would be better to cancel the visit. "They said we wouldn't be able to fly you in. I said, 'That's okay. I'll just come in the next day and I'll still be able to go to the basketball game,' and they said, 'Uhh, really you want to fly all the way across the country?'" Jim said. "I said yes that I was really excited and looking forward to it, and they said they didn't think it was a good idea. So I said I could come the day after the basketball game, and they said no. Finally, they had to come out and tell me they weren't going to recruit me. They didn't have a spot for me."

N.C. State had recruited a junior college quarterback and brought him in that year and recruited Erik Kramer, another junior college prospect, a few years later, so the staff didn't want to spend the scholarship on Jim at the time. The visit never happened, and the communication with N.C. State fell off.

He took his official visits to Wisconsin and to Arizona but still hadn't heard much from Michigan. At least no official scholarship came through, and even in the middle of January—only weeks before the signing period—he still did not have an invitation to visit. Even in early January when Schembechler was in California coaching the East-West Shrine game, Jim remembers putting on his khaki pants, a sweater, and going over to Stanford where practices were taking place. He mustered up the courage to ask Bo if Michigan was interested in him and if he thought Jim could play at Michigan. "Bo said, 'Ahh, Jimmy, we'll talk about it,'" Jim recalled. That was all that came of the conversation, and Schembechler went back to Michigan after the All-Star Game was finished.

Then, with only one weekend left for official visits to take place before Signing Day in the beginning of February, Schembechler called Jackie to tell her that Michigan wanted Jim to take a visit. Being the protective mother that she was, being a wife of a football coach, and understanding how the recruiting process worked, she expressed her doubts to Schembechler as to why it had taken so long to even invite Jim for a visit. "He said he wanted Jim to visit, and I said, 'You're absolutely positive about that, right?' Bo asked what I meant and I said, 'Well, Jack coached there for seven years. You're not recruiting him because Jack coached there—are you?'" Jackie said. "'Are you recruiting him because you believe he has a chance to play there? Because Wisconsin is recruiting him, and they will probably offer him to start.' And Bo said, 'I've gone around the table and asked every coach, and they all believe he can play and start at Michigan at some point.' So I said, okay, you can talk to Jim now."

Jim was happy with Wisconsin and Arizona recruiting him and, with his father the head coach at Western Michigan, he figured if all else failed he could play for his dad in Kalamazoo. He always loved the idea of playing for his dad, and now that Jack was a head coach, that seemed as though it could be a reality. Jack Harbaugh always had a special relationship with his children, and they all hold him in high regard, and it would've created a unique bond had Jim been able to be his father's quarterback.

But with this sudden invitation to visit Michigan, the potential of a scholarship offer coming from Schembechler while on the visit was creating some real conversations as to how his recruitment should conclude. When Schembechler invited Jim to Ann Arbor, he called Jack shortly after to offer a proposition. Schembechler knew the Harbaugh family was close knit, and since Jim was still in California, he hadn't had many opportunities to speak with his father in person about his recruitment and where he wanted to go. So Schembechler offered to Jack that Michigan would fly Jim out to Ann Arbor, Jim would take his visit to Michigan, and then Jim would be able to drive to Kalamazoo to see Jack and talk about the opportunity to play at Western Michigan for his father. Jim would then return to Ann Arbor and finish his visit at Michigan before flying back to California.

Before the trip took place and with only a few weeks before he needed to sign, Jim, Jack, and Jackie all got on a phone call together to discuss what Jim was thinking, which school he wanted to play for, and what his parents thought. Jackie picked up the landline phone in her bedroom. Jim was on the phone in the kitchen, and Jack was back in Michigan. The three discussed his options, weighing the pros and cons of each school and talking about all the different scenarios that could play out. Jackie again expressed her concerns if Michigan really wanted her son or if they were doing Jack a favor. Jack listened intently and asked Jim what he wanted to do to. Jim replied he really didn't know. Because he didn't know if Michigan would offer him a scholarship, most of the conversation was between Wisconsin and Arizona.

Jim could see himself at either school, but then he asked his father where he thought he should go. Despite knowing that his son would listen to his wishes and come play at Western Michigan if he expressed that desire, his father told Jim that if Michigan offered him a scholarship, he should play in Ann Arbor. Jack spoke confidently that Jim could win a national championship at Michigan and maybe have a shot at the Heisman Trophy. Taking his father's word and opinion, Jim said that it was settled then. If Michigan offered, he would be a Wolverine. As he said that, his mother walked into the kitchen and told Jim to get off the line, so she and Jack could talk privately. "I'm going to pick it up and hang it up, but they're already talking, and it's kind of heated. It's kind of back-and-forth, so I started listening and covered up the part you talk into," Jim said. "So then finally my mom goes, 'Jack, where do you honestly want him to go?' And my dad goes, 'I want him to go to Western Michigan. That's what I want him to do.' I took the phone and kind of slid my finger on top of the button and hung up. I didn't tell my mom and dad until years later that I overheard that."

Jack knew that the opportunity to play at Michigan would provide his son more than he could at Western Michigan, so he adhered to the advice that Elway had given him at the beginning of his recruitment. Although it was difficult to pass up coaching Jim and spending time with him, Jack knew the best thing for him was to join the Wolverines if they were to have him.

It was a selfless act and it put to end the conversations. Jim was headed to Ann Arbor to visit, hoping he would come away with the opportunity to play for Schembechler and don the winged helmet, the same helmet that Leach had worn when Jim was just a young kid, roaming the halls and picking up gloves in the locker room.

Jim made the trip to Ann Arbor, saw everything he had seen as a 10-year-old boy, but he was now seeing it through the eyes of someone who could one day step on that field inside The Big House and someone who could use the locker room for its proper purpose. On the trip Bill McCartney, an assistant coach at Michigan, told Jim of a dream he had the night before Jim arrived on campus. "He said I was playing at Michigan, that I was the starting quarterback. I can't remember the opponent, but that was his dream," Jim said. "I remember thinking at the time that he probably hadn't had a dream, and it was probably a sales pitch."

Jim eventually made his way to Kalamazoo to see his father and talk about the potential to play at Western Michigan. At this point, however, Jack knew that Michigan would not have flown out his son unless they were intending to offer a scholarship. It would have been great to see his son under center, and he knew that if he told Jim directly that he wanted him to play in Kalamazoo, Jim would have said yes in a heartbeat. But Jack knew that wouldn't be right. "I told Jim that I loved my time at Michigan. I loved Bo Schembechler, I loved my son, and I thought Michigan would be the perfect place for him. We were in agreement that if Michigan was where he wanted to be, that's where he belonged," Jack said. "This wasn't a decision about what my career was. It was a decision about his career. I know the influence Bo had on so many different people, and my thought was I wanted Jim to be a part of that program if that's what he wanted to do."

Back in Ann Arbor, Jim found himself sitting across from Schembechler in his office, nearing 9:00 AM on a Sunday. The two spoke about what Michigan had to offer and that Schembechler wanted Jim to come play at Michigan. In the excitement of the moment and the vague wording of it all, Jim was unclear whether Schembechler was offering him a full scholarship or a walk-on role. Before he told Schembechler of his intentions, Jim wanted it to be crystal clear what he was accepting. "I asked him: 'Coach, is that a full scholarship?' Because I didn't know. There was no, 'we want you to come to Michigan; you have a scholarship until that moment,'" Jim said. "It was a full scholarship, and I accepted it right then and there. The rest of the story behind that—what I didn't know at the time—was I was probably their second or third choice."

Jim later found out that Dave Yarema, an in-state quarterback from Birmingham Brother Rice High, was being recruited ahead of him at Michigan. Yarema committed to play at Michigan State, however, which left the Wolverines looking for another quarterback in the class to go along with Dan Decker, who also signed with Michigan.

The scholarship was offered, though, and in late January of 1982, Jim had committed to Michigan. "For me it came down to: I was sitting in that chair, and Bo said he wanted me, and all I could say was yes. It was the only thing I could think of saying, and I was excited about it," Jim said. "The only thing that was weighing on my mind after that was that I wouldn't play for my dad. Leading up to Signing Day, and for years on…what if I had played for my dad, because my dad is the best coach I've ever had in my entire life. Bo is right next, but I always wondered about it the day after…should I have played for my dad?"

He went back to what his father told him, though, and the opportunity that he had to play at Michigan. He stuck with his decision and signed with Michigan. Schudel flew out to Palo Alto, so that he could get Jim's signature on the letter of intent for Signing Day. The coaches weren't allowed to be present when the letter was signed, but they were able to go and collect them in person. Schudel describes it as the best recruiting visit he has ever been on. He was picked up from the airport by the Harbaughs, taken to Ming's Garden Chinese restaurant—a spot Schudel still lauds as one of the best restaurants he has eaten at—and was able to stay with the Harbaugh family. Jim signed his letter of intent at his school and then gave it to Schudel, and the assistant coach made his way back to Ann Arbor.

Back at Michigan, Falk got word that Jim was signing with the Wolverines and chuckled to himself, thinking of Bo's proclamation before the recruitment started. *Jim Harbaugh would play for Michigan; he just didn't know it yet.* "After Jim signed, I went into Bo's office, and Bo said, 'Falk, Jim Harbaugh is coming to Michigan.' I said, 'You mean that little kid that ran around the locker room?'" Falk recalled. "Bo said, 'Yes, and he's going to be a great player for Michigan.'"

Jim made his way to Michigan and, being the son of a coach, he knew to some effect what the transition to college would look like. He had been around college practices and inside locker rooms his whole life, but now he was a part of the team. He showed up on campus and asked Falk for No. 10, but Falk replied that he would wear No. 4. Jim explained that he was No. 10 at Ann Arbor Pioneer and No. 11 at Palo Alto. The No. 11 was retired at Michigan at the time, so Jim knew he wouldn't be able to get that number. He wanted 10. "I repeated that he was going to be No. 4, and if he had a problem with it, go see Bo," Falk said. "Jim laughs now because he saw Bo and mentioned he wanted No. 10. After that conversation Jim says he never asked again."

Schembechler was notoriously stern and held his players and coaches to high standards. Jim was unflappable, though, and typically took any harsh comments or tough love in stride. He found out early on in his time at Michigan that Schembechler was serious about his rules, especially about being punctual. For Schembechler, being on time meant being five minutes early. That rule made itself known during Jim's first team meeting he participated in as a freshman. "I looked out the window of the team meeting room, and here comes Jim walking down the sidewalk to the meeting, and it's already started. I turned to somebody sitting next to me and said this is going to get real interesting in a second," Schudel said. "Jim walks in, and Bo just rips him. Jim just goes in and sits down like it was an uncatchable pass that went right over his head. I'm sure it registered with him, but it was just so funny that Bo ripped him and said he was calling his dad, and it was only the first meeting."

Jim redshirted his first year on campus, but it was difficult to stay on the sidelines for a full year. He had fought and battled to get to where he was, and it was already a difficult enough year, which had featured three losses heading into the Rose Bowl. Then in December of 1982, as Michigan was practicing for its bowl game, a familiar face showed up on the sideline on a visit to Ann Arbor. "Lo and behold, who comes out for a visit? Who do I look over and see standing there but John Paye being recruited to Michigan?" Jim said. "He was like the No. 1 All-American high school player in the country. It was like, oh, here we go again. John Paye again."

Luckily for Jim, he would not have to live in Paye's shadow in college as Paye eventually signed with Stanford. Jim eventually assimilated and after his redshirt year he started to grasp what was required of him. He took to Schembechler's teaching style and could relate to his competitive nature, which helped his progression. As was the case with many of his players, the more time Jim spent with Schembechler, the more his attitude changed toward the team. Schembechler's famous speech about The Team, The Team, The Team, that no man is more valuable than the team, wasn't just a speech to his players. That was a mentality that he instilled, and it was something that Jack started to notice in his son.

During Jim's first year on campus, he called his father and told him about his performance in the spring game, describing his personal stats and how he fared in the competition. But after his second year on campus, Jack noticed a subconscious change in how his son was describing the events. "All at once the conversations got: 'I was in four series, we scored a touchdown, we got a field goal, we picked up X number of first downs.' It hit me about what Bo used to talk about," Jack said. "What happened in two years here at Michigan under Bo Schembechler, it was no longer an individual. It was: 'What I did as a quarterback to help our team win.' When he made that transition, all at once, now he became the quarterback at the University of Michigan."

Jim started for three years at Michigan, accumulating 5,449 passing yards and throwing for 31 touchdowns over his career from 1982 to 1986. During the 1986 season, he completed 65 percent of his passes, a mark that sits in second place for a single year. He is still in seventh place in Michigan history for career passing yards and number three in average yards per game over his career, averaging 175.8 passing yards.

The Chicago Bears drafted Jim in the first round of the 1987 NFL Draft, and he went on to have a 14-year career as an NFL player. Once his playing career was over, Jim went into coaching, guiding the quarterbacks with the Oakland Raiders before taking the head coaching position at University of San Diego in 2004. He was then hired as the head coach at Stanford, where he coached from 2007 to 2010 before becoming the San Francisco 49ers' head coach.

After the 2014 season was over, Jim was presented with the opportunity to take over as head coach at the University of Michigan, the program he had grown to love so much, starting as a 10-year-old kid who roamed the halls and locker room. He now had the opportunity to follow in his father and Schembechler's footsteps and coach for the Wolverines. Jim was announced as Michigan's head coach on December 30, 2014. Now, as Jim works in Schembechler Hall with his father, Jack, and special assistant to the head football coach, Falk, Jim's children are roaming the locker room and building memories of their own.

FATHER'S NAME _Jack Harbaugh_ OCCUPATION _Football Coach_ COLLEGE _Bowling (_

MOTHER'S NAME _Jackie Harbaugh_ OCCUPATION _Housewife_ COLLEGE _Bowling Gr_
(1969 Champions[?] team)

SPORTS IN WHICH HE/SHE PARTICIPATED (Honors) _Football, Baseball in college; Football,_
Basketball in H.S. // _(she) Basketball, Volleyball, Swimming_

BROTHERS _John_ SISTERS _Joan_

RELATIVES WHO PARTICIPATED IN COLLEGE ATHLETICS OR ACHIEVED PUBLIC DISTINCTION _____

John is defensive back at Miami of Ohio

HIGH SCHOOL TEAMMATES PLAYING IN COLLEGE (List sport and college) _____
Reid Johnson - Football (Cal-Berkeley) Mike Beasly - Football (Washington St. (

HIGH SCHOOL HIGHLIGHTS (Best game, etc) _Basketball 36 pts vs Monteray H.S._
Football 252 yds passing vs Mills H.S.

HOBBIES/OUTSIDE INTERESTS _golf, history_

FAVORITES (Books, movies, music, sports teams, athletes, etc.) _T.V. show (Rockford Files)*_
sport teams (Western Mich U. - S.F. 49ers - Detroit tigers); James Garner (Movies);
favorite sports Personalities - Bobby Knight; Music Rock Bands ACJDC and Sammy Hagar

GOOD LUCK SPORTS SUPERSTITION _____

GREATEST SPORTS MEMORY _Playing in CIF-CCS Basketball_
State playoffs

COLLEGES WHICH YOU CONSIDERED SERIOUSLY IN ADDITION TO MICHIGAN _Stanford,_
Wisconsin, Arizona

WHY DID YOU CHOOSE MICHIGAN? _Coaching Staff, winning tradition,_
play in front of 100,000 fans, chance to play in Rose Bowl

TOUGHEST OPPONENT YOU'VE EVER PLAYED _____

HOMETOWN NEWSPAPERS YOU WOULD LIKE INFORMATION SENT TO: _____
Penninsula Times Tribune, SAN Jose Mercury, SF Examiner

I authorize use of the above information and related athletic material about myself
by the Michigan Athletic Department and Board in Control of Intercollegiate
Athletics.

Jim Harbaugh
Signature

Jim Harbaugh

UNIVERSITY OF MICHIGAN SPORTS INFORMATION OFFICE

This form will serve as permanent record in your athletic file. Please fill it out neatly, accurately and completely so that it may be used to its best advantage. Feel free to use extra paper. Any newspaper articles about yourself and your achievements would be much appreciated.

NAME _James_ (First) _Joseph_ (Middle) _Harbaugh_ (Last) _Jim_ Nickname/preferred CLASS _1982_

SPORT _Football_ POSITION _QB_ HEIGHT _6'3"_ WEIGHT _195_

DATE OF BIRTH _12/23/63_ WHERE BORN _Toledo OHIO_

HIGH SCHOOL _Palo Alto_ LOCATION _Palo Alto CA._

HOME ADDRESS ███ (No.) (Street) (City) (State) (Phone Number)

LOCAL/CAMPUS ADDRESS ███ LOCAL PHONE ███

PREVIOUS VARSITY ATHLETIC EXPERIENCE

YEAR	SPORT	POSITION	COACH	AVERAGES/STATS (Yardage, PPG, RBIs, etc.)
1980	Football	QB	Chuck Ritter	Starting QB Pioneer H.S. (soph)
1980	Basketball	G	Art Lee	Lettered Varsity B.B. Pioneer H.S.
1980	Baseball	P. of	Palmer	Lettered Varsity B.B. Pioneer H.S.
1981	Football	QB	Earl Hansen	1523 yds 19 td passes (passing)
1981	Basketball	F	Clem Wiser	14.3 ppg
1981	Baseball	P of	Doug Gieger	417 BA 5-W 2-L
1982	Football	QB	Earl Hansen	1380 yds 15 td passes 59% comp
1982	Basketball	F	Clem Wiser	19.8 ppg 10.3 Rebound pg

DESCRIBE ANY AWARDS, HONORS OR RECORD YOU MAY HAVE ACHIEVED IN HIGH SCHOOL. LABEL EACH ITEM BY SPORT AND YEAR ATTAINED. (All-League Basketball - 1980; School Record 19 TDs - 1980, etc.)

All-League, Basketball, Football, Baseball - 1980; 1981 & 1982;
All-Peninsula Basketball, Football - 1981; 1982;

CIF - ALL CCS (central coast section) Football - QB All Bay area QB

LIST ANY NON-ATHLETIC HONORS AND AWARDS WON IN HIGH SCHOOL (National Honor Society, etc.

CHAPTER 3

Jamie Morris

An undersized running back recruit hoping for a Michigan offer, Jamie Morris sat in a hallway in Michigan's athletic facilities next to other high school recruits seeking the same thing. He was next in line to meet with legendary coach Bo Schembechler about the chance of a scholarship to Michigan when linebacker Chris Spielman headed in to talk with the head coach. Spielman was from Ohio and was heavily considering Ohio State, so he and Schembechler butted heads during the meeting, an argument broke out, and Schembechler cancelled the remaining visits with recruits.

Morris was heartbroken, thinking he might have missed his only shot to impress the head coach and wear that winged helmet he had dreamed about so often. But given Morris' backstory, the fact that he'd gotten this close was something of an upset.

In the mid-1970s to 1980s, the Morris family was very well-known in the small town of Ayer, Massachusetts. Situated an hour northwest of Boston, the family took the town by storm through their athletic prowess. Joe Morris, the eldest of four boys, excelled at nearly everything he did athletically, garnering most of the attention at Ayer High on the football field. He was so successful in high school that he went on to play running back at Syracuse and set record after record from 1978 to 1981 before going on to have a successful career with the New York Giants.

The oldest Morris brother still holds the Syracuse record for most rushing yards in a game, season, and career. His totals impressively outrank names like Ernie Davis, Larry Csonka, and Jim Brown. Joe set the pace for his younger brothers—Larry, Mike, and Jamie—and blazed the trail that led most of his talented siblings to continue his legacy at Syracuse. All four were on the small side, which turned some programs away. Joe stood at 5'7", 180 pounds in high school but boasted a drive, will, and heart that were greater than anyone that stood on a field with him.

Their spirit, work ethic, and desire were engrained in each one of the brothers through their father, Earl, and mother, Addie. Earl, a former army sergeant, taught the boys about being the best versions of themselves and that nothing came for free. They all took that to heart and never let their size get in the way of their accomplishments on the field.

Larry is three years younger than Joe and one year older than Mike but was held back in the fourth grade, so Larry and Mike were a part of the same graduating class. Both boys picked up where Joe left off at Ayer and both were recruited to play at Syracuse themselves. The brothers decided to follow in Joe's footsteps and went on to play for the Orange. That left youngest brother, Jamie, with the whole town's gaze on him and expectations stacked as high as his three brothers on top of each others' shoulders. "It was hard because I played with my brothers Larry and Mike my freshman year, then they moved on," Jamie said. "When they moved on, we were a good team still, but we were looking for a leader. It was my sophomore year and my coach, Chet Steele, decided to make me a captain."

Before accepting the responsibility, Jamie consulted with Mike on whether he should take on the role. Jamie believed in himself but knew it would be difficult for a sophomore to try to lead seniors while trying to live up to the expectations his older brothers had forged ahead of him. Mike told Jamie if he was to accept the captaincy that he needed to bring the seniors together because they wouldn't be happy about a sophomore taking one of the few captain roles. Jamie decided to accept the captaincy and the responsibility and weight that came along with it—as long as Coach Steele named at least two other senior captains alongside him. He was ready to lead and ready to create his own path within those white lines spread out 100 yards from end to end.

His recruitment hadn't yet started to pick up, but Jamie was starting to get attention through his older brothers. The four were featured in a *Sports Illustrated* article in August of 1981 at the beginning of Jamie's sophomore season. "The article was called 'The Fearsome Foursome.' It was mainly about Joe, but Joe is very family-oriented, so he said, 'You think I'm good; you should see my brothers behind me,'" Jamie said. "We threw my dad in the pool for a picture with the article. We threw Earl Morris in the pool! I was afraid of my dad, and you don't throw him in the pool, but he was willing to do it for the article and for us."

And Joe was willing to take some of the spotlight off of himself because Jamie was about to embark on a journey he had already taken and because their mother and father had taught them that family comes first.

The first recruiting letter Jamie received was from coach Dick Crum at North Carolina after that sophomore season. The Morris family was originally from Southern Pines, North Carolina, so it was an exciting letter for the youngest Morris brother. Michael Jordan was about to start his sophomore season as a Tar Heel, and the basketball program was creating buzz for the university.

Jamie's junior year in 1982 was when his recruitment really started to pick up and schools started showing interest. The town the Morris family lived in was only a few miles from Fort Devens, a military base primarily used for training purposes in World War II. The University of Massachusetts and Harvard eventually used the 1,200 barracks at the base because the G.I. Bill of Rights brought more students to the universities. Ayer High also used the barracks during Jamie's junior year as the school closed down due to asbestos issues. So he and his classmates attended class in the army barracks and even lived at the fort during football training camp. "We were lucky we were right next to that military base because they cleared out the barracks, and they had a gym and field. I finished my high school in those barracks," Jamie said. "Football camp was kind of cool because you go away for 10 days, and you're in the military barracks doing training with the troops."

That junior year, Jamie heard from Syracuse, Boston College, and North Carolina but hoped that Michigan would come calling. Despite having three brothers play for Syracuse, something about the Wolverines always intrigued the youngest Morris brother. He grew up watching Michigan on television and loved the famous winged helmets the players wore while flying around the field. He first remembers falling in love with Michigan at eight years old after watching the Rose Bowl and Orange Bowl games the Wolverines often played in. Jamie had high hopes of attending Michigan, but standing at 5'7", 160 pounds, he didn't think that would ever truly happen. "Plus, I didn't think my mother was going to let me go that far away by myself," he added.

So it came as a shock to Jamie when Michigan assistant Bob Thornbladh called him toward the end of his junior year to express interest in the undersized back. While on the phone, Jamie continuously asked who Thornbladh really was and why he was calling. He was in disbelief that the Wolverines would be recruiting him. "I called him and said this is Coach Thornbladh from the University of Michigan, and he refused to believe that I was actually representing Michigan," Thornbladh said. "He said, 'No, who is this? Why are you calling me?' I said this is Coach Thornbladh from Michigan. We're interested in you and we want to come up and discuss the University of Michigan with you and talk to your coaches."

Coach Schembechler made the final decision on scholarship offers, so Thornbladh couldn't offer him anything except for an evaluation. Schembechler wanted to understand who the recruit was and how he conducted himself, so he typically waited to offer scholarships in person after a personal interview with the prospect, according to Thornbladh. Schembechler's thought process was that he didn't offer a scholarship to a prospect until he visited campus. He figured if they didn't come to campus, then they lacked interest anyway.

Thornbladh recruited New England, New Jersey, and Chicago at the time for the Wolverines, so Jamie was in his recruiting area. During that time the coaches typically sent surveys to high school coaches prior to spring recruiting. The surveys consisted of questions to help the college's assistants recruit their territory. They asked if the high school coach had any prospects on his team they should look at and if there were any other football players in the area they thought were top prospects. "The best indicator was asking about other players. Because when you cross-index the coaches, you'd see names pop up more than once," Thornbladh said. "If you got back six or seven guys that said this kid is a great player, that was usually a good indicator. Back then there was no Internet, so you'd go out in the spring and look and go to each high school to talk to coaches, principals, and guidance counselors and pull transcripts."

Thornbladh would typically greet a prospect on their visit but wouldn't really initiate the recruitment until he watched the film and sent letters to the recruit. The early letters weren't typically anything specific but more marketing letters to generate interest about the school among the recruit and his family. Since Jamie was from such a small town in a relatively quiet area, there wasn't a lot of foot traffic from coaches. But because his brother, Joe, had created such a buzz at Syracuse and eventually in the NFL, Jamie and the area were on the radar of a few programs.

It was difficult for one college coach to scan his entire area for prospects such as Jamie, so they often received help from alumni in the area. "They couldn't talk to kids, and Bo was very strict about that because he knew the potential for abuse," Thornbladh said. "They were sort of our eyes and ears in the region, and there was a wonderful guy named Dr. Lintz, whose father was a Michigan grad. He lived in Milton, Massachusetts, and he, along with two brothers, Jim and Larry Cedar, were sort of my eyes and ears up there in the Boston area."

So Thornbladh's eyes and ears were on the lookout, but once again big brother Joe was looking out for his family. Prior to that first phone call in January 1982, Joe was playing in the East-West Shrine

Game in California. He played for the East team, which featured Alabama's Paul "Bear" Bryant as the head coach and Michigan's Schembechler coaching the offense. "They were in San Francisco for the game, and Joe went up to Bo and said, 'My little brother loves Michigan,'" Jamie said. "Bo came home from that game and asked who they had in Massachusetts that could get film on me. Former Michigan quarterback B.J. Dickey was out there, so B.J. went and got my film and got it to the Michigan coaches to watch."

Jamie eventually believed Thornbladh that Michigan really was contacting him on the phone and started to think that maybe his dream of being a Wolverine wasn't so far-fetched. But this was the spring before his junior season, so there was still a long way to go before an offer would even be extended or anything firm was going to happen.

Thornbladh knew Jamie was a Michigan fan, but he did feel as though the Wolverines had a little catching up to do. Thornbladh's former teammate at Michigan, Chuck Heater, was now coaching with Dave McClain at Wisconsin, and the Badgers also had their sights set on the shifty back. "He was our main target," Heater said. "I went to one of his basketball games, and he played a team up in New Hampshire. I watched him goaltend. He got called for goaltending at 5'7", so I said this kid is a freak, and he was a great kid."

Along with football, Jamie was also the point guard of his high school's basketball team. He wasn't flashy and, because of his height, he wasn't a big basketball prospect. His stats weren't off the charts because Morris managed the game and usually saw his assist total as the highest number on the stat sheet.

Although Thornbladh thought he might have a little catching up to do, Heater knew that Jamie always wanted to go to Michigan and felt that he and Wisconsin were actually behind Michigan. But that didn't stop him from putting the full-court press on Jamie and trying to secure a commitment. Heater also knew that Schembechler wasn't completely sold on the smaller back just yet. "The problem was Bo didn't go see the kid. Bo was not convinced that he was that good of a player," Heater said. "Obviously Bob was, so my whole recruiting pitch was that I played at Michigan, and if Bo wanted you, he would be in your home. Truth of the matter was that Jamie was better than anybody else that year."

Thornbladh knew he had some convincing to do when it came to Schembechler and he sold Jamie's speed and shiftiness that could be useful as a return man and change-up running back. Michigan had a few smaller backs on the roster, but the Wolverines' leading rusher in 1983, the season before Jamie's freshman year, was Rick Rogers, who stood at 6'2", 200 pounds. "Most of our tailbacks were big, strong guys, so [for] Bo, there was this thing about [how] he didn't like short-armed backs," Thornbladh said. "Bo would say, 'I don't want short-armed backs. They're fumblers and they can't hold on to the ball.' So I tried to convince Bo that Jamie could be a great return guy to get over that."

While all of the convincing and recruiting pitches were happening, Jamie was primarily focused on his senior season as a captain and leader of his team. He knew that most of what matters in recruiting—his visits to campus—wouldn't happen until after that 1983 season was over so he was able to focus on what he did on the field and put recruiting out of his mind for the most part. But once that season was over recruiting picked back up, and Jamie started his trips to his top schools: Boston College, Syracuse, Michigan, and Wisconsin. Boston College wasn't as highly thought of in Jamie's mind as the other three. And despite having three brothers play at Syracuse, the school wasn't that appealing to Jamie.

In fact, having his three brothers as standouts for Syracuse might have hurt the coaches more than it helped them. His brother Joe was already gone from Syracuse, and brothers Larry and Mike would have been in school with Jamie for only two years had he gone to Syracuse. "I asked someone, 'You know what the roughest time of my life has been these last three years?'" Jamie said. "I got to play with my brothers for one year, and when they left, everybody expected the same thing to continue happening. When it didn't happen, when we lost, I was the loser."

People around town would say that Jamie's older brothers would have pulled out the win and Jamie didn't play as hard as his brothers would have. So he rationalized that it would be much of the same if he were to attend Syracuse once he was the lone Morris on the roster.

But feeling obligated to show the coaching staff some respect for how they had treated the family over the years and for recruiting his brothers, Jamie took a visit to Syracuse in December of 1983. He had not gone in depth with his brothers and mother and father about how Syracuse factored into his recruitment, but that would have to take place after this visit. "Syracuse was playing North Carolina in the dome, and Michael Jordan was coming, so it was a great game," Jamie said. "It was a good visit, but I knew everything about Syracuse, the good and the bad. When I had my coach-player meeting with Dick MacPherson on the visit, he threw the papers in front of me and was like, 'Are you ready to go?' I said, 'No, I need to take my visits and I told my mother I wouldn't sign anything.'"

Jamie's mother wanted to make sure he got all the facts from all the schools he was considering, which is why she didn't want him to sign any paperwork committing to a school without taking all of his visits. At Syracuse it was easy because Jamie knew he wasn't going there anyway.

He also took a visit to Boston College partially because it was close to home. On the trip Jamie hung out with quarterback Doug Flutie and running back Troy Stradford. The pitch from the Boston College staff was that Flutie would be back the following season when Jamie hit campus. He thought that was a great thing for Boston College but didn't know how much it would truly impact him because the great quarterback would be gone for the remaining years of his time on campus. He quickly dismissed that offering and figured he shouldn't consider it for his final decision.

That left the two Big Ten teams with former teammates battling over this Massachusetts speedster. Each school waited for its turn at a visit and a chance to show him what it had to offer. Michigan would be up first in January 1984. Because he was still selling Schembechler on the idea of Jamie joining the team, Thornbladh tried to prep Jamie for his visit. He told him that Schembechler loved to recruit the best athletes and liked to see big, dominating performances in every sport from their recruits. Jamie and his basketball team had an undefeated season on the line, and Thornbladh knew that his prized recruit probably would stick to what he knew best in his next game. He wouldn't put up any big numbers and would do everything he could to help his team win the game. But Thornbladh had something else in mind. "I said, 'Jamie, I have a problem. The old man is going to ask how many points you're averaging,'" Thornbladh said. "If this is a superior athlete that wants to come to Michigan, then most guys are averaging 20 points a game. I said, 'You gotta score for me and come up with a big game, so I can go to the old man and say he got 28 the other day.'"

Jamie obliged despite knowing he would be putting his team's record and No. 1 state ranking on the line. He talked to Thornbladh after that January game, and Thornbladh asked him how many points he scored. Morris replied that he had 26 points in the game. The Michigan assistant coach was excited, but Jamie didn't have a matching excitement in his voice. "He told me he got 26 and said that was the good news," Thornbladh said. "The bad news is: 'My coach is really mad at me, we lost the game, and my coach said I was a selfish player that didn't distribute the ball, and it caused us to lose the game.'"

Thornbladh apologized but said his team could still win the state title and that the performance would help with Schembechler. The point total made its way back to Schembechler, and he was indeed impressed by what Jamie could do on the hardwood.

Days before his visit to Ann Arbor, the anxious running back had prepped himself for the trip by reading a *Sports Illustrated* article on Michigan wide receiver Anthony Carter and researching the university as much as he could. Michigan strength and conditioning coach Mike Gittleson picked Jamie up at the airport, and the high schooler was impressed that the staff would send the strength coach to escort him around. They toured the campus and went to The Big House to allow Jamie the chance to see the historic stadium in person. Just standing on that turf where the Michigan players had stampeded for years, Jamie was sold that Michigan was the place for him. "That week Michigan played Indiana in basketball, and I went to the game and sat next to Bo Schembechler, eating popcorn," Jamie said. "It was a big recruiting weekend, and I could tell because Chris Spielman was there. We're at the recruiting weekend, and I'm sitting next to Bo, and he's like, 'This is a great game, isn't it?' I was like, 'Yeah, I'm talking to you!'"

Jamie was also sitting next to Gerald White, a player already on the roster at Michigan. Jamie took note of the 6'2", 205 pounder's size and asked White what position he played. When the words "running back" were spewed out of White's mouth, Morris instinctively blurted out, "Wow! Oh my God, you do?"

All the recruits headed to the old wrestling practice room where hot dogs and beverages were served for the visiting prospects. Jamie and Schembechler had a little more time to talk, and the coach, as he usually did, got straight to the point. "He says, 'How big are you?' I told him that I was 5'7" and I don't know how that registered, but it seemed okay," Jamie said. "He then told me, 'People said I could stop on a dime,' and I told him that I was all right and that, yeah, I can do that."

He felt at home on the visit because the Michigan coaches strategically paired Jamie with other players on the team that were from the East Coast. Jeff Akers and Bob Perryman were two of the bigger names that he spent time with on the trip, and it made him feel as though he could fit right in at Michigan. That said, he still didn't know if Schembechler thought he would fit and if he would help the program. An offer had not been extended. Schembechler liked to personally interview each visitor in his office.

So all the recruits lined up outside of the head coach's office to wait their turn to be interviewed by the legendary coach. Jamie was among the first five in line to see Schembechler and sat just behind

Spielman outside the office doors. "I'm looking at how Spielman is dressed, and he has on acid-washed jeans and a T-shirt, and I had a golf shirt on," Morris said. "Spielman goes in, and next thing I know, there's screaming and yelling going on. All of the sudden, they cancel the rest of the meetings with Schembechler, and he storms out. I know the story now that they got into an argument, but at the time it was like, *What?* I was next."

The rest of the coaches scrambled after the meeting went south with Spielman. The visiting prospects, including Jamie, still wanted their chance to meet with Schembechler. "I had Jamie all prepped to do a good job with Bo, and he has Spielman in his office, going hard on Spielman," Thornbladh said. "The meeting is going over the time, it's going forever, and someone comes up and tells us we're going to have to move Jamie back and do the meeting on Sunday."

Jamie was heartbroken, thinking he might have missed his only shot to impress the head coach. Thornbladh did his best to console him and reassured him that Schembechler was going to love him. He reminded the running back that if he was going to get a scholarship to Michigan that it would happen in that meeting, so he needed to impress the old coach.

Since the rest of the meetings were cancelled, the recruits were all rounded up and taken out to dinner. Jamie went to bed early. Having grown up in a military family, he was up at 5:45 the next morning. That was fortunate. Because not long after he rose from his sleep, the telephone rang in his room. It was Bo looking to hold the meeting they missed the day before. "Morris, it's Schembechler," the coach said. "Come on down here."

So Jamie swiftly put his clothes on and ran downstairs to find the head coach waiting for him on the ground level. The two headed to

Schembechler's office, and the future of Jamie Morris' football career hung in the balance. "I couldn't believe I was sitting there talking to Bo Schembechler. He says all the right things and is honest," Jamie said. "He says to me, 'We're looking at some other guys, but I want to keep you in the back of my mind. If I offered, are you here?' I said, 'No, I told my mother I wouldn't make any decisions until I got back home.'"

Jamie wanted Bo to offer him a scholarship in this meeting, so he sold himself to the legend sitting in front of him. He told him he thought he could be the next Heisman Trophy winner for Michigan. Tears welled in his eyes, as Jamie poured his heart out, pitching his shot to be a Wolverine. "Bo looks back at me and says, 'I'll tell you what, Morris. You are a son of a bitch,'" Jamie said. "He said it with a smile and said, 'Son, I think we have something for you, but you can't take it because you have to talk to your mother.'"

Jamie had earned his scholarship to Michigan. The dream was now a reality, but he hadn't yet made his commitment official. He wanted to honor his mother's wishes, so he headed home to tell his family about the unbelievable visit to Michigan. He got home, and his parents saw the gleam in his eye. He told them, sheepishly, that he hadn't yet made a decision. His mother knew him too well and accusingly asked if he was sure about that.

Jamie still had the Wisconsin visit to take, and it was now getting close to February and the time he needed to make a final decision. He wanted to respect Coach Heater and the other Wisconsin coaches, so he took the visit to Madison, Wisconsin. The Badgers' coaches had a jersey out with his No. 23 on display. Heater met up with his recruiting target, and the two had a frank conversation about his options and which school Heater felt was best for the running back. "Chuck said that they really wanted me and that he didn't want to say anything bad about Michigan, but Michigan is about numbers," Jamie said. "They take the best of the best, and then the best play, but you can get caught up in numbers. He said he wasn't saying it was going to be me, but just keep that in mind."

Heater continued to harp on the fact that Schembechler wasn't sold on him at first and that he was the top target at Wisconsin. The Badgers coach hoped that he could be persistent enough in his message that it would eventually wear on Jamie. His persistence made a dent, and Jamie did start to wonder if he would just be another number at Michigan and if he would ever see the field ahead of the other 6'2" monsters.

After his Wisconsin visit, his brother Mike called him and asked how the Michigan trip went. "I told him he should see the backs at Michigan," Jamie said. "They're 6'2", 226 pounds, and he said, 'Stop. He's not as fast as you and he can't do the stuff you can do.' He made me realize that I'm something special, too."

His eldest brother Joe said opportunity is going to knock, and you're not always going to know when it will. The youngest Morris brother finally realized that if he went to Wisconsin despite having a scholarship offer from the University of Michigan that he would always wonder if he could have been successful as a Wolverine.

So in February 1984, Jamie got a phone call from the coaches at Michigan, and when they put Schembechler on the line, the diminutive back made his commitment to be a Wolverine and finally get his chance to wear the winged helmet. Although he felt relief and his mother was happy that recruiters would stop calling the house, it still didn't mean his process was over.

Heater and Wisconsin still wouldn't give up. "In the old days, there wasn't the same rules, so I went out there and spent a whole week in Massachusetts. I wouldn't leave," Heater said. "I came to his school every day and tried to come up with something every day. In the end he wanted to go to Michigan."

He wanted that since he was eight years old, to be exact. The helmets, the stadium that held 100,000 fans, the coach he convinced to offer him a scholarship—it was all a part of why he wanted to go to Michigan. Heater and Wisconsin tried one last time before Signing Day and came to the Morris house with Coach McClain. The visit didn't change anyone's opinion, though, and Earl Morris kindly told the coaches it was time to go. And when Earl Morris says it's time to go, then it's time to go.

Three reporters from the local newspaper came to watch Jamie sign his paperwork binding him to Michigan on Signing Day. They gathered at the Morris house and asked a few questions of the local star. "I signed the papers and then I answered their questions," Jamie said. "Once I was done, my mom told them they had to go so she could clean her house. She congratulated me, then looked at my dad and told him to drop me off and go to work."

The whole process had led to this moment as he was finally, officially, a Wolverine.

Schembechler wasn't always convinced that Jamie could play running back at Michigan, but the decision to offer the undersized kid from Massachusetts eventually paid off. Schembechler told *The New York Times* before the 1987 Rose Bowl game that he had told Jamie he was too small to be a running back. "I did, however, promise him the chance to try to be a running back for us," Schembechler said in the article. "Good thing I did, isn't it?"

He would go on to break rushing records at Michigan and still ranks No. 3 in rushing yards in a season and No. 4 in career rushing yards and rushing attempts. He is tied for seventh most touchdowns during a season (14) and ranks No. 5 for 100-yard games in a career at Michigan. Jamie Morris was a captain during his tenure and a two-time All-Big Ten selection.

CHAPTER 4

Mark Messner

Take a dive into Michigan's football record book, make your way to the defensive stats, and there you will find Mark Messner's name splattered throughout the various categories. Whether it's tackles for loss or sacks, Messner's career at Michigan is still one of the best statistically for any Michigan defensive lineman. The four-time, first-team All-Big Ten lineman and unanimous All-American terrorized opposing quarterbacks from 1984 to 1988. During that time he racked up statistics that are still standing today in Michigan's record books and could stand for quite some time.

His five sacks in one game against Northwestern in 1987 are still the most for any Wolverine in one game, his 36 career sacks are the most for any Michigan player since 1980, and his sack yardage of 273 yards still stands as the most anyone at Michigan has ever accumulated in their career. Although he was a local, Michigan kid, his recruitment was never pointed straight at the University of Michigan, at least not until the very end. His process and high school career were winding and—despite his dominance in college—riddled with self-doubt that almost led him to another Big Ten team.

Growing up in Hartland, Michigan, a small town to the north-west of Detroit, Messner attended Detroit Catholic Central High from 1981 to 1984. He lived with his mother, Sharon Pretty, and his stepfather, Del Pretty. Messner's biological father, Max, played linebacker in the NFL in the 1960s, but Messner's stepfather was the main father figure in his life. Pretty was there for his stepson in every aspect of his life but really loved to watch Messner in his high school football games. The family never thought much about college football mainly because Messner wasn't sure how he stacked up. He didn't know if he was big enough—or if any schools would even show interest.

That all changed, however, toward the end of his junior year when he started to receive recruiting letters from across the country. Michigan, Notre Dame, UCLA, Boston College, Michigan State, Ohio State, Tulane, and Purdue, among others, sent him mail. But the one school that really started the actual recruiting process for Messner was Indiana. He played tight end and defensive tackle for Catholic Central and was starting to turn some heads with his play. At the time in 1983, Sam Wyche was the head coach of the Hoosiers, and Ed O'Neil had just joined the staff as the linebackers coach. After having played football together in the NFL with the Detroit Lions, Wyche and O'Neil had reunited at Indiana.

O'Neil was tasked with scouting the state of Michigan and inadvertently found Messner while watching film. "I was hired at Indiana in January 1983 and I went straight to Michigan to recruit kids. I was watching film on a senior who would've been coming in with that '83 class and I saw a junior playing defensive tackle, and it was Mark Messner," O'Neil said. "Here I am watching the senior who people were recruiting, but the player that caught my eye was this defensive tackle on the other team."

This was the first full year that O'Neil had coached in football. After a short stint at Eastern Michigan in 1982, the whole staff was let go, which led him to join Wyche at Indiana. Despite not having much experience coaching, O'Neil had been in football his whole life and knew that he needed to land Messner. He figured that it would be a heck of a challenge to get a talented player like Messner to choose a place like Indiana. But he tried to recruit him anyway because the potential he saw on that film as a junior was too much to pass up. "The two best high school football players I ever watched on film were Chris Spielman and Mark Messner," O'Neil said. "As a junior he far exceeded the young man I was watching on film as a senior. That's what stuck out in my mind."

The ironic part is while O'Neil thought Messner would be out of his league, Messner figured Indiana would likely be the best he could do and immediately became interested in the Hoosiers. Plus, it was in the Big Ten and relatively close to home, so his mom and dad would have the opportunity to see him play. "I really started to think they were the first school, and here's this guy, me, who's not big enough, strong enough, fast enough, but a Big Ten school like Indiana is recruiting me," Messner said. "I think I should really give them a shot."

Indiana continued to court Messner as his senior season was fast approaching. As he got closer to fall camp, Messner started to hear from more and more schools, and the recruiting mail picked up. All was going well for the senior-to-be until one day in camp before the season. Messner was lined up as a tight end and went up for a pass without pads on. He came down awkwardly and broke his collarbone.

He would miss the first three games of his senior season due to the injury and started to wonder if the broken bone would hurt his chances at getting recruited. Indiana was still the only school showing a lot of interest, but he had received recruiting letters from other programs and didn't want that progress to stop. His mother, Sharon, knew that Indiana would be an option and was happy with wherever her son chose. It would be an added bonus for her if he chose a school like Indiana that was within driving distance, so she could easily watch his games. "He really liked the coach at Indiana and he thought he could be a big fish in a little pond instead of a little fish in the ocean," she said. "If he went to a smaller college, he felt assured he could get a place there. He wasn't cocky. He was worried that he would even be able to play."

After taking time off because of the injury, he fully healed. He sat out the three games and by the fourth he was ready to show everyone what he was capable of. "Game 4 I had a lot pent up," Messner said. "I had to make up lost ground. So for the final six games, I played like a man possessed and put myself back on the radar. I ended up being a high school All-American tight end and nose tackle."

He was back on track. And now that his senior season was ending, he was ready to focus on choosing a college. Because he had healed properly and performed so well during his senior season, the floodgates opened with his recruitment. To keep control of the process, he had to tell some schools no right off the bat. Pitt was one of those schools that was told no almost immediately. Messner didn't have any interest in the Panthers, so he told them right away rather than dragging it out.

He went back to O'Neil and Wyche and told them he wanted to take an official visit to see the Hoosiers and find out if that was the right place for him. The coaches were excited that they were going to get such an exceptional athlete on campus for a visit because it wasn't the typical prospect they were able to recruit at Indiana. In late December of 1983, Wyche and O'Neill came to Messner's house and solidified their message that they were building something special at Indiana and that Messner—if he were to choose the Hoosiers— would play early and often. That weekend Messner went to a friend's cottage for a weekend trip.

He happened to read the newspaper on Saturday, and one of the articles in the paper was about Wyche's decision to leave Indiana for the Cincinnati Bengals. Wyche had been in Messner's home the same week he was hired by the Bengals, and now Messner didn't know who he could trust with the recruiting process. "I called Ed O'Neil and asked what was going on, and he said, 'I don't know. I'm out of a job,'" Messner said. "If he's in my house Wednesday, and Saturday he's leaving for the NFL, how truthful are the other ones saying wonderful things about you and their future school?"

To cut down on any trust issues and to make the process easier on himself, Messner decided he should narrow his choices down to five schools. Initially, Indiana was on that list, but because of Wyche leaving, the Hoosiers were now out of the picture. Now he was considering UCLA, Boston College, Notre Dame, Michigan, and Michigan State. "When I narrowed down my five, coming out of Catholic Central, Doug Flutie was at Boston College and being a Catholic university, I said I would go there, go to Notre Dame, get all the religious schools out of the way," Messner said. "I wasn't even going to take a Michigan State visit. I had both schools in my backyard, and back in those days, Bo was always going to bowl games.

When Sam Wyche at Indiana fell off, I said I'd look at Michigan State and evaluate both the in-state schools."

Despite growing up in Michigan, Messner wasn't sold on either Michigan or Michigan State early on in the process. Hartland was about equidistance from both programs, and neither really stood out to him. Michigan initially made the list because of Schembechler and its academic reputation. Michigan State really only made the list because Indiana was bumped out.

Now that he had his list narrowed down, he needed to take his official visits. It was December 1983, and Boston College got the first visit. Flutie was the quarterback at Boston College at the time and was the player host for Messner on his trip. Although the visit went well and Messner described Boston College as a wonderful place, he felt ultimately it was too similar to his high school. It was a smaller school, and Messner already had gone to a small, all-boys Catholic school. Boston College was out.

His next visit was Notre Dame, which was also a Catholic school but wasn't as small as Boston College. While at Notre Dame, Messner went out to dinner with then-head coach Gerry Faust. That practice often takes place, as it gives the coaches an opportunity to spend one-on-one time with the prospects and it gives the recruits a chance to have a good meal at a nice restaurant. Normally, those dinner experiences are positive, but for Messner, it didn't go as planned, and he found out quickly that he wouldn't fit in at Notre Dame. "I was excited about Notre Dame and going there until I got there. I met Faust and said I can't do this," Messner said. "He was out of his league and he acted like an 18-year-old kid. He was exuberant and loud in a really nice restaurant and was making a spectacle. I was embarrassed that this was the leader of Notre Dame football, and if he embarrassed me in a restaurant like this, I can't imagine what the seniors think."

It was disappointing for Messner because he went into the visit thinking that Notre Dame would be the school he would choose. It seemingly had all the positives from his high school experience but none of the negatives. He, however, came back from the visit and eliminated the Fighting Irish. The coaches and the fans turned off Messner by displaying a cocky attitude that he wasn't used to. The small-town kid wasn't familiar with the arrogance he felt from the Irish fans, who were telling him that Notre Dame was the only place to be and the only university that mattered. So his list of five became a list of three. Michigan, Michigan State, and UCLA were the schools still in contention. There was still a long way to go, though, as he wanted to visit all three remaining schools.

The Michigan visit was next, and since the school was so close to home, it didn't take much to set up the trip. He was intrigued by what Michigan would show him but hesitant because of how his last two visits had gone. He got to Ann Arbor and was immediately impressed. "I saw everything I wanted to see. [Offensive lineman] Jumbo Elliott scared the living crap out of me as he walked through the dorm room door and introduced himself," Messner said. "I thought, *Oh my God, I'll never player here. These people will kill me.* I thought I would never stack up and play at Michigan because they had All-Americans three deep."

His player host at Michigan was Kenny Higgins, a wide receiver whom Messner describes as brilliant. Messner was grateful to have an intelligent host that he got along with. Higgins showed him around campus and looked after him for the weekend. "All the football players hung out together, so I'm a defensive lineman, and Kenny takes me to a party. We meet Jumbo and Doug English," he said. "It's like shaking a baseball mitt when you shake their hands. Then there was Harbaugh, sitting in a chair surrounded by his minions of linemen."

It was intimidating seeing the players, and Messner had his doubts about himself, but the way the coaches recruited him and the players treated him reassured him that Michigan could be the right home. He still had two more visits, though, and wanted to make an educated decision based on all of them. Michigan had risen up the board, but he still wasn't exactly sold on the Wolverines just yet. He wanted to give Michigan State and UCLA their fair shot and had his visits lined up.

Michigan State was next, and following up the Michigan trip was a tough break for the Spartans. In Messner's mind they didn't stack up to what the Michigan program was all about. "I visited Michigan State, and as I anticipated, it didn't hold the caliber as Michigan did," Messner said. "If I'm going to stay in Michigan, I'm going to go to Michigan because I'll get a great education and I'll go to bowl games every year. I may never step on the field, but I'll come out of there in a much better situation than comparatively something else."

While he was in Ann Arbor, Bo Schembechler drove it home to Messner that he was a Michigan Man and the type of player that Michigan builds itself around. He said that Messner belonged and that he would be part of history. Schembechler didn't promise playing time—he never did—but Messner found out very quickly that he and Schembechler were on the same page in terms of personality and what Messner was hoping for in a coach.

All the local visits had been completed, and by January 1984, he had one trip left. It was the dead of winter in Michigan, and he was about to take off for sunny California—Los Angeles to be more specific—to see what UCLA had to offer. "So then I go to UCLA, and oh boy. All-guys Catholic school, grow up in Michigan, January, and I get off an airplane in California," Messner said. "I get picked up by Coach Donahue, and we go right to Venice Beach first where there's bikinis, roller skates, boom boxes, muscle beach. I just couldn't believe it."

Messner recalls the drive up to UCLA's campus, turning left into Brentwood and seeing *The Beverly Hillbillies* mansion and an incredible gated community as you pull into campus. He saw students sprawled across campus, lying on the grass, reading books in January, which is normally freezing cold and snow-filled back in Michigan. The visit had just begun, and it was already off to a fast start. It was shocking in a good way. During the month of January, he was used to seeing people in large, insulated jackets and bundled up from the snow. He was now staring at bathing suits, the beach, and a whole different lifestyle. It was a lifestyle that Messner thought he could enjoy.

Donahue sold the UCLA depth chart to Messner, saying if he were to choose the Bruins he could play early. Everything was flashy and new and exciting, and it was all drawing Messner in. There was no snow, and it was as far from an all-boys school as you could get, but he could still get a great education and join a great football team. "I committed to UCLA with Coach Donahue while I was there. How can you not come to school here when it's an option?" Messner asked. "I said, 'I've spent my whole life in Michigan, and if I sit on the bench here, if I'm not good enough, but you're going to pay for me to come to this school, then I'm in.'"

Messner committed to the Bruins but never consulted with his mom and dad. He had to come back home after the visit and discuss the decision he just made with his parents. Before the recruiting visits happened and well before his recruitment ever picked up, Messner's stepfather had been diagnosed with cancer. The two were very close, and the relationship meant a lot to Messner, which is part of why most of the schools he was interested in were close to home. He wanted Del to have the chance to see him play, and because the games weren't broadcast on television nearly as much as they are now, it wasn't guaranteed that would be the case for UCLA.

But UCLA just felt different and felt right at the time. Messner thought he could deal with the distance and deal with being on his own in California. He flew back to Michigan and thought about how he would break the news to his parents, who were so close to him, that their son would be playing college football all the way across the country. His mother and father picked him up from the airport, and he told the two that he decided he would play for UCLA. His mother cried, and his dad smiled because he understood that this was a dream, and his son had the chance to fulfill something special. "He had never been to California. So the beaches, the bikinis, he came home thinking, *I'm a UCLA man*," Sharon said. "It's beautiful out there. The winters aren't like Michigan. I told him this is your choice completely, and you're so lucky to have this opportunity so you need to do what you need to do."

The three packed into their car and made their way home. As the drive began, the family thought Messner's recruitment was over but found out shortly that it had only just begun. As they made their way back to their house, they noticed a car, a Delta, parked in the driveway.

Messner, his mother, and father pulled in the driveway, got out of the car, and two doors opened from the idled Delta. It was Schembechler and assistant Gary Moeller. "Coach Moeller gets out of the driver side, and Bo gets out of the passenger side. They walk to our car, and Bo hands me a VHS tape and said, 'You're a Michigan Man. You belong at the University of Michigan,'" Messner said. "He hands me the tape. They both get back in the car and they leave. That was the extent of their visit with me after getting home from the airport—just the face-to-face, him walking up with that voice. *Holy Crap! Why are you in my driveway, and how did you know I'd be here?*"

Stunned at what had just happened, Messner and his parents went inside to relax and settle in for the night. Sharon told her son that there were robins and eagles in this world. When eagles grow and get to adulthood, they take off and make their life wherever. A robin stays close to home and nests around the area. So she told her son he had to decide if he was a robin or an eagle.

Messner didn't watch the tape, which was a Michigan hype video showcasing bowl games and well-known Michigan players, but that night he laid in his bed until one or two in the morning, thinking about the decision he had made. His father was fighting to get his cancer in remission and, not wanting to try chemotherapy, he was using experimental treatment to try and beat it. He thought about that visit from Schembechler, and in true Bo fashion, little was actually spoken, but it made such a big impact on Messner. He started to think about Michigan being in his backyard, that his mother and father could see him play every home game, and it hit him as hard as he hit opposing players: Schembechler was right. Mark Messner was a Michigan Man.

"I did what any 18-year-old in my shoes would do, and that's dial the phone in the middle of the night—to ensure there would be no coaches in that coaching facility at UCLA—to leave a voicemail," Messner said. "I called to explain to Coach Donahue why I was reneging on my commitment, and because it was my dad, suffering from cancer, and he loved to see me play. I wanted to stay home, giving him as many opportunities to go to games that I'm playing in."

Donahue called Messner back the next day and was supportive of the decision and understanding in the reasoning. He wished Messner's father well and hung up the phone. Beyond the glitz and glamour, Messner committed to Michigan that day and finally knew that he had found his future home.

Messner went into his parents' bedroom, crawled into their bed, told them he called all the schools, and that he was going to be a Wolverine. His mother sat up and said, "I thought they were the Bruins." He looked at his mother and told her he was a robin and that he would be attending the University of Michigan. His mother cried again, and his father smiled again—for completely different reasons this time. They knew they would get to see their son play football, and the family would stay close. "My heart was racing. I was just so delighted because if he had gone to UCLA, it would have been like losing him," Sharon said. "You don't get those games on TV, so we wouldn't have been watching him. His going to Michigan kept us a part of his life. It was a real joy."

Now, finally, his recruitment was over. After traveling all over the country to Boston, Indiana, and California, Messner realized that home is where the heart is and would spend the next five years as a Wolverine. He was a humble person and never wanted any real fanfare with his recruitment, so he signed his paperwork, put a stamp on it, and mailed it back to Michigan. It was so uneventful that Messner himself doesn't truly remember what happened.

Messner redshirted his freshman season in 1984 at Michigan. Schembechler never promised playing time, and it had to be earned. Messner already felt as though he wasn't good enough to play at Michigan, and those concerns intensified after seeing how big some of his new teammates were. "That was the year I questioned if I made the right decision. We were 6–6 and lost in the Holiday Bowl to the national champions, BYU," he said. "Spring ball was hell. I couldn't wait for the regular season because Jumbo Elliott was making my life hell."

Messner stuck with it, though, and played in the 1985 season, recording 71 total tackles and 11 sacks on the year. He acclimated himself well for a small-town kid who thought he was too undersized and not good enough to compete at that level. Messner helped the Wolverines to a 10–1 record, beating Nebraska 27–23 in the Fiesta Bowl. He earned All-Conference honors that season, along with defensive tackle Mike Hammerstein, defensive back Brad Cochran, and linebacker Mike Mallory. But maybe more importantly, his parents were in the crowd at the home games and got to see every play that Messner made. "I think so much of it is fate. I don't know if I had gone into the UCLA program with their style of defense that it would've meshed the way Michigan did with smaller, more agile linemen," Messner said. "I could use my intelligence and quickness, not my brawn, and they needed that at Michigan early. UCLA may never have needed that. They might have said we want you to be a linebacker, and I may never have had the right time to present itself."

Messner finished his career at Michigan with 36 total sacks, 70 tackles for loss, and 281 total tackles. In the 1989 NFL Draft, the

Los Angeles Rams selected Mark Messner in the sixth round, and after five years, Messner finally made his way to play football in Los Angeles. His stepfather was able to see his first NFL game against the Atlanta Falcons, but that would be the last time Messner would see his father healthy and alive. Del Pretty died of cancer in the middle of Messner's rookie season. Then, even more so than before, he knew that his decision to stay home and play in Ann Arbor was the right choice. Del made it through his entire college football career and had the opportunity to be a part of it all before passing on. Messner's NFL career was cut short after tearing his ACL in 1990. After the knee injury, he retired from football and now resides in Tampa, Florida, where he is a vice president of a business solutions company.

DEPARTMENT OF INTERCOLLEGIATE ATHLETICS
University of California, Los Angeles
405 Hilgard Avenue • Los Angeles, California 90024
(213) 825-3236 or 825-3326

May 2, 1983

Dear Mark:

At this time I am sure you are giving very serious thought to
your academic and athletic future. We here at UCLA understand
that concern and want to help you in every possible way. You
owe it to yourself to fully investigate how UCLA can help you
achieve your personal ambitions. You will find that our interest in your individual development goes far beyond the playing
field. We want to help you reach your full potential in every
possible area.

UCLA has a rich tradition of excellence in both academics and
athletics. An education at UCLA means that you will graduate
from one of the top ten schools in the entire country. Your
academic goals can be completely met at our University. The
atmosphere at our school is unique, and there is a very special
warmth that comes from growing and learning in our program.
Our campus, located in an exclusive suburb of Los Angeles, called
Westwood, is surrounded by both Beverly Hills and Bel Air. The
Pacific Ocean lies only five miles to our west, and our average
temperature is 72°. It is undoubtedly one of the most beautiful
and attractive campuses in the country.

Over the past 18 years, UCLA athletic teams have claimed 35
NCAA championships. This statistic is unparalleled in intercollegiate athletics. Under Terry Donahue, one of the youngest
and most dynamic head coaches in major college football, the
Bruins will be one of the top teams in both the Pacific-10
Conference and in the country year in and year out. The UCLA
roster is comprised of some of the most outstanding players on
the West Coast and throughout the United States.

Please complete the enclosed questionnaire so that we may get to
know you better. We want to gather all pertinent information
about you so we are better able to meet your goals, both academically and athletically.

My best wishes to you, and I trust that this will be a winning
year for you in every way. If I can be of any assistance to you,
please do not hesitate to call upon me.

Sincerely,

Bill Rees
Recruiting Coordinator

enclosure

University of Notre Dame
Notre Dame, Indiana 46556

Gerry Faust
Head Football Coach

May 3, 1983

Mr. Mark Messner
c/o Coach Thomas Mach
Catholic Central High School
14200 Breakfast Drive
Redford, MI 48239

Dear Mark:

We at the University of Notre Dame are very interested in
you as a possible student athlete for our football program.
We would like to find out more about you and your interests.

Enclosed are two questionnaires for you and your coach to
complete and return to me. These will enable us to begin
compiling information about you. If you feel your interest
in Notre Dame to be genuine and sincere, I urge you to
return these as quickly as possible.

Our format of evaluation is based on several items: grades,
overall transcript, playing film, personal interviews, etc.
Primarily it all begins with these questionnaires.

Please request your high school coach to send a film of your
play along with the blue questionnaire he will fill out. Be
sure the jersey color and number are indicated. I assure
you, the film will be returned to your coach without delay.

Looking forward to hearing from you in the very near future.

Yours in Notre Dame,

TOM LICHTENBERG
RECRUITING COORDINATOR

TL:gd

Enclosure

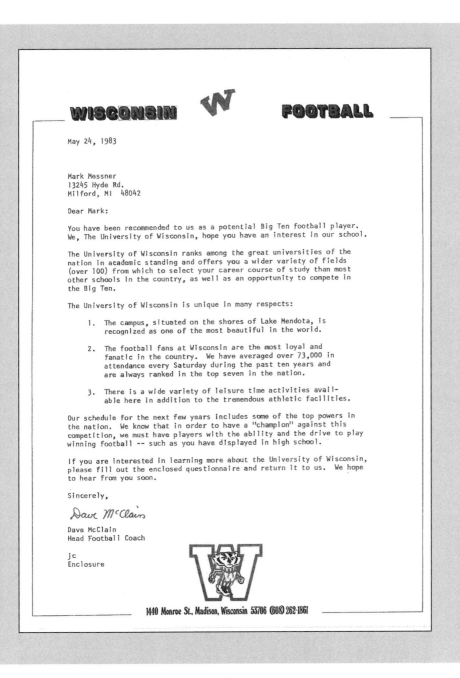

WISCONSIN W **FOOTBALL**

May 24, 1983

Mark Messner
13245 Hyde Rd.
Milford, MI 48042

Dear Mark:

You have been recommended to us as a potential Big Ten football player.
We, The University of Wisconsin, hope you have an interest in our school.

The University of Wisconsin ranks among the great universities of the
nation in academic standing and offers you a wider variety of fields
(over 100) from which to select your career course of study than most
other schools in the country, as well as an opportunity to compete in
the Big Ten.

The University of Wisconsin is unique in many respects:

1. The campus, situated on the shores of Lake Mendota, is
recognized as one of the most beautiful in the world.

2. The football fans at Wisconsin are the most loyal and
fanatic in the country. We have averaged over 73,000 in
attendance every Saturday during the past ten years and
are always ranked in the top seven in the nation.

3. There is a wide variety of leisure time activities available here in addition to the tremendous athletic facilities.

Our schedule for the next few years includes some of the top powers in
the nation. We know that in order to have a "champion" against this
competition, we must have players with the ability and the drive to play
winning football -- such as you have displayed in high school.

If you are interested in learning more about the University of Wisconsin,
please fill out the enclosed questionnaire and return it to us. We hope
to hear from you soon.

Sincerely,

Dave McClain

Dave McClain
Head Football Coach

jc
Enclosure

1440 Monroe St., Madison, Wisconsin 53706 (608) 262-1861

WESTERN MICHIGAN UNIVERSITY

DIVISION OF INTERCOLLEGIATE ATHLETICS

KALAMAZOO, MICHIGAN 49008

BRONCOS

May 27, 1983

Mark Messner
c/o Coach Tom Mach
Detroit Catholic Central
14200 Breakfast Drive
Redford, MI 48239

Dear Mark:

Your coach has recommended you as a prospect for our football program at Western Michigan University. We would appreciate it if you would complete the enclosed card and return it at your earliest convenience.

Western Michigan has a great reputation academically as well as athletically. Several of our academic departments are rated the best in the entire Midwest. The football team has had one of the best records in the Mid-American Conference over the past ten years.

We will start to evaluate all our prospects this spring and will continue throughout the fall. In this evaluation process, we look at your improvement in the classroom as well as on the athletic field. It is important for you to give your best effort in both areas.

Best wishes for continued success!

Sincerely,

Jack Harbaugh

Jack Harbaugh
Head Football Coach

Enclosures

MEMBER
MID-AMERICAN
CONFERENCE

AREA CODE 616
383-1930

THE UNIVERSITY OF MICHIGAN **Football**
DEPARTMENT

1000 South State Street, Ann Arbor, Michigan 48109   **Bo Schembechler**, Head Coach
Phone: (313) 663-2411/763-4443

MICHIGAN STADIUM (101,701 Capacity)

June 7, 1983

Mark Messner
c/o Head Football Coach
Catholic Central
14200 Breakfast Dr
Redford, MI 48239

Dear Mark,

Your performance on the athletic field and in the classroom has
impressed my University of Michigan football staff. We will be
following your progress in your senior year both on the football
field and in the classroom. Work hard and the fruits of your
efforts will be most rewarding.

Selecting a school to continue your education and play football
can be a difficult and confusing ordeal for some, and yet - is an
extremely rewarding experience for others. Largely, it depends
upon whether or not a young man knows what he is looking for in a
school. During the next few months my staff and I will be
sending you literature on all phases of The University of
Michigan. I hope that you and your parents will take time to
look over this valuable and interesting material.

There will be two ideal opportunities for you to personally look
at The University of Michigan. We will hold our Nationally
recognized and attended football camp July 5-10 and then, we will
hold an "Open House" on July 30. You will receive more
information on each of these in the future. Both events provide
an excellent opportunity for you to evaluate our university in a
very informal manner. Should you wish to visit Ann Arbor any
other time please give us a call.

My Recruiting Coordinator is Fritz Seyferth. Don't hesitate to
give Fritz a call anytime you have a question about Michigan or
the recruiting process in general.

Congratulations on your fine achievements thus far. Work hard to
have a great senior year both on the football field and in the
classroom. We, at Michigan will follow your progress with great
interest and are looking forward to getting to know you better.

Sincerely,

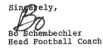

Bo Schembechler
Head Football Coach

BS:dlm
103 Years • 31 Big Ten Championships • 82 All Americans • 11 Rose Bowls • 640 Victories

INDIANA UNIVERSITY
FOOTBALL
Assembly Hall
Bloomington, Indiana 47405
812/335-9618

June 29, 1983

Mr. Mark Messner
13245 Hyde Rd.
Milford, MI   48042

Dear Mark,

I just wanted to write you a short note to reiterate what I said last week. It is extremely important that you prepare harder than you ever have before to make this your most outstanding season.

To help you in your preparation I have enclosed the work-out book that we send to all of our current players. We believe that it is the best way to ensure that you will be in great shape for football. I encourage you to "hit" the weights hard and run faster and farther that any other summer in your life.

If we can answer any questions you might have please contact us. Good luck this summer.

Sincerely,

Sam Wyche
Head Football Coach

SW:bt
Enclosure

UNIVERSITY OF NOTRE DAME

Football Office

GERRY FAUST
Head Football Coach

June 29, 1983

Mr. Mark Messner
13245 Hyde Road
Milford, MI 48092

Dear Mark:

I hope that you are having an enjoyable summer and that you are keeping yourself mentally and physically ready for the coming season. As a senior you have a great responsibility for the success of your football team.

I am mailing to you under seperate cover two Notre Dame posters, one is our schedule poster and one depicts the Notre Dame football tradition. We hope that you will find a place for our posters in your room or den and refer to our schedule during the season.

Enclosed you will also find the spring issues of Inside Irish. They give a good account of spring practice and a capsule evaluation of next Fall's returning personnel. I hope you find the articles pertaining to the other athletic interests on campus informative.

If you have any questions, please feel free to contact me.

Yours in Notre Dame,

Tom Lichtenberg

TOM LICHTENBERG
ASSISTANT FOOTBALL COACH AND
RECRUITING COORDINATOR

TL:gd

Enclosure

ATHLETIC AND CONVOCATION CENTER • P.O. BOX 518, NOTRE DAME, IN 46556

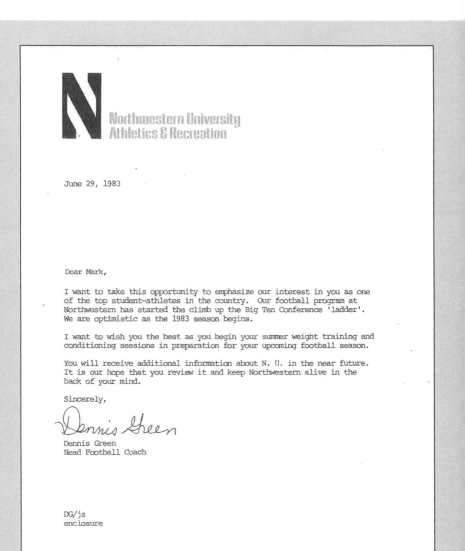

Northwestern University
Athletics & Recreation

June 29, 1983

Dear Mark,

I want to take this opportunity to emphasize our interest in you as one
of the top student-athletes in the country. Our football program at
Northwestern has started the climb up the Big Ten Conference 'ladder'.
We are optimistic as the 1983 season begins.

I want to wish you the best as you begin your summer weight training and
conditioning sessions in preparation for your upcoming football season.

You will receive additional information about N. U. in the near future.
It is our hope that you review it and keep Northwestern alive in the
back of your mind.

Sincerely,

Dennis Green
Head Football Coach

DG/js
enclosure

Dennis Green, Head Football Coach

1501 Central Street   Evanston IL 60201
312 · 492 7274

THE UNIVERSITY OF MICHIGAN

M

DEPARTMENT

1000 South State Street, Ann Arbor, Michigan 48109   Bo Schembechler, Head Coach
Phone: (313) 663-2411/763-4443

MICHIGAN STADIUM (101,701 Capacity)

July 6, 1983

Mark Messner
c/o Head Football Coach
Catholic Central
14200 Breakfast Dr
Redford, MI 48239

Dear Mark,

     I trust your summer is going well and that you are looking forward to your senior year. We are all trying to rap things up so we can get some vacation in before our meetings begin to prepare for our 1983 season.

     I want to send on to you the enclosed brochure that covers all aspects of The University of Michigan and our football program. Take your time to read through it carefully and share it with your parents. I think you will find the facts most interesting.

     Enjoy your summer and call if we can answer any questions for you.

Best Wishes,

Bo Schembechler
Head Football Coach

BS:dlm

P.S.   Please note error on the Open-House mailing it will be
       held on July 30, 1983.

103 Years   •   31 Big Ten Championships   •   82 All Americans   •   11 Rose Bowls   •   640 Victories

UNIVERSITY OF NOTRE DAME

Football Office

GERRY FAUST
Head Football Coach

J.M.J.

July 6, 1983

Mr. Mark Messner
13245 Hyde Road
Milford, MI 48092

Dear Mark:

I would like to express again our interest in you as a prospective student athlete for the University of Notre Dame. We are pleased that you are interested in our fine University and I hope that I can reinforce your interest over the next few months.

Notre Dame can offer you a very unique opportunity: a combination of one of our nation's finest academic institutions and traditionally, the top football program in the country.

Enclosed you will find a copy of IRISH EYE, which is a review of the 1982 Notre Dame football season, and a copy of the 1983 Spring Football Prospectus. We hope you find them both interesting.

God bless you always.

Yours in Notre Dame,

GERRY FAUST

gd

Enclosure

ATHLETIC AND CONVOCATION CENTER • P.O. BOX 518, NOTRE DAME, IN 46556

THE UNIVERSITY OF MICHIGAN **Football**
DEPARTMENT

1000 South State Street, Ann Arbor, Michigan 48109   Bo Schembechler, Head Coach
Phone: (313) 663-2411/763-4443

MICHIGAN STADIUM (101,701 Capacity)

July 11, 1982

Mark Messner
c/o Head Football Coach
Catholic Central
14200 Breakfast Dr
Redford, MI 48239

Dear Mark,

You are about to embark on perhaps the most exciting, demanding, and most important six months of your life. The decision you make in the next six months will determine the school you will attend and play for the next four years, as well as, the school that will be a part of you for life.

"The school to attend" is a big decision and one that deserves much consideration. I have enclosed a decision matrix that should aid you in evolution of each school against several key points you should be looking for in a school.

Determine what the school you are going to attend <u>must have.</u> Then eliminate those that don't meet <u>your musts</u> and compare the remaining schools by what <u>you want</u> your school to have. This is a decision process used by managers of some of the most successful corporations in the world in evaluating alternatives. You can begin using it now with the enclosed decision matrix.

The next six months are going to be fun for you and your family if you take time to determine what it is in a school 1)<u>you must have</u> and then 2) comparing what <u>you want</u> in a school.

Seek answers and be informed in making your evaluations. Don't hesitate to call me <u>collect</u> anytime you have a question. I'll be happy to talk with you.

Read the enclosed carefully. The sooner you start, the more objective your criteria will be. Work towards completing it over and the next six months with the aid of your parents and it will be a great help in your decision process.

Sincerely,

Fritz Seyferth
Coordinator, Athletic
Recruiting

103 Years • 31 Big Ten Championships • 82 All Americans • 11 Rose Bowls • 640 Victories

INDIANA UNIVERSITY
FOOTBALL
Assembly Hall
Bloomington, Indiana 47405
812/335-9618

July 30, 1983

Mr. Mark Messner
13245 Hyde Rd.
Milford, MI   48042

Dear Mark,

T e football season is drawing near and in less than three weeks we will begin practice for the 1983 season at Indiana. If you are facing the fall with the same excitement as the Hoosiers, 1983 will be a great one for you.

We hope that you enjoy the poster we have enclosed. The new look of Indiana football is evident with our new uniforms, as well as in other areas. I can assure you that you will have the best in every way at Indiana, as we are totally committed to excellence. T is excellence includes improvements in every facet of our football program from facilities and equipment to academics.

We have fewer than 30 scholarships available so we are looking only at the best athletes in the country. We trust that you will work hard to be included in that select group. Also, we hope that you maintain a strong interest in Indiana football. We will continue to evaluate you and keep a close watch on your final high school season.

Indiana is building for a championship program, and we won't settle for anything less. Continue to work on your physical characteristics as well as the mental aspects of football in order for you to reach your full potential.

Again, enjoy the poster and if we can be of help, let us know.

Sincerely,

Sam Wyche
Head Football Coach

SW:bt

UNIVERSITY OF NOTRE DAME

Football Office

GERRY FAUST
Head Football Coach

J.M.J.

August 1, 1983

Mr. Mark Messner
13245 Hyde Road
Milford, MI 48092

Dear Mark:

We would like to wish you the very best in your football
endeavors during your senior year of high school.

Being a former high school football coach, I know that the
senior year is one that you will always remember -- so give
your very best, and have a great year.

We at Notre Dame feel that you are the type of student- athlete
we would like to recruit. We will not be bothering you during
your football season for we believe your concentration should
be completely on the goals you want to achieve for your high
school.

So remember, this does not mean that we are not interested in
you. As a matter of fact, we are very interested in you, and
we will be getting in touch with you again in December or early
January.

If you have any questions concerning Notre Dame football or
scholastic requirements before you hear from us, please contact
Coach Mike Stock, our new Recruiting Coordinator, by calling
collect 219/239-5476.

Best of luck to you for an outstanding football season, and may
God bless you and your family always.

Yours in Notre Dame,

GERRY FAUST

gd

CHAPTER 5

Tripp Welborne

Tripp Welborne was one of the most prolific safeties to play for Michigan and is still known today as one of the best to don the winged helmet. Versatile in his ability with athleticism to match most receivers to come his way, he was a strong presence in Michigan's secondary from 1987 to 1990. That's partially because Welborne was one of the top wide receiver prospects in the country out of high school and knew the position well. He went on to become a two-time All-American with the Wolverines as a safety, but there were two schools and a different sport that nearly stole him away from Michigan football during his recruitment.

Sullivan Anthony Welborne III and his brother, Keith, grew up in Reidsville, North Carolina, where they were widely known as some of the best athletes in the area. Their school, Walter Hines Page Senior High, regularly put out excellent baseball, football, and basketball teams, all of which Tripp played on during his time at Page.

Two years older, Keith was a senior when Tripp was a sophomore. Todd Ellis was the quarterback for the football team and was highly regarded by college coaches. Ellis helped bring in coaches to practice, which almost always led to eyes on the Welborne brothers. The brothers were then ranked as the No. 1 and 2 wide receivers in the state, which was the first time such a tandem came from the same household. Tripp was nearly five inches taller than his older brother, who only stood at 5'6", 165 pounds, but Keith was quick and could take a five-yard pass and turn it into a 50-yard gain. "Everything I would catch was 50 or 60 yards down the field because it was all bombs," Tripp said. "They would say, 'Wow, that guy is just like this guy, except he's five inches taller,' because my brother was shorter. Oddly enough, he was the No. 1 receiver in the state, and I was No. 2, and he still reminds me of that all the time."

Because of Ellis, the Welborne brothers, and other teammates, Clemson, North Carolina, N.C. State, Wake Forest, and South Carolina were just some of the schools that regularly made their way to the Welbornes' high school to scout the players. While those schools were coming by the school and regularly sending mail, Tripp's high school coach, Marion Kirby, often kept the recruiting letters in a box in his office. Every now and then he would let some of the players know which schools were watching them, but he tried to keep everyone level-headed by keeping much of the recruiting process out of their everyday thoughts. So little did Tripp know, the letters were piling up by the dozen.

Kirby was an old-school coach that came to Page in 1973, and his teams won the state title in 1980, 1983, 1984, and 1985. At one point in the 1980s, Kirby's teams won 46 consecutive games, earning national prominence during that stretch. Keith was a big part of those teams and eventually went on to play at N.C. State, leaving Tripp as the lone Welborne at Page.

Since he grew up in hoops crazy North Carolina, basketball was actually his first love and the sport he thought he would end up playing in college. A lot of coaches said he would have the opportunity to play both basketball and football, though some of that was veiled in the fact that they just wanted to get him on the football field. Heading into his senior season in 1986, Tripp was ranked as the No. 1 wide receiver and No. 1 defensive back in football as well as the No. 1 guard in basketball in the state of North Carolina. The football scholarship offers started to roll in. But Tripp still wasn't sure if he wanted to play basketball or football despite the plethora of colleges offering him an opportunity in football. "At the time I did have offers in basketball but not near as many as football," he said. "The problem was that all the schools that offered for basketball also wanted me to play football. So football was really the drive, I believe...The football program at North Carolina, at the time, was horrific. I was struggling because I really wanted to go play basketball there, but [with] football I had more opportunities. So I got to see more schools and think about more options."

There were so many football scholarship offers that Tripp can't remember them all. And when his high school coach finally revealed the number of letters and mail he had received over the past year, he was overwhelmed. Tripp recalled nearly 200 letters from colleges all over the country being dumped in front of him. With Tripp wide-eyed and not knowing where to start, his high school coach told his star pupil that he needed to focus on narrowing his list down to a top 20. Once he narrowed it to 20, he could then find the 10 that he could really see himself at. "That was done in one day because I basically already knew what kind of school I wanted to go to," Tripp said. "That was during my senior year during football season, and then I narrowed it down to five during basketball season. I actually made it to six because I included North Carolina, but I didn't need to take an official visit to Carolina."

He narrowed the list to five because high school football recruits are allowed to take five official visits, which are recruiting trips where the university pays for travel and accommodations for the prospect. Since North Carolina was so close and he had already seen plenty of the school, he didn't need to use an official visit on the Tar Heels. His brother was at N.C. State, so he was already going to those football games and didn't want to use the in-state schools on official visits.

So he narrowed it down to Alabama, Florida State, UCLA, Michigan, and South Carolina as the programs that would get his official visits. His old quarterback, Ellis, was at South Carolina and told his coaches that Tripp would visit. Tripp is a loyal man, so he wanted to honor that request and visit South Carolina for his old teammate. "I wanted at least one basketball school in there, and that was UCLA. They had a great basketball program and football—because Troy Aikman had just transferred in, so I knew they would have a fantastic quarterback," Tripp said. "My strategy was also: when I narrowed it down, I narrowed it by geographic location. I'm going to pick a school in each region that I felt like was one I could see myself at and then go to those schools."

Tripp narrowed his list down to five during basketball season, and his official visits started in December of 1986. Before the visits, though, college coaches were regularly coming by his school to watch him play basketball and get any face time they could. That included Michigan head coach Bo Schembechler, who always liked multi-sport stars like Tripp. "I would notice him in the stands. And it was funny when I talked to him the first time. He looked at me," Welborne said. "He told me, 'I watch you playing basketball, and you shoot too much.' I thought to myself, *I like this guy*. I said, *If he's trying to recruit me, that's the exact opposite of any other coach*. Every other coach is telling me how great I am and everything, and he just wanted to say that I shoot too much. I thought that was great."

The odd way of recruiting him and Schembechler's personality hit home for Tripp as it was somewhat similar to how his high school coach kept all his recruiting letters. Trying to prevent him from getting an ego or thinking he was better than anyone else, both coaches would prefer toughness to someone who thought they could come in right away and make a splash without putting in the work. Despite his interest in Schembechler's style, though, Michigan just was not as appealing yet to Tripp as some of his other options.

Florida State had legendary head coach Bobby Bowden and was on the verge of putting together a dominating program. Tripp was fond of Bowden and was also keen on an emerging star for the Seminoles in Deion Sanders. He saw a little bit of himself in Sanders, who did a little bit of everything. Sanders played defense, offense, special teams and played baseball and basketball in high school. Chuck Amato recruited the state of North Carolina for Florida State at the time and knew that Tripp would relate to Sanders. He and the rest of the Florida State staff weren't shy about using Sanders to their advantage. "Deion was special, and we had a lot of great players," Amato said. "For us to go to North

Carolina—with all the speed we had in Florida—to recruit a skill player, we were very interested in him. If he wasn't that dynamic, we weren't going to go up there, but he was."

Amato recalled that he went all out for prospects he truly wanted, and Tripp was a target he went after as hard as he could. He felt as though Florida State had a chance, but for some reason, he always felt that he was a little behind in the race. "I knew some other schools were there, but I never understood why Michigan was," Amato said. "Do you like cold weather? Well, we ain't got it. Do you like warm weather? We have it. Do you like to walk to class in the winter time and see people and all you can see is their face? You walk to class in winter time in Tallahassee, and you see girls walking across campus in bikinis. I mean, what the heck do you need?" Amato would later find out, though, that Tripp was about much more than girls or weather.

Tripp took his visit to Alabama but knew he wouldn't end up choosing the Tide. He had an old teammate who played for Alabama, but the Tide didn't have the combination of academics and athletics he was looking for. So he knew almost immediately that it wouldn't be a school in the final running.

The third visit was to Florida State, and on the visit, Amato and Bowden paired him up with Sanders as his player host for the weekend trip. It was close enough to home that Tripp felt comfortable and knew his parents would be able to visit for games. Having Sanders there to take him around campus made him feel that much more comfortable. "I'm not going to say I verbally committed, but I pretty much said I'm coming," he said. "Tallahassee was good, and I was like, I'm there."

And he likely would have been there had it not been for one problem. His father, Dr. Sullivan A. Welborne Jr., worked in academia, and both parents stressed the importance of an education. Tripp was mature for his age and enjoyed learning and knew that he wanted to study engineering in college, which Florida State was lacking. "They did not have an accredited engineering program. They were doing a joint co-op with Florida A&M," Tripp said. "Because they didn't have a heavy interest in math and science, I started to shy away from Florida State, and that was the only reason."

Florida State was out, Alabama was out, and South Carolina was seemingly a kind gesture to a former teammate. So it was down to UCLA and Michigan, schools both highly regarded for academics and football, and it would come down to where he felt most comfortable.

His parents didn't travel to any of the previous trips. But on his visit to UCLA, his parents decided to make the trip, not wanting to miss out on a trip to Los Angeles. Because UCLA had also offered for basketball, Tripp had two player hosts on this visit. One was Greg Foster, a center on the basketball team, and the other was Roman Phifer, a linebacker on the football team. "When I went out to California, my parents went, and the first thing we wanted to do was we wanted them to take us to *The Beverly Hillbillies* house," Welborne said. "It's not nearly as big as it is on TV, but it was pretty cool. After that, I split up from my parents and I didn't see them for the rest of the weekend."

His parents were escorted around campus by the coaches for the remainder of the weekend, while Tripp made his way around with his player hosts. He also spent time with the coaches, discussing the program and the university and what they had to offer. One of those coaches was his area recruiter, Greg Robinson, who was the defensive line coach for UCLA at the time. "I can tell you that he was a very gifted athlete. And on top of that, like a lot of the guys we recruited at UCLA, we didn't go all the way across the country to get a guy who couldn't handle the academic world," Robinson said. "He was a bright guy, good sense of humor, but not a flashy guy. I knew it would be very competitive because he had everybody talking to him, but I tried to paint a picture for him that he's comfortable with."

The UCLA coaching staff knew that the Welborne family prioritized academics and made sure to emphasize how well-regarded UCLA was academically. The staff used every positive the Bruins had to offer to try to convince the family that this was the right place for the youngest Welborne. Robinson felt good about the Bruins' chances because of the relationship he had built with the family, how well the school fit with Tripp's personality, and what Tripp was telling the coaches. "I told the staff that I'm here for sure, and they already had my jersey hanging up with my name on the back. They gave me the No. 4. That was my brother's number in high school, so that was cool," Tripp said. "The conversation wasn't I am committing. This is a verbal commitment. It was: I can see myself here, I think I'm coming, but there was still recruiting going on and no announcement yet."

He wasn't quite ready to make anything official as he still had one more visit left—to the University of Michigan. He didn't know much about the Wolverines, so Tripp wanted to take the visit to make sure he gave every school a fair shot. He was set to visit in the middle of January in 1987. Coming from mild-weathered North Carolina, Tripp was about to set foot in a Michigan winter. The biggest jacket he had was a light leather jacket, which was not sufficient.

He went to the mandatory activities throughout the visit, touring the facilities, meeting with the coaches and players, and learning about the university, but when there wasn't a mandatory event, Tripp found himself back in his hotel room because it was so cold on the trip. That blistering cold initially turned him off—even while he was on the visit.

What seemed like a negative, though, quickly turned into a positive for the Wolverines as Tripp didn't have much to do in his hotel room. He decided to dive in to the pamphlets and reading materials the Michigan staff left in his room, all detailing what the University of Michigan had to offer. "As a high schooler, what I knew about Michigan was that they had a good athletic program, it was a great academic school, and they have an iconic coach," Tripp said. "I knew they were on TV, I knew Anthony Carter with the No. 1, and they had a good running back in No. 23, which was Jamie Morris. Once I started learning more and more, reading the material, I started to realize how robust a university it was. I was reading everything they had, talking about the campus, the legacy. Throughout that experience, I actually learned much more about Michigan than any other school."

As a teenager, Tripp was fond of learning and research, so the time spent in the hotel was well worth it. It helped Michigan's chances and certainly gave him more information about what the university had to offer him. What he had learned through the pamphlets and Schembechler's personality were starting to ring true for Tripp. He always had interesting conversations with Schembechler and he always felt as though the legendary Michigan coach was different from the other coaches recruiting him. "Bo said, 'We have a lot of great players that have come to Michigan and we're a championship team. If you work hard, too, you're a fantastic player, but if you work hard, maybe by your junior year, you'll be on the field and a contributor to our team,'" Tripp said. "I'm looking at him thinking, *Did he just say by my junior year? Has Bo even read my press clippings? I'm planning on going and wrecking shop right now.* But he was the only coach that ever said that. Every other coach said you can play whatever position you want, you'll play right away, you'll be great."

Tripp loved a good challenge, and that's what he felt Schembechler was doing. Schembechler wasn't the only coach who helped Michigan in Tripp's recruitment, though. The Wolverines had another ace up their sleeve in defensive line coach Tom Reed, who was previously the head coach at N.C. State. Reed recruited Tripp's older brother, Keith, while at N.C. State and had already established an excellent relationship with the family. Because of that prior relationship, the family trusted Reed and confided in him to help guide Tripp as he did for Keith at N.C. State.

Before he left Michigan, Tripp got the chance to take a tour of Michigan Stadium, The Big House. He had seen it on television and heard about its enormous size and capacity, holding more than 100,000 people, but he had never seen it in person. It had recently snowed, so the field and seats were covered in snow, giving the stadium a unique look. But once again, the cold and snow provided a surprising perspective that left a mark on Tripp. "Everything was covered in snow except for one thing. Somebody had walked out to the field, and you saw some footprints coming from the tunnel," Tripp said. "A pair of feet going out, walked around the block M with their feet, and then walked back. I thought, *Wow, all this snow and they still did that.* Michigan's brand is so much bigger that nothing can overshadow it, nothing can take the place of it in people's hearts, and I felt that."

Getting closer and closer to Signing Day in February, Tripp went back home—still torn and undecided. Michigan had made a good impression, but the shock of the weather was still weighing on him and was weighing heavier than any positives that Michigan showed him on the trip. "I had a great time, but leaving the visit, people would ask if I knew where I was going and I would say, 'I don't know, but I know where I'm not going, and that would be Michigan because it's too cold,'" Tripp said. "That's all I was think-ing at first because it was a shock. But after that every day it became more apparent that Michigan, athletically and academically, pre-sented opportunities that the other schools did not. Michigan started to move up."

As Tripp contemplated his options, Florida State was out because the school didn't have the proper engineering school, and now the Wolverines were starting to move past UCLA. Tripp reflected on his time in California when he visited the Bruins and he started to realize that maybe he had too good of a time on campus. He felt as though he would want to get involved with the movies and what Los Angeles had to offer and wouldn't be focused on his academics, which was his main goal.

Schembechler's personality came back into play as well because Tripp felt comfortable with his style and approach. Schembechler reminded him of his father and high school coach, and it was refreshing. Even on an in-home visit where Schembechler came to the Welborne household, he impressed by being unorthodox and going against the grain. "Growing up, we never heard curse words because we grew up in a strict family. So Bo comes in and Bo is sitting there, and his normal talk is cursing," Tripp said. "My mom almost had a fit. My dad went by Sticky, so she said, 'Sticky come in the other room.' She said, 'He is cursing in my house, and there is no way we can send our son somewhere where he curses like that.' My dad looked at her and said, 'Be quiet, he's fine, our boy will be fine.' Bo didn't know that he was cursing in the Welborne household. He was real genuine, though, and that's what my parents loved about him: that he was real."

Despite his affinity for cursing and gruff demeanor, Schembechler won over the Welbornes as he did with so many of his other players and their families. Plus, Reed was still on staff and was likely what put it over the top for Michigan. His decision still wasn't made, though. He was still not 100 percent sure, and Signing Day was fast approaching. Many of his friends and people close to him believed he was headed to UCLA, and that included Robinson and Bruins head coach Terry Donahue. He wore UCLA-branded clothes in the last week before Signing Day because he figured—despite Michigan's best efforts—that he was likely going to be a Bruin.

His family sat down that night before Signing Day and talked through all of his options. His mother and father told him to come to a decision and sleep on it before letting any of the coaches know.

"As the night progressed, I kept thinking about where I would thrive best and I could just focus on my studies and play and enjoy myself. Michigan just continued to bubble up," Tripp said. "It was about the challenge, and because it was about the challenge, I felt as though that was the place for me because it was a precursor for what the school was going to do for me. It was going to push me and be better than what I could be. That's what tipped it. I'm a blue-collar guy. Deep down I'm a North Carolina boy, a country boy, hard worker and I grew up knowing how to go to work. So I felt as though L.A. might be a little too much flash and dash, and Michigan, to me, was just go to work."

He realized late at night—the night before his press conference to announce what school he was choosing—that Michigan was where he was supposed to be. His mother told him to sleep on it, though, so he did. Tripp woke up, and it was still Michigan. So the Wolverines would get the versatile athlete from Reidsville, North Carolina, and Tripp would need to upgrade his winter jacket. The decision was made, but now he needed to tell the coaches who would miss out.

Tripp called Robinson at UCLA before his press conference to tell him the bad news. He thanked Robinson for all the hard work and for his interest in him but told him that he was headed to the University of Michigan. "He would have been a darn good player for us. When he decided to go to Michigan, I was real disappointed, but in my own mind, I thought he made the choice," Robinson said. "I knew he would've done well at UCLA and when I think of it I don't think, *What a jerk for not picking us.* I think, what a good guy that I wish I could've coached at UCLA."

Tripp didn't call the coaches at Florida State because he figured they knew they were out of the race. He did call the coaches at Michigan, though, just before the press conference to tell them the good news. If Schembechler was excited on the phone call with his newest commitment, he didn't show it. He told Tripp he looked forward to getting to work and for the second time in his recruitment reminded him that there were a lot of great players in front of him and that it would take a lot of hard work to see the field at Michigan. "They had three receivers coming back—John Kolesar, Greg McMurtry, and Chris Calloway. My thought process was always: last year you played with three; this year you're going to have to play with four," Tripp said. "I'm going to make it so I have to be on the field. Either you're going to have me on the field, or someone is going to have to not play."

With a Michigan shirt underneath his sweater at his press conference, Tripp Welborne announced that he would play football for the University of Michigan. He never revealed the undershirt to the crowd, but after sporting UCLA and Florida State apparel up to this point, Tripp knew the last shirt he put on was the right shirt and the right choice for him.

He enrolled at the University of Michigan and almost immediately saw his athletic ability cause confusion as to what position he should play as a Wolverine. Tripp still had Kolesar, McMurtry, and Calloway in front of him, and it was looking more and more like those three would stay ahead of him. In 12 games during his first season, Tripp caught two passes for 45 yards and no touchdowns. He played special teams, so he was already making tackles on kick and punt returns.

Michigan lost to in-state rival Michigan State 17–11 that season and threw seven interceptions in the game. Tripp believes he had four tackles in the game and joked that without quarterback Demetrius Brown throwing all those interceptions he never would have switched to defense. The coaches would not have discovered his tackling ability.

After that first season, the coaching staff decided to move Tripp to defense where he would start as a cornerback. "Bo said, 'We think that maybe you'll be good for us at corner, maybe you can do both. What do you think about that?' I said, 'Do I have a choice?'" Tripp said. "He said, 'Sure, what's your choice?' I said, 'I choose offense,' and Bo said, 'Great, I'm glad you told me that. That means a lot.' I show up to practice the next day and I have a defensive jersey in my locker. I was like, wait…we just had a conversation about this."

His first practice as a cornerback was a scrimmage in the spring of 1988. From playing receiver he had some idea of what he was supposed to do as a defensive back, but he didn't know any of the plays or technique. The coaches reassured him that they would tell him what to do and where to be, and it would work itself out. He sealed his fate as a defender in one play on the first day of practice as a defensive back.

The very first play, Brown called a streak on one side and a companion route that had a running back coming out of the backfield to run a route. Tripp might not have known the defensive plays, but he knew the offensive plays and knew where the receivers and the back were supposed to be. "I knew the call and I knew the reads, too. He's supposed to go through his progressions, so I'm sitting as a corner. I didn't backpedal much," Tripp said. "He goes through his progressions and then he turns and throws the ball to running back Jarrod Bunch. I'm standing there thinking to myself, *I know Demetrious is not about to throw the ball out here because Coach said a million times you have to read the corner and make sure he's not sitting."*

The ball came to Bunch, and Tripp didn't move because he was shocked that Brown was throwing his way. Had he moved or known what he was doing at corner, he could've intercepted the ball. Instead, the ball arrived in Bunch's hands, which he had to turn to grab. Bunch ran straight in the flat, and Tripp finally reacted—as if he were shot out of a cannon. "Jared takes one step, and I'm coming at him full throttle. I blow through him as nobody has done this spring because Bunch was a terror," Tripp said. "I didn't mean to do it and I probably couldn't do it again, but he turned, and I knocked him out. It was such a big collision, the ball went flying, and he was laid out on the ground."

All the defensive players ran out onto the field and dove on top of Tripp to celebrate his big hit and his initiation to the defense. Tripp claims it was a clean hit, though the offense jokingly declared him a traitor for leaving them to help the defense. The hit was so big that they replayed it several times the next day while watching film, and each time the defense would cheer.

Tripp was a cornerback until a week before the opening game of the season against Notre Dame. His roommate, Otis Williams, was slated to start at safety, but Williams had some issues throughout the week, and the coaches asked Tripp to slide over to safety for the game. David Key filled in at corner for Tripp, and Tripp never moved back from his new safety position after that game.

Tripp ended up recording 238 tackles and nine interceptions throughout his career at Michigan. He returned 67 punts for 773 yards, was a part of three Big Ten championship teams, and was a two-time consensus All-American at safety before being selected in the 1991 NFL Draft by the Minnesota Vikings. The talented defender fell to the seventh round after tearing his ACL his senior year at Michigan and saw his NFL career cut short by another ACL tear in his rookie season. He is now the athletic director at the Lawrenceville School in Lawrence Township, New Jersey.

UNIVERSITY OF MICHIGAN ATHLETIC QUESTIONNAIRE FooTBall   3/28/87
                                               sport   date

NAME Sullivan   AnThony   Welborne III   (Tripp)
     (First)   (Middle)   (Last)   (Nickname preferred)

WEIGHT 189   HEIGHT 6'1   DATE OF BIRTH 11/20/68   CLASS Freshman

WHERE BORN Reidsville, N.C.   HOMETOWN GReensboro, n.C.

HIGH SCHOOL Page High School

HOME ADDRESS ██████████   CITY GReensboro   STATE N.C. ZIP 27405

HOME PHONE ██████████   LOCAL PHONE SAME

LOCAL ADDRESS SAME

SCHOOL ENROLLED (LS&A, Engineering, etc.) Engineering   Major Industrial
                                                               Administrator
FATHER'S NAME Dr. Sullivan A. Welborne Jr. OCCUPATION University Professor COLLEGE A+T, UNG-G

MOTHER'S NAME Gloria D. Welbome   OCCUPATION Primary Teacher   COLLEGE WSSU

HIGH SCHOOL SPORTS YOU PLAYED FooTBall, BasKetBall, Baseball, Track

NO. VARSITY LETTER WON PER SPORT FooTBall (3), BasKetBall(3) Baseball (2)
Track (2)
HONORS WON, ATHLETIC (all-league, all-state, etc.) AND NON-ATHLETIC (Honor Society, etc.)
FooTBall MVP (1986)(1985)   FooTBall (1986 Parade-All American)
FooTBall Conference Player of The year (2), All-State OFFense+Defense) Shrine Bowl
BasKetBall -All Conference -Player of year(1)1986, All-State (1986) MVP (1985-86)
Mc Donald All American nominee - Eagle Scout (1987) Honor Student
NON-ATHLETIC ACTIVITIES, HOBBIES, INTERESTS
Scouting, Music, young LiFe ((hristian Organization) Tutoring + Volunteering

GREATEST SPORTS MEMORY 1985- STate FooTBall Championship

GOOD LUCK SUPERSTITION #Boot Towel (FooTBall)

RELATIVES IN ATHLETICS OR OTHER AREAS OF SPECIAL NOTE Hornsby Howell
Asst. ATHletic Director University of Georgia

CAREER PLANS To be successful in the field of Engineering

(Continued other side...)

PREVIOUS HIGH SCHOOL VARSITY ATHLETIC EXPERIENCE

YEAR	SPORT	POSITION	COACH	AVERAGES,STATS,RECORD, etc.
1984	FootBall	WR - DB	Kirby	47 catches - 950 yds 5 T.D's, 1 INT.
1985	FootBall	WR - SlotBack - DB	Kirby	28 " — 10 TD's, 9 INT
1986	FootBall	SlotBack - DB	Kirby	31 " — 12 T.D's, 9 int.
1984	BasKetBall	guard	Morris	11 pts per game
1985	BasKetBall	guard	Morris	15 pts per game
1986	BasKetBall	guard	Morris	18 pts per game
1985-87	Baseball	Centerfield	Mckeel	Most runs scored, Most Steals
1986-87	Track	Sprinter	Kirby	400 + mile relay (Regionals)

DESCRIBE ANY AWARDS, HONORS OR RECORDS YOU MAY HAVE ACHIEVED IN HIGH SCHOOL. LABEL EACH ITEM BY SPORT AND YEAR ATTAINED (For example: all-league, basketball - 1986; School record, 19 TD's - 1985; etc.)

FootBall 1984 - 47 catches - 5 T'D's - 950 yd

FootBall 1985 - Conference player of year 10 T.D's - 9 int. (Defense) MVP 28 catches Shrine Bowl

FootBall 1986 - Conference Player of year 12 T.D. 31 catches 9 int Defence All State Offense + Defense

BasKetBall 1985-86 - MVP - 15 pts per game , BasKetBall 1984-85 11 pts per game

BasKetBall 1986-87 - 18 pts per game - All State

FootBall 1986 - Parade All American ＊ 106 Catches (FootBall - School + State Record Career)

BasKetBall 1986-87 McDonalds Nominee

HOMETOWN NEWSPAPERS Greensboro, News And Record

I authorize use of the above information and related athletic material about myself by the Michigan Athletic Department and Board in Control of Intercollegiate Athletics.

Sullivan A. Welborne III
Signature

"Tripp"

CHAPTER 6

Desmond Howard

Desmond Howard was one of the most electric players to step foot in The Big House. As a receiver and return man, Howard racked up yards and touchdowns in a multitude of ways from 1989 to 1991. The Cleveland, Ohio, native finished his career with 2,146 receiving yards and 32 receiving touchdowns. He still holds the Michigan record for most receiving touchdowns in a season (19 in 1991). The next closest is Braylon Edwards, who caught 15 touchdowns in 2004. But Howard's recruitment came down to the final hours before Signing Day and almost went in a different direction than Michigan. There was some uncertainty and late drama that had an opposing coach sitting in Dayton, Ohio, hours away from Howard's home in Cleveland, waiting to see if he would be able to reel in the speedy athlete.

At St. Joseph High, which is now known as Villa Angela-St. Joseph High, Howard participated in track, basketball, and football and excelled at all three. The Catholic school had some good athletes, but Howard stood out among them all. He was naturally gifted in whatever sport he played and, while the 5'9" 170-pounder wasn't the biggest prospect, he made up for his lack of height with toughness, speed, and pure athletic ability.

He is the second youngest of four boys and, as much athleticism as he possesses, Howard said his brothers did not inherit the same genes. He was the only sibling recruited by a college for athletics, so the whole process was foreign to the family. On his football team, Howard started out as a tailback and a cornerback, but prior to his junior season, his coach asked him to switch from cornerback to safety. "My coach had a lot of confidence in me as a football player and he wanted me to be the last line of defense because not only was I fast, but I was tough and physical," Howard said. "I wasn't afraid to come up and get in the mix, and he knew I would tackle, so he said I would be the safety. I can cover a lot of area because I was fast, and he knew I was tough because I was our tailback and carried the ball 28 or 30 times a game."

When Howard says he carried the ball 30 times a game, he's not referring to jet sweeps or pitches to get him out in space. He's talking about I formation, downhill, between-the-tackles, smash-mouth football.

He describes the offense as a wishbone/I formation offense, and despite having quarterback Elvis Grbac, who would also sign with Michigan, the high school team only passed the ball a few times a game. The offense was predicated on the run, and Howard was featured in that ground attack. His junior season started in 1986, and that was when Howard really started to come into his own, and the recruiting process started to pick up. Back then, it wasn't unusual for a recruit to start hearing from programs either during his senior season or after, but Howard was such a good athlete that he had a few programs reach out during his junior season. "I had an explosive year my junior year, especially my first game," Howard said. "That's when I started getting letters, and it started off as smaller schools… You would get them from the high school. They didn't send them to the house. So I would meet with one of the assistant coaches, and he would give me a letter, and I was excited."

In that first game, Howard scored five touchdowns for his team and started to wonder if football could take him somewhere. Initially, Howard heard from Ohio, Kent State, and Toledo, as well as a few other schools that are now in the Mid-American Conference (MAC). It was still early, so it made sense that the local, smaller schools were trying to get a jump on his recruitment. It's more difficult for the smaller schools to compete with the larger, more prominent schools in recruiting, so they try to compensate by beating them to the punch. The coaches were hoping that if they could get in first that they might be able to make an impact and stay in the race until the end.

But Howard was special, and despite the wishbone offense, his raw talent was on display in full effect, and coaches eventually came to see just what he was capable of. "After my junior year, I was on a lot of people's radar," Howard said. "Going into my senior year, the expectations were pretty significant, so that's when people understood who I was as a football player and started sending me offers."

Based off his junior season, word had gotten out, and Howard was becoming a well-known prospect. He knew what the expectations were now, heading into his senior season and he was more than happy to take on that challenge. If Howard had an exciting junior year, his senior year was even better. On offense he had 18 touchdowns and on defense he had 10 interceptions. His high school team was ranked nationally, which helped Howard get even more attention among college coaches and brought more coaches to his high school to see what the team had in talent and prospects.

John Storey, the defensive coach for St. Joseph's, always came away impressed with what Howard could do on the field. "He's not a big man of stature, but when he played on the field, he was," Storey said. "It was amazing how good he was in high school. It was fun to watch in practice because we were a big school and had a lot of players, so we scrimmaged a lot."

Howard would put on a show in practice and in those scrimmages, and Storey joked that the star player was a running back, defensive back, punt returner, and kick returner who only came off the field during halftime and when the game was over. He was a true do-it-all prospect who had the respect of all his coaches and teammates.

But what was so remarkable about the fact that he was receiving offers as early as his junior year is that Howard had never once gone to a football camp. A lot of times a prospect would go to a college camp to work out for the coaches in person and give the staff a good look at the player's ability. Howard had been to a basketball camp but not one for football. He believes the interest must have been from word of mouth and from his coach sending out his VHS highlight tapes.

His mentality was that if you're good enough, they'll find you. And they indeed found him. As he went through his senior season, more and more schools started to show interest, but Howard wanted to keep control of his process and narrow it down to just five schools that he would really consider. "I wasn't a big college football fan. I was a huge NFL fan, so I loved the Dallas Cowboys," Howard said. "I would watch college football, but it wasn't my thing. My buddies did, though, and they'd be like, 'Wow, Georgia Tech wants you. That's Coach Ross down there. Michigan wants you. Man, that's Bo Schembechler.'"

So Howard worked to narrow his list down, trying to distinguish the schools that met his academic and athletic needs. He targeted Michigan, Michigan State, Georgia Tech, Syracuse, and Purdue. Despite the fact that he lived in Ohio and grew up in Cleveland, Ohio State never offered Howard. Whether it was his size or another reason, the Buckeyes didn't get involved with Howard's recruitment.

Georgia Tech was an interesting choice because it was a school well-versed in academics, was in the culturally diverse city of Atlanta, and had a new coach in Bobby Ross. Chuck Priefer was the defensive backs coach for Ross at Georgia Tech and was originally from Ohio. Priefer attended high school in Ohio, coached at Padua Franciscan High in Ohio, and eventually went on to coach at Miami (of Ohio) as well. Because of his ties to the state, Ross gave Ohio to Priefer as one of his recruiting territories. They knew there was no way to pull any prospects out from Ohio down to Georgia if there wasn't a tie to the state, so Priefer was a natural fit.

Priefer knew about Howard and his quarterback teammate, but Grbac was more of a pro-style quarterback. At the time Ross was looking for more of a dual-threat quarterback, so the staff was only interested in Howard.

Ross and his staff had just finished their first season in 1987 with a 2–9 record, so recruiting the right players to help turn the program around was crucial. "We were at St. Joe's watching basketball practice, and at that time, Desmond was 5'9", 170 pounds," Priefer said. "I watched film during the day and then watched practice and I was convinced that they were both—Desmond and Elvis—Division I players. I didn't have any doubt about either one of them."

Priefer wanted Howard and was going to show him that not only was he wanted at Georgia Tech, but he also was needed.

Since Howard had his list narrowed down and his senior season was done, it was time to take his official visits. It was January 1988—just after his senior season—and Howard made his way to all the schools on his list. He went to Syracuse and was hosted by one of his former teammates, Turnell Sims. Howard recalled that he thought Syracuse had a rich history of running backs and felt the staff ran the ball quite a bit. But because of the offense his high school team ran, college coaches still weren't completely sure where he would project once he got to college.

Many coaches told him running back, some said defensive back, and a few saw the ability at receiver. According to Storey, the team only threw the ball in the neighborhood of 50 times the entire season, so there wasn't much film on him as a pass catcher, which made it difficult for coaches to really evaluate what he would be in college. "We didn't know. We thought defensive back, but he would've ended up at wide receiver because defensive backs are guys that can't catch," Priefer said. "They ran the ball, so Desmond was a receiver on a team that never threw, so you had to evaluate him on what you saw defensively. Then I watched him play basketball, and you can tell after 10 minutes that he's a special athlete."

There was one play on the football field that really stood out to Priefer. Howard was playing safety in the playoffs, and his team was backed up to the goal line. The ball carrier on the opposing team came over to his side of the field, and Howard squared up and smacked the offensive player, standing him up at the goal line. Despite his size, he played bigger than he was, and that play showed Priefer and other coaches that Howard was tough enough to play at the next level. They might not know his position yet, but he had the athletic ability, speed, and toughness that you couldn't teach.

Howard continued on in his recruitment and also took a visit to Purdue. The Boilermakers were coming off of a 3–7–1 season in 1987 and could have used an infusion of athleticism in the form of Howard. Although the Boilermakers made his list, it always seemed as though Purdue was behind when it came to the other schools. "Purdue was fun. It was different. I enjoyed it but from a different standpoint," Howard said. "The guys I spent time with, they had a level of substance to them. That part was very different to me, but I appreciated it. When I was at Michigan State, it was wild, but I went to Purdue, and it was mature, and the conversation had substance to it, in-depth stuff."

A big reason why Michigan State was in the picture was because of Nick Saban, who was the Spartans' defensive coordinator. Michigan State was then coached by George Perles, who had rejoined the Spartans in 1983 and coached in East Lansing, Michigan, until 1994. The Spartans had an excellent season in 1987, going 9–2–1, beating in-state rival Michigan, and eventually winning the Rose Bowl 20–17 against USC. The team was loaded with big-name players, including running back Lorenzo White and offensive lineman Tony Mandarich.

Michigan State was winning on the field, and the Spartans had their secret weapon in Saban. Howard and Saban developed a close relationship through recruiting, and Saban was striking all the right chords for the Ohio prospect. "He used to drive down from East Lansing to Cleveland to recruit me," Howard said. "Nick was my guy. That's why—even today as a broadcaster—he knows me way before then, and we go way back. We have a little history."

Saban was a defensive coach and was after Howard relentlessly. He knew Howard was a good player and would be someone who could keep Michigan State in the forefront. As was the case with many of the schools, Howard wasn't positive as to where he would play at Michigan State and what position would get him on the field. It's a question Howard, who now works as an analyst on ESPN's *College GameDay*, asked Saban many years later. "Nick Saban was on our show, and I was on the bus with Nick," Howard said. "So I asked Nick, 'When you were recruiting me, what were you guys recruiting me at? Were you going to put me at defensive back?' He said, 'No, our best athletes, we put them on the offensive side. You would have played offense.'"

Howard took his trip to Michigan State and recalled the visit being a lot of fun. Although that was good for a few visits, Howard was a serious kid who was always interested in academics. He was more mature than a lot of kids his age and took a business approach to his schooling. A former Michigan coach even said that Howard would often wear a tie at Michigan and carry a briefcase to class. Part of that might have been because of the Catholic school dress code he was used to, but it also spoke to the fact that Howard was looking for more than just a fun time in college. He knew his education would be important.

Saban kept the Spartans involved, but it seemed as though the opportunities at Georgia Tech and Michigan outweighed what the Spartans could offer. "It really came down to Georgia Tech. Nick Saban was a hell of a recruiter, and I enjoyed Michigan State, but Michigan and Coach Schembechler, I really liked," Howard said. "Georgia Tech really wanted me, and they were on the verge of being more relevant nationally."

So he and his mother made the trip to Atlanta to see just what exactly Georgia Tech could offer and what the surrounding environment was like. Being from Ohio, he didn't really know all that much about the school other than what he had learned through Priefer and what he had seen on television. This trip would be instrumental in finding out if Georgia Tech was a good fit. "They got there Friday afternoon, relaxed for a little bit, then took him and his mom to dinner, then he went out on the town with some of our players. Atlanta is a great African American city, and Desmond liked the culture of the city, and his mom did, too," Priefer said. "We talked to him about postgraduate work and business connections. Some guys are all about football, and Desmond had deep thoughts about what he wanted to do with his life. Bobby [Ross] made the official offer to him Saturday afternoon, and we had told him before the visit we weren't just checking him out; there was an offer."

Howard described his time in Atlanta as fantastic and confirmed he did like the city and its environment. That feel of the city would be the complete opposite of Ann Arbor and the Michigan campus. But both schools offered an education that meant a lot nationally, and that was important to Howard, his father, and his mother. Priefer was doing his best to lure Howard, recruiting him as hard as he could within the rules and taking advantage of every opportunity he could to have communication with him. "I felt like we had a chance, but only because Michigan was hemming and hawing," Priefer said. "Because Bo was the only one who could make an official offer, the assistant coaches couldn't make the offer. The head coach had to, and that had not happened yet."

Howard was heading into his Michigan visit without an offer, which was normal back then, but it seemed as though most of the other schools made it fairly obvious a scholarship offer would be waiting for him once he got to campus. Michigan and Schembechler made no such suggestions. Typically, Schembechler liked bigger running backs, and that's not what Howard was. Schembechler was known for saying that small backs have small arms and hands and fumble a lot. Between his small size and not knowing where he would play on the field, there was some hesitation on the part of Michigan. But Howard took the visit and saw what Michigan was all about. He knew who Schembechler was but wasn't fully aware of the history and tradition at the university.

At the time, Schembechler seemed larger than life. Even though he was more of an NFL fan, Howard had seen him on television coaching in big games and he was aware of the Rose Bowl, so sitting down and meeting with the legendary coach stood out for the teen from Cleveland. "He had this persona and perception that he was a rough, no-nonsense gruff guy, but he really had a nice smile and could make you feel at ease when you sit down with him. You wait your turn sitting outside his office in the hallway with the other recruits," Howard said. "You're waiting to go in and you're like, *Man, on the other side of that door is Bo Schembechler.* There was a nervousness involved. The thing I can probably try to compare it to is when you're in trouble, and you get sent to the principal's office, and the door is shut. You're waiting, trying to visualize how this conversation was going to go. Even though I wasn't in trouble, I was like, *What am I going to say to this guy? What is he going to say to me? Is he going to be this mean guy?* I'm just playing that out in my head."

Howard waited in line, along with the other recruits, for his turn to sit face-to-face with Schembechler. Many great players had sat in those chairs before him and had similar conversations with Schembechler about what Michigan had to offer and how difficult it was to come to a place like Michigan. Schembechler and his assistants never sugarcoated what it was like to play for Michigan. He didn't guarantee playing time and stressed that it had to be earned, and regardless of what type of high school player you were, you wouldn't see the field unless you worked hard for it.

The whole team was filled with top high school prospects from across the country, so it didn't mean much to stroll in with stats and awards. Schembechler looked for grit and a hard-working mentality. "You get in there, and he has this rough edge to him. He said, 'Sit down, Howard. You want to come play for Michigan?' He talked about what Michigan has to offer and what opportunities would come from Michigan," Howard said. "We talked about football, and he looked at me and said, 'Are you tough? Are you tough? You're just a little bitty fella.' He wasn't going to stroke your ego and he's not going to say you need to come here or our program is going to fold. It's more: it's a privilege to come here."

Howard left his Michigan visit without a scholarship offer. That didn't deter him, though, as the communication was still open, and he knew that Michigan was interested. It was January, though, and getting closer to Signing Day in February, so he also knew the Wolverines would have to make a decision quickly. After the visit Michigan was out in front of Georgia Tech, but without a scholarship offer, he wouldn't be able to commit to the Wolverines. Priefer knew Michigan was yet to offer and made sure that Howard knew how badly he was wanted at Georgia Tech, that he already had the scholarship offer, and that he could help propel their program forward.

No decision was announced publicly, but as Signing Day approached, Howard knew that Michigan was where he wanted to be. On the Sunday before Signing Day, Priefer made one last in-home visit to try to sway Howard. Priefer felt he only had a shot because he knew Michigan hadn't offered yet. A couple of days went by. It was now Tuesday, the day before Signing Day, and Howard still had not spoken with Schembechler about an offer. It was terrible timing as Schembechler was attending to a funeral. Howard spoke with assistant Gary Moeller and told him he wanted to be a Wolverine, but it needed to be cleared by Schembechler, who was unreachable.

Priefer was sitting in Dayton, Ohio, a little more than 200 miles from Howard's home in Cleveland. He was meeting with Georgia Tech commit Marco Coleman, who would go on to be an All-American for the Yellow Jackets. Moeller and Priefer happened to be friends, so Priefer called Moeller Tuesday night just to gauge where Michigan was at with Howard. But Priefer knew where Howard's inclinations were. "I talked to Desmond about 5:30 that night, and he was still hemming a little bit. He said, 'Coach, I want to be honest with you. I'm leaning toward Michigan,'" Priefer said. "I said I understand that, but if you want me to, I'll drive up to Cleveland right now."

At 8:00 PM, the night before Signing Day, Howard still hadn't heard from Schembechler. So Priefer was waiting in Dayton just in case. Then at 9:30 PM, Priefer got the final phone call from Howard with the definitive news. He was a Wolverine. "He says, 'Coach Schembechler just called me and he made a full offer to me.' I think they had another guy in Texas that I found out later about, but they got Desmond," Priefer said.

That phone call was difficult for Howard. Having to turn down coaches he had built real relationships with didn't sit well with the teenager. He wanted to tell every coach yes, but he knew that Michigan was where his heart was. Priefer was especially hard for Howard to turn down because the two had a great relationship. Howard remembers Priefer asking him if he was sure he wanted to go to Michigan. After Howard said yes, Priefer reiterated that Georgia Tech still had an offer for him.

Michigan just had everything Howard and his father wanted in a school. It was close to home—but not too close—and the education combined with the athletics made it the perfect school. "To have the opportunity to play for a living legend in Coach Schembechler, that doesn't come around every day. To be guaranteed that if you stay, you're going to get a degree and you're probably going to play in two or three Rose Bowls," Howard said. "It was the Granddaddy of them all, so those were the deciding factors. Coach Ross was a good coach, but he didn't have the aura that Coach Schembechler did, and Michigan State was a solid program but nowhere near Michigan. It was one of the best decisions I've ever made."

Though his recruitment almost went to the final hour, it was officially over. That next day (Wednesday), Howard signed with Michigan and would soon be on his way to Ann Arbor to start his next journey. The Michigan coaches still didn't know what position was best for Howard—even once he made his way to campus. He showed up in 1988 for freshman camp, which was three days before the veterans showed up. That extra time allowed the youngsters to get in some independent work with the coaches.

Coach Moeller had been leaning toward offense because of what Howard was able to do at running back in high school. But on the first day of freshman camp, Howard went out with the defensive backs and played on defense. "If you talk to Coach Moeller, he would say, 'Where the hell is Howard going? What is he doing?' Then the second and third day, I played running back and receiver," Howard said. "Coach Schembechler and [Cam] Cameron sat me down and said, 'We think you could help the team faster and more effectively at wide receiver.' They said they had three receivers on the way out—Chris Calloway, Greg McMurtry, and this kid named John Kolesar—and they thought I could be an effective player at wideout. I didn't bat an eye and I said, 'Okay, Coach, I'll be in the receivers room tomorrow.'"

Howard redshirted his freshman season and had nine catches for 136 yards the next season. After that second year, Howard and Priefer had somewhat of a reunion in Ann Arbor.

Given his friendship with Moeller, Priefer came up to Michigan to study its defense and take something back with him to Georgia Tech. "There's Desmond on the sideline, and by that time he was playing, but he wasn't Heisman Trophy yet," Priefer said. "And Mo and I are laughing about the whole recruiting story, and even Desmond was laughing about it."

In 1990 Howard burst onto the scene with 63 receptions for 1,025 yards and 11 touchdowns. He was on his way to an outstanding career and helped Michigan to a 9–3 record with a win against Ole Miss in the Gator Bowl. That same season Georgia Tech went 11–0–1 and won a share of the national championship after a 45–21 win against Nebraska in the Citrus Bowl.

Howard could have had a national championship but still to this day doesn't regret passing on Georgia Tech. The national championship would have been a big deal, but the experience Howard had at Michigan was invaluable for the speedy receiver from Cleveland. He won some hardware himself in the 1991 season. During that year he hauled in 62 passes for 985 yards and 19 touchdowns, 412 kick return yards, 282 punt return yards, and two touchdown returns.

Howard had 1,211 career yards returning kicks, 337 yards returning punts, and three touchdown returns. One of those touchdowns will always be remembered because Howard struck the Heisman pose in the back of the end zone after returning a punt against Ohio State in 1991. The punt return put Michigan comfortably ahead in a game the Wolverines would win and also cement Howard's position in the Heisman Trophy race.

As Howard was making his way toward the end zone, ABC broadcaster Keith Jackson famously narrated Howard's race down the field, declaring, "One man…good-bye…Hello, Heisman." As if it had been dramatically planned by the two, Howard struck the pose shortly after Jackson uttered the word "Heisman" and was then gang tackled by his teammates.

It is the most well-known play of Howard's career at Michigan, but there were plenty more that stood out. As a result of such plays, he received All-American honors and won the Walter Camp Trophy and Maxwell Award. That performance in his final season at Michigan earned him the Heisman Trophy and a place in college football history.

Despite having one more year of eligibility, Howard graduated from Michigan and was selected with the fourth overall pick of the 1992 NFL Draft by the Washington Redskins. He played for the Redskins until 1994 and eventually made his way to the Jacksonville Jaguars, Green Bay Packers, Oakland Raiders, and then back to the Packers. After accounting for 244 return yards, including a 99-yard kickoff return, Howard was named MVP of Super Bowl XXXI, which the Packers won 35–21.

In 1999, however, Howard was cut by the Packers, and once again he and Priefer would have a chance at a reunion. Priefer was now the special teams coach for the Detroit Lions under Ross, the head coach. The two Georgia Tech coaches stayed together in the NFL and even added an old friend to the staff in Moeller, who coached the linebackers for the Lions. "The Packers cut Desmond on a Tuesday. Well, Saturday morning, Terry Fair, who returned kicks and punts for us, comes in Saturday morning, and his hand is bandaged up, and he says he fell down the stairs," Priefer said. "We found out later that was a lie, and he was in a fight at a party Friday night. So he's done for the year, and we're scrambling. So I know Desmond and I know he's released and I know Bobby knew him and liked him."

Priefer told Ross that Howard was available, and Ross asked if he knew where he was. Priefer went and found an old teammate of Howard's in Corwin Brown, who had Howard's number. The coaches talked to Howard on Saturday morning and told him he needed to be in Detroit and signed by 4:00 PM or he couldn't play in the game the following day.

Howard got in at the last minute, but unlike his recruitment, Priefer got his man and signed Howard right at the wire. "We're playing the next day at home in the Pontiac Silverdome," Priefer said. "So we're playing and we stop the other team, and they're going to punt to us. They announce over the Silverdome PA: 'Now returning for the Detroit Lions, No. 18, Desmond Howard.' The place goes crazy."

That other team was the Redskins, who drafted Howard. The Redskins had just scored, and Matt Turk kicked the ball off with 1:52 left in the second quarter. Howard was back to receive the ball and, as if he were transformed back to his Michigan days, he cradled the ball and raced 68 yards for a touchdown. The Lions won that game 33–17, and Howard revived his career in Detroit, where he made his only Pro Bowl appearance as a kick returner in 2001. Howard retired after that season in the state where his incredible career began and in front of the fans who loved him so dearly when he donned the winged helmet in maize and blue.

Desmond Howard

MICHIGAN ATHLETICS INFORMATION SHEET

NAME Desmond Howard   SPORT Football

ID # (10 DIGITS)   CAMPUS PHONE 764-6606

w/ Marc Jacobson
CAMPUSS ADDRESS S. Quad Fred. #1814

PARENTS FIRST NAME James Howard   PARENTS PHONE ███████

PARENTS ADDRESS ████████████ Ohio 44128
STREET   CITY   STATE   ZIP

HIGH SCHOOL ATTENDED St. Joseph

DATE OF GRADUATION June 1988

YR IN SCHOOL: FR (SO) JR SR   SCHOOL/COLLEGE ENROLLED LSA

MAJOR/CONCENTRATION: Communications (JR & SR MUSH HAVE ESTABLISHED)

ENTRY DATE AT MICHIGAN Sept. 1988

ENTRY DATE AT ANY OTHER COLLEGE/UNIVERSITY _____

YEARS OF VARSITY COMPETITION IN **THIS** SPORT: 0̶ (1) 2 3 4

I AUTHORIZE THE DEPARTMENT OF ATHLETICS AND/OR ITS REPRESENTATIVES TO ORDER AND OBTAIN COPIES OF ALL SCHOLASTIC, MEDICAL OR OTHER RECORDS WHICH ARE PERTINENT TO ESTABLISHING MY ATHLETIC ELIGIBILITY FOR THE 89-90 ACADEMIC YEAR OR OTHER MATERIAL RELATED TO MY ATHLETIC COMPETITION.

_____
STUDENT-ATHLETE''S SIGNATURE

PLEASE MAKE SURE FORM IS COMPLETED AND LEGIBLE!!!

CHAPTER 7

Jarrett Irons

Many Michigan fans remember Jarrett Irons as a hard-hitting, smart linebacker in the 1990s. One of the best defenders to play for the Wolverines, he ranks No. 2 in career tackles with 453. From 1992 to 1996, Irons was a no-nonsense, academics-oriented player, who fit with what Michigan was and he flourished on the field for the Wolverines. He grew up in a football family. His father, Gerald Sr., played nearly 10 years in the NFL; his older brother, Gerald Jr., played at Nebraska; and his younger brother, Grant, eventually played at Notre Dame. But perhaps Jarrett's recruiting path to Michigan was preordained, a way to take advantage of an opportunity his grandfather missed out on.

As a young teenager, Jarrett Irons had the chance to see the recruiting process firsthand from his older brother, who was recruited by nearly every major program in the country. His parents understood the magnitude of the recruiting process and also saw the potential that Jarrett and his younger brother had on the football field, so everyone in the family sat in recruiting meetings with coaches that came by to see Gerald Jr. The family lived in The

Woodlands, Texas, and at times there were 10 to 12 coaches lined up in their cars down the street to come see Gerald Jr. and the Irons family. When the coaches met with the family, the two younger brothers were encouraged to ask questions as well, so they would be prepared for the process when it came time for them to look at colleges.

Gerald Jr. is three years older than Jarrett, so Jarrett was only a freshman when his older brother was going through the process. Gaining that experience and building those relationships would later make the recruiting process that much easier for Jarrett. All three Irons boys were similar but unique in their own right. All three were homecoming kings, and all three took after their father as captains of their high school football teams.

Jarrett had a strong personality and was confident beyond his years. Being mature in his mental makeup meant he knew how to get what he wanted and what to say to get it. "My husband was on the school board, and Jarrett wasn't all that happy with him being on the school board. One day we had to go to the school for Jarrett because the teacher said that Jarrett wasn't answering the questions," Jarrett's mother, Myrna, said. "I said, 'What do you mean he's not answering? I know Jarrett has the knowledge base.' She said, 'Well, he told me he wasn't a morning person, that he knew the answer, but he didn't want to talk before 12.' So, of course, we went to the school and we had a little come-to-Jesus meeting with Jarrett."

Gerald Jr. saw coach after coach come in to his home and eventually told coach Tom Osborne that he would commit to Nebraska to play for the Huskers. Because those coaches had also spoken with Jarrett during their time spent with his older brother, Jarrett got his recruitment off to a fast start. Clemson was the first school to send him a letter during his sophomore year, which kicked off his recruitment. His high school was a prominent school known for producing quality players, so it was no stranger to college football coaches. Because spring ball is a big deal in Texas, a laundry list of coaches would come out to evaluate the talent, including Jarrett.

He knew that coaches were there for him and now Jarrett admits that he was a little arrogant because he knew what he brought to the table. He knew that those letters that started rolling in were just canned letters or pre-printed and shipped off to every recruit that program was targeting. Each school did the same thing, and the letters became very impersonal and lacking in meaning. At first he liked the idea because he would get a stack of letters in home room in front of all his classmates, then he'd get home, and there would be another stack waiting for him. But as more mail started to roll in, Jarrett wanted to see just how serious the coaches were about recruiting him and how personal they could make it. "I started telling coaches, 'Look, the same letter you're sending me, you're sending to a thousand other kids like me around the country. So, I started telling guys, 'If you're going to be interested in me and sending me things, you need to be handwriting my letters,'" Irons said. "'I want to know that you mean it, and it's not someone else getting this same letter.' So I started getting a lot of handwritten letters from coaches."

He went through his sophomore and junior seasons and continued to rack up more personal recruiting letters and interest from various programs across the country, including Nebraska, Texas A&M, Florida State, Notre Dame, and Colorado, among others. At the time Cam Cameron was the assistant coach for Michigan who recruited Texas, so Cameron would make his way through the state and scout various high school programs, eventually making it to The Woodlands. "Michigan hadn't recruited Texas a lot, so they sent me down there when all the other schools were going on probation. I went down there and realized they're probably not going to get a lot of kids to go to Michigan unless they want a college degree," Cameron said. "The first practice I went to, Jarrett didn't know I was going to be there, so he wasn't putting on for me. It was one of the most impressive practices from a leadership standpoint I have ever seen."

This practice was the spring before Jarrett's senior year, so there still wasn't much contact or communication between him and the schools, but he was now on Michigan's radar, whether he knew it or not. That performance at practice led Cameron to believe that Irons was a target who should be recruited by the University of Michigan.

Jarrett was very motivated, mature, and had a good head on his shoulders, so heading into his senior season he already had a good idea of what he was looking for in a school and what he needed to hear from the coaches in order to convince him their program was the right place for him. Academics would be paramount—not only because his parents reinforced the idea that he needed to get an education, but also because he saw the impact up close and personal that a lack of education could have on a football player.

When his father was playing for the Cleveland Browns, Jarrett went into the locker room postgame to spend time with his dad and be around the team. He noticed one player at his locker in tears and asked his father what had happened. "You're a kid and you see a grown man, a tough football player, crying. It really messes with your psyche a little bit. So I tapped my dad and said, 'Why is he crying?'" Jarrett said. "My dad waited until we got in the car and said that's why you need to get your education. That guy has a family at home and he was just told he was cut and no longer playing. He doesn't have a degree and he has kids at home. That's why education is very important."

That experience stuck with him for his entire life and was a big part of why he was such a stickler in the recruiting process, ensuring that every school recruiting him laid out their academics, graduation rates, and plans for their student-athletes on how they would succeed outside of football. Cameron didn't know it just yet, but Jarrett was exactly the kind of Texas recruit that Michigan could have a shot with.

Michigan wasn't the only school recruiting him, though, and there would be plenty of competition for the middle Irons brother. As his parents had done for his older brother, they insisted that Jarrett sit and meet with every coach who wanted to come by the house for an in-home visit because he never knew where his scholarship would come from, and they didn't want to burn any bridges.

His parents also made it very clear early on that this was Jarrett's decision to make—not theirs. They would help him through the process, but he had to be happy with the choice he made because if it ever got difficult at the school they didn't want it to be on them. "During the recruiting time when they could come to our house, everybody would come to the house, and we had to sit there and listen to them. Every team comes in and they show you a videotape of the campus and the players and the whole happy-go-lucky, warm, fuzzy video of your experience," Jarrett said. "The BYU video was nothing but black people. Knowing good and well that BYU didn't have that many black people, I was like, *Dude, there's no way there's this many black people at BYU*. It must have been a tape catered to certain families, but nonetheless, I wasn't going there, but my mom and dad made us sit through all of that."

His father likely knew his son wasn't going to BYU as well, as he dozed off during the meeting and had to be nudged by his son to wake up.

While this was going on with other programs, Cameron and Michigan prepared for their in-home visit to ensure they made a better impression than BYU. Cameron knew Jarrett's father had played in the NFL, specifically for the Oakland Raiders, and had some connections to people within the NFL. Through his diligent research before his visit, Cameron found out some information about the family and mainly that they were very academically-oriented. Jarrett's father went to law school at the University of Chicago during his time in the NFL and got his MBA, so many around him knew that the family would be focused on education. "I had only seen Jarett from a distance and I think you only got one phone call, so I had a phone call. A young man answers the door, and I thought, *Holy smokes, this guy is even taller than I thought he was*," Cameron said. "It was his younger brother, Grant, who was 12. So I go in the house, and there's Dad, who was smart, a leader and tough. Back then, I don't think I ever recruited a kid that academics wasn't either No. 1 or on par with being a great player, so I knew he was a perfect fit for us."

Cameron sat down with the family, but rather than pop in the warm and fuzzy videotape, he sat and asked questions of the family for nearly two hours. He didn't describe the university or what it had to offer but learned about what made the Irons family tick and what they were looking for in a university. The family had questions themselves but hadn't had the opportunity to ask them just yet. Cameron wanted to make sure he covered every aspect and knew everything he could about Irons and this family. Once he was done and he felt he couldn't ask any more questions of them, he asked them if they had any questions for him.

Shocked that this was Michigan's recruiting speech, Myrna spoke up and said that they would like to know what the University of Michigan is all about and what they have to offer her son. Cameron reached into his sport coat pocket and pulled out a folded up piece of paper. From the research he had done, what was written on that piece of paper would make a bigger statement about Michigan than any videotape ever could. Cameron unfolded the piece of paper and handed it to Jarrett's parents. Written on the paper was the graduation rate for Michigan athletes at the time, and that was it. "He handed the paper to my parents and was like, 'Listen this is the graduation rate of Michigan athletes. Your son is going to come here and play in front of 110,000 people. He's going to be on television every week, he's going to graduate, and we're going to make sure he gets everything he needs to be successful outside of football,'" Jarrett recalled. "My mouth dropped. I wasn't prepared for it because you go through all these recruiting pitches, and it's like a canned speech, and everyone has their thing that they talk about how great their school is and the big finish at the end. Cam didn't do that. He got to talk to us and he did his homework and he knew we're about academics and life after football."

121

Before that visit Jarrett knew very little about the Wolverines and what they had to offer. Now, as Cameron was leaving his home, Jarrett felt that Michigan had most of what he was looking for in a school. He had never been to Ann Arbor, though, and wasn't 100 percent on board just yet. There were some other schools still in the mix. Texas A&M, Colorado, Oklahoma, Nebraska, and Notre Dame were the main other players.

Cameron left the meeting very confident that he struck a chord with Jarrett and the family. He didn't know exactly how Jarrett felt, but he was sure that Michigan would have a shot because of his homework and the fact that Michigan sells itself. "I learned a lot from Bo in terms of how to talk to kids. Parents would sit down with Bo and say, 'Help us decide this recruiting. How do we decide on a school?' He would say it's simple," Cameron said. "Bo would tell them to take five schools that you're interested in, rank them one through five, and then go to the first school and say, 'Do you want me?' If they say yes, stand up, shake their hand, and say recruiting is officially over. I would tell that story, not jokingly, but you knew they weren't going to stand up and end it."

Notre Dame was still lurking as the Irish could offer many of the same benefits as Michigan. In Jarrett's mind the tradition, the academics, and the football program were all on par with what he knew about Michigan. Head coach Lou Holtz was recruiting Irons for the Irish and had a little help in his corner within the Irons family. Jarrett's grandmother lived in Gary, Indiana, and loved Notre Dame. She had such love for the school that she was upset with Gerald Jr. for picking Nebraska instead of Notre Dame. So when it came time for Jarrett to go through the process, his grandmother told him he had better pick Notre Dame. That was in jest, of course, but it came with a little sincerity behind it.

So while Holtz had Grandma on his side, he now had to compete with the meeting that Cameron had with the family. The bar was set high since Cameron did his research and set Michigan apart from the pack. Jarrett knew a little more about Notre Dame than Michigan simply because the Irish were on television more than the Wolverines. He knew of their prominent players like Tony Rice and Raghib "Rocket" Ismail. That wouldn't be enough to impress Jarrett, though, and he wanted to know how Notre Dame stacked up against a school like Michigan.

Holtz came in for a visit and spoke about the program, gave his recruiting speech, and endeared himself to the family. Jarrett acknowledges that Holtz was an outstanding recruiter, someone who just made you feel comfortable in person as if you had known him for years. Plus, the coach had built up his profile as one of the best coaches in the country and was now sitting in their living room. That alone was impressive, and the family already felt comfortable with Holtz because he had recruited Jarrett's older brother as well. Much of the speech was what they had heard before, but true to who he was, Jarrett had a question about Notre Dame that was unique to the recruiting process. "I said, 'Coach Holtz, I have a question. From my understanding if you have sex in the dorms, you get kicked out of the university. Is that true?' He said that was true, that they have a strong Catholic foundation, and that they have rules against that in the dorms," Jarrett said. "My mom sight unseen didn't even hesitate, just said, 'Yeah, that's probably not going to work for Jarrett.' It was true. I was like, yeah, I'm not going there."

That question probably wasn't what his grandma had in mind, and she would have to deal with being upset once again because Notre Dame was out for another Irons boy. Regardless of the rules against sex in the dorms, Jarrett still felt Michigan had more to offer him than Notre Dame.

Jarrett had tired of the recruiting process earlier than most because he had already heard many of the recruiting pitches from when his brother went through the process. He had nearly every school in the country after him and he knew it was getting out of hand when he had to take refuge from the phone calls and visits by spending time at his girlfriend's house. He then knew that it was completely out of hand when college coaches somehow found his girlfriend's home phone number and started calling him at her house. He had no way to get away from it and, being a person who didn't want to play around with the process or lead anyone on, Jarrett knew that he needed to get serious about figuring out where he wanted to go to school.

He happened to have some family that lived in Michigan, and he and his immediate family were taking a trip to the Midwest the summer before his senior season. They used that opportunity to take an unofficial visit to Michigan to help Jarrett see if Michigan was what he thought it was and if Ann Arbor was a place he could see himself for the next four or five years.

He and his family still only really knew what Cameron had told them about Michigan, so this would be an excellent opportunity to familiarize themselves with the program and find out the type of players that were already on Michigan's roster. Luckily for

Michigan, two of the best representatives of the program happened to be around when Jarrett and his family were taking their visit.

Desmond Howard and Tripp Welborne were both on campus and both very similar to Jarrett in terms of how serious they took their academics and life after football. "I always felt our players would always sell our program. Once a recruit decided to come up, you didn't really structure it and make sure a guy bumped into him, but once you knew they were on campus, you made sure they had a chance to meet them," Cameron said. "Similar-minded people, they think in terms of four years and 40 years for their career. Jarrett saw the big picture like those guys, and I think Jarrett fit well with us."

So Jarrett spent some time with two players he had some familiarity with by way of television and immediately felt comfortable around the two Michigan athletes. He saw a little bit of himself in them from the football aspect but also with what they were saying about the academics. Welborne had just injured his knee and was rehabbing the injury at the time.

That was certainly a negative for Michigan and for Welborne, but what Welborne told him about his mentality when it came to his injury always stuck with Jarrett. It struck a chord and was another notch on the belt for the Wolverines. "Tripp was talking about his injury and that he had insurance. He said, 'I'm going to rehab and try to come back, but if not, I have insurance and I go to Michigan,'" Jarrett said. "He was so cavalier about it…He said he'd try to get back, but if he didn't, he would be fine because of what a Michigan degree meant. That resonated because I was all about life after sports."

That conversation and that injury were a turning point for Jarrett in his recruitment. He now had the information he needed about Michigan and stories corroborated with like-minded players, so this was looking more and more like the place for him. After that unofficial visit, Jarrett felt it would be very tough to beat out Michigan for his commitment. But true to his parents' wishes, he still entertained the other coaches and made sure he was making the choice on his own at the right time. He tried to lay low and focus on the start of his senior season, but once the season started up, he knew that he would need to take his official visits and finish the recruiting process.

A number of schools, including Texas A&M, Colorado, Nebraska, and Oklahoma, were still after him. He had considered Florida State at one point but felt it wouldn't fit with what he was looking for. So those four schools, in addition to Michigan, were the five that he would focus on and eventually take recruiting visits to during his season.

Texas A&M wanted to keep him in-state and tried to do everything they could to land him in its class. During Thanksgiving weekend head coach R.C. Slocum even called Jarrett from the locker room before his rivalry game against Texas to try to show him just how badly he wanted him. "I'm watching right before the game, and he called me and was like, 'Hey, Jarrett, how you doing? This is R.C. Slocum.' I was like, 'Coach I'm watching the game, I'm about to watch you,'" Jarrett said. "He said, 'I just wanted to call you. I just gave a fiery pregame speech to my team, we're ready to play, and I just wanted to call you and make sure you're watching the game.' I was like, *What*? That was special."

In his senior season, he figured out the visits he wanted to make and set them up. He would officially visit Nebraska, Texas A&M, Michigan, Oklahoma, and Colorado. His brother was currently playing at Nebraska, so the trip was more of a fun vacation for the middle Irons brother.

Being able to spend some time with his brother was great, but the visit solidified for him that Nebraska was not where he wanted to be. His brother was there, but as his mother noted, all three boys were unique and liked to lead in their own way. None of them wanted to follow in the footsteps of the other. The visit to Nebraska ended, and the trip to A&M also removed the more local school from the competition. He simply thought an A&M degree wouldn't take him as far as he wanted in the business world.

So that left his official visit to Michigan on December 21, 1991. As a senior in high school from Texas, Jarrett made the haul up to the cold, wintry state of Michigan. His player host on the visit was tailback Ed Davis, who remains a close friend to this day, and linebacker Bobby Powers. Jarrett felt a close bond with Powers because the two played the same position, so he could relate to his experience and could ask him specific football questions.

The time he spent in Ann Arbor was increasing his love for Michigan and reinforcing everything that Cameron had told him and his family throughout the process. But being the confident, outspoken individual he was, Jarrett still had a question for then-head coach Gary Moeller about his future. "I said to Gary, 'Listen, one of the things I'm looking at with the schools I want to go to: I want to graduate in four years.' Gary was like, 'Listen if you redshirt, you'll have a five-year scholarship, but you don't need to graduate in four years. We can stagger it out for you, and it won't be that difficult,'" Jarrett said. "I said, 'That's not going to work for me because in my mind I wanted to graduate in four years, and if I stay for my fifth year, will you pay for my master's because I have to be there and play.'"

Moeller told Jarrett that not many players do that at Michigan, but he would agree to honor a five-year scholarship, and Michigan would pay for his first year of his master's program if he was able to graduate in four years. Saying it and promising it wasn't enough for Jarrett, though, so he asked Moeller to put it on paper and officially write that the offer would be honored. Moeller obliged. That promise, and putting it to paper, sealed the deal for Jarrett. He knew at that point that Michigan was the school for him and, as soon as Moeller offered him a scholarship on the visit, he accepted and committed while on his recruiting visit.

He felt there was no need to extend the process if he knew this was the place for him. Everything lined up with what he was looking for, and the kid from Texas, who initially knew nothing about the University of Michigan, was now committing to spend the next five years in Michigan as a Wolverine.

The commitment was sentimental for Jarrett. Not only was his recruitment over and he would have the chance to earn an outstanding education from a top notch university, but also in the back of his mind, he had accomplished a goal for someone who had been very close to him.

Jarrett's grandfather passed away from a boating accident on Lake Michigan at 56 years old in the 1980s. He passed away when Jarrett was young, but the two had a close bond and special relationship. Before he passed away, his grandfather had told Jarrett his dream was to attend the University of Michigan as a student, but he was unable to because he was an African American. His grandfather instead attended Eastern Michigan University and always spoke about how he had wished to be a Wolverine.

So when Jarrett chose the Wolverines, he wasn't just choosing it for himself. He would be attending Michigan with his grandfather in his heart and in his mind. "When I committed, I did it for us. We made it. We always called him 'Buddy,' and I would always say a prayer and say, 'Buddy, we made it to Michigan,'" Jarrett said. "You couldn't get there, so I got there for us. We're there together. And I made something of myself there, getting two degrees, two time All-American, two-time captain. I did him proud."

His journey was complete. With his grandfather in mind and his family behind him, Jarrett told the Michigan coaches he was a Wolverine. His player hosts, Davis and Powers, joked that he made it too easy on the coaches, that he didn't make them sweat it out at all, but that wasn't his style. He felt that he was meant to be a Wolverine and he would now be fulfilling a dream his grandfather never got to see.

Jarrett finished his senior season, signed with Michigan with a small amount of fanfare, and prepared for his first season as a college football player. He was under the impression that he would likely redshirt and was perfectly fine with that, but part of him felt there was still a possibility he could play that first season because Michigan didn't have a lot of linebackers on the roster. Plus, he was a high school All-American, All-State, and All-Everything player. He admits that he was a little arrogant about his abilities at the time. "It's a tough year, away from home, away from my girlfriend, and during two-a-days, I'm practicing my ass off. I'm thinking I should be getting more reps. Just like any other arrogant high school football player, I think I should be playing," Jarrett said. "And when I got to Michigan, they said I would be like three deep, but when I get there—the freshmen enroll two days earlier to get reps—but when the vets get there, I realize I'm really 10 deep. They have all these linebackers ahead of me, so I'm not happy as it is and then I'm not getting reps and I'm not playing."

It was a tough adjustment for a kid who had the power to tell prominent college coaches to write him handwritten recruiting letters. To go from top of the world with college coaches telling him how great he was to being unable to sniff the field as a freshman was something that didn't sit well with him. He felt slighted and felt as though he was told he would have a better shot than what he was given. He started to develop a bad attitude and was resentful that he wasn't getting the same shot some of the other linebackers were. It started to spill over into his relationships. He wasn't getting along with defensive coordinator Jim Herrmann because he felt that Herrmann was treating him unfairly.

Since Cameron was his main recruiter, he heard that Jarrett was starting to act poorly and his attitude had gone south. So Cameron decided to have a talk with the touted freshman about his position at Michigan. Cameron saw Jarrett in the hallway inside the facilities and approached him. He looked at Jarrett and said he had heard he was unhappy. Cameron said he knew he was an All-American in high school, that he was All-State, and a really good player. He told him to look around the locker room and the facilities, that everyone here was an All-American, and that now at Michigan it means nothing. He looked at Jarrett, the recruit he spent so much time trying to get to Ann Arbor, and told him if he wanted to transfer then he could, but Michigan would just go back to Texas the next year and get another Jarrett Irons and do it again the following year. If he transferred, it would impact Jarrett more than it would Michigan. "I was a young coach back in those days, and the one thing I always felt like, this was our style. I challenged him, but there was no chance I would have let him go. There would have been a follow-up conversation, patting him on the back," Cameron said. "That was a kid from Day One I felt like he would eventually captain the Michigan team. He couldn't see it and he wasn't the fastest guy, and school was hard for him, so he's getting hit from both sides. I knew what he was made of and I knew he wouldn't quit."

Jarrett stayed, but he was still unhappy. He redshirted that freshman year and, though his attitude had changed on the outside, he was still uncertain if Michigan was where he should be anymore. Once that first school year was over, he decided to fly back home to Texas to be with his family and regroup. The family drove up to Nebraska from Texas to see his older brother at school and spend some time together. On the drive back to Texas, Jarrett's mother was asleep in the backseat, and Jarrett was in the front passenger seat. Jarrett and his father had a serious conversation about his reservations with Michigan and his potential to play in Ann Arbor.

For most of the drive, the two went back and forth on the pros and cons as his mother was quiet in the back. At the end of the conversation near the tail end of the drive, Jarrett's father felt his son was unhappy and said if he wanted to transfer that he would make the necessary calls to Michigan and other programs when they got home. At this time Jarrett's mother, who had heard some of the conversation from the backseat, was asked by her husband what she thought about the matter. His mother's first remark was that she didn't raise any quitters and neither did her husband.

Both men perked up and listened as Myrna began to speak her mind and remind her son why he was at school in the first place. "I kept on thinking to myself over and over, *What does happiness have to do with this? You made a commitment, and when you left home, we said whatever school you pick, you'll be there until you graduate,*" Myrna said. "I just let him and his dad talk it out, and then when he was ready to talk to me, I said no. I said, 'What is your last name?' He asked what that meant, and I said, 'You represent us, and I didn't raise any quitters. You made a commitment, and they made a commitment to you.'"

She went on to say that she didn't care if he played another down at Michigan, that he was there for his education, and he would honor his commitment. She also believed he could be one of the best players Michigan ever had if he would show some humility and trust the process. She thought her son was a leader and would stay at Michigan. That was the end of the conversation, and Jarrett never mentioned the possibility of transferring again. He had never seen his mother put both him and his father in their place so sternly, so he knew it was serious and he respected his mother's wishes.

She told her son he would go back to Michigan that summer and he wouldn't be allowed to travel back home anymore. She told him he would work harder than he ever has and he would have to do whatever the coaches ask of him. He took that conversation to heart, changed his attitude, and started putting in the work to fulfill the potential he had shown in high school.

"Coming into two-a-days, I'm 10 deep again, not expected to play. But [I] come to find out all the linebackers ahead of me get hurt except for myself and Bobby Powers, so I had to play," Jarrett said. "I started that first game against Notre Dame, and my mom still brings it up to this day that I was going to leave Michigan. I started that first game and started for the next four years."

Even though he was now starting, he felt as though it was just out of necessity, and doubts started to creep into his mind about whether he could sustain the success. If the injured players got healthy, would he just go back to the bench? His father reminded him that he was a leader, that all he could do was focus on what he could control. He told his son to make every tackle, to make every play, let the media sing his praises, and make it difficult for the coaches to ever replace him.

And that's what he did. That redshirt freshman season in 1993, Irons earned Freshman of the Year honors, racking up 95 total tackles in the 12 games he played. Irons would average more than 100 tackles per season over his career, eventually being named a two-time captain and an All-American for Michigan. He accomplished what he wanted on the field, but maybe more importantly, he also accomplished what he wanted off the field as well. Irons graduated in four years, and Michigan honored their commitment to his fifth year on scholarship, paying for his first year of graduate school at Michigan. He earned two degrees at Michigan—in sports management and management—and left the university making his family and his late grandfather proud of the legacy he was leaving behind. Buddy never made it to Michigan, but Jarrett did, and he will live forever in the history of Michigan football as one of the best linebackers to come through The Big House.

University of Michigan Athletic Public Relations
Student-Athlete Biographical Information

This biographical information is a permanent record in your athletic public relations file. Please complete the form neatly, accurately and completely. Supplemental information (newspaper articles, etc.) may be included to complete background information.

Date ___5-1-92___ U-M Sport ___Football___

Personal Information

Legal Name (first, middle, last) ___Jarrett David Irons___

Preferred Name / Nickname ___Iron-Man___

Date of Birth (month/date/year) ___12-14-73___ Height ___6'3"___ Weight ___220___

Home Address (address/city/state/zip) ███████████████

U-M Address (address/city/state/zip) ___South Quad___

Home Phone ████████ U-M Phone ████████

Academic Class (fr., so., jr., sr., grad.) ___Fr.___ Athletic Eligibility (fr., so., jr., sr., 5th yr.) ___Fr.___

U-M School Enrolled In ___Literature, Science and the Arts___ Major ___Communication___

Family Information

Father's Name (first/last) ___Gerald Irons Sr.___ College ___Univ. of Maryland / Univ. of Chicago M.B.A.___

Father's Address (if same as yours, omit) _____

Mother's Name (first/last) ___Myrna Irons___ College ___Univ. of Tennessee___

Mother's Address (if same as yours, omit) _____

Parent's Marital Status: married ___✓___ divorced _____ Number of: brothers ___2___ sisters ___0___

Parent, sibling(s) who are now or have been members of intercollegiate varsity athletic team (indicate school/sport/years)

___Gerald (Jerry) Irons Jr. Univ. of Nebraska - Football 3 yrs.___
___Gerald Irons Sr. - Univ. of Maryland - 1966-70 - Football___
___Oakland Raiders - Linebacker - 1970-76 Cleveland Browns 1976-80___

Hometown Media Information
Name(s) of Newspaper(s) which regularly cover your high school. Give complete name and location, if possible.

___Houston Post - Houston Chronicle - Houston, Tx___
___The Villager - 2250 Buckthorne - The Woodlands, Tx 77380___
___The Woodlands Sun - 2220 Buckthorne - " " " "___
___The Courier - 100 Ave. A. Conroe, Tx 77301___
___People Scene - 1755 Woodstead ct, Tx 77380___

University of Michigan Athletic Public Relations
Student-Athlete Information Release

Name _Jarrett David Frons_

Note: This form comes under the purview of the Family Educational Rights and Privacy Act of 1974.

Principle Specification of Records: This consent statement authorizes administrative personnel of the University of Michigan Athletic Department and its Athletic Public Relations office to review and to disseminate to third parties information in my personal "educational records," including information contained on this release form and any other education information, bodily injury/health data, or family tragedy facts collected and/or maintained by this institution, for public relations purposes.

Purpose(s) of Disclosure: Information obtained from these records will assist in compilation of personal information for use in official athletic department/athletic public relations publications for dissemination to legitimate news media, for purposes of nominating me for athletic and academic honors programs, awards and scholarships, and for general public relations purposes.

Party or Class of Parties to Whom Disclosure May Be Released: By signing this consent statement, I authorize administrative personnel of the University of Michigan Athletic Department and its Athletic Public Relations office to review and disseminate any information per Principal Specification of Records (above) to third parties for general public relations purposes.

Jarrett David Frons   _5-1-92_
Signature (legal name only; no nicknames)   *Date* (month/date/year)

FootBall   _1992-93_
Sport(s)   *Commencing Academic Year*

High School Information

High School (name/city/state) *McCullough – The Woodlands, Texas*

Year Graduated *1992* Athletic Conference (spell out) *Fifteen – Five – A*

Academic Honors, Clubs (i.e., National Honor Society, Honor Roll, etc.) *Honor Roll – HONOR Courses – Jack and Jill of America Teen of the Year – Homecoming King – 1991*

By Year, list sports competed in, honors received, varsity letters earned, season-ending statistical information, team achievements. Be sure to give complete name of each award/honor (i.e., All-West Central Conference Football First-Team; All-Putnam County Girls' Track - selected by Putnam County Banner-Graphic).. List coach's complete name with sport. Use an additional piece of paper if necessary.

Freshman Year, 1988 - 1989 (9th grade):

Freshman Football – Weldon Willis
" Basketball – Coach Priest
" Track – Dan Creek

Sophomore Year, 1989 - 1990 (10th grade):

Varsity Football – Weldon Willis
All District in Football
Varsity Track – Dan Green
Earned Letters in Football + Track

Junior Year, 1990 - 1991 (11th grade):

Varsity Football – Varsity Track – *Weldon Willis Junior + Senior yrs / Dan Green*
All District First Team All Greater Houston
Super Prep Team –
Bi-District Champions – Regional Champions

Senior Year, 1991 - 1992 (12th grade): – 1991 – First season in history to go undefeated! *District Champions!*
First Team on all Honors Captain of Football Team — Parade Magazine All-American
All-State *First Team* All Greater Houston All-District – A.P. Super Team
Montgomery Co. Defensive Player of the Year - 1991 - Houston Chronicle - Top Fifty *in State*
Super Prep All-American - Tom Lemming's All-American - Max Emfinger's Top *Linebacker*
Most Tackles (316) of Any Player in McCullough's history
Longest Touchdown in McCullough's History - 88 yard Interception Return *Touchdown*
1991 – 24 Tackles for Negative yardage (most in McCullough's history)
1991 – 146 Tackles (most in Season of Any Player in McCullough's history)

CHAPTER 8

Brian Griese

The University of Michigan has been the landing spot for top quarterback recruits year in and year out, producing some of the best signal-callers in college football. At various periods of time, the program was bringing in some of the elite quarterbacks in each recruiting class and stacking the roster with the next best thing. Because of that Brian Griese saw himself on the outside of the recruiting picture for Michigan.

Griese grew up in Miami, Florida, the son of Hall of Fame quarterback Bob Griese. Brian wasn't a highly touted prospect, so he saw very little activity—only a few scholarship offers—when it came to his recruitment. Being the son of a well-known quarterback, Brian never wanted to follow in his father's footsteps, even though his dad's alma mater was one of the few schools to offer him a scholarship.

The elder Griese had starred at Purdue before heading off to the NFL, and Purdue assistant coach Dino Babers had offered the younger Griese a full-ride scholarship to become a Boilermaker. "He was our No. 1 target. We would have taken him. Obviously his dad, Bob, was an All-American at Purdue, but we offered Brian because he could flat-out play," Babers said. "He was playing at a smaller school, but he had all of the tools and skills that we wanted at Purdue. We thought he could be a very good player for us."

Part of it was that Brian didn't want to go on the same path his father did, and part of it was that he also didn't want to be an engineer, which is primarily what Purdue is known for academically. Because of his father's success, Brian was afforded the opportunity to turn down a full-ride to a Big Ten school. Had he and his family not been able to afford college without a scholarship, he admitted that he likely would have wound up playing for Purdue. But the circumstances and his situation gave him the opportunity to look elsewhere and find the right fit. Since he lacked many scholarship offers, Brian figured he shouldn't have any aspirations to make it to the NFL. If he couldn't make a college team, why should he think that he could eventually make an NFL team? "Honestly, when I tell you it was the academics I was looking at, it was the academics that sold me," Griese said. "I wanted to study political science, and honestly and truthfully, the furthest thing from my mind was becoming a professional football player. I know a lot of kids now that's the forefront of their mind, but for me there were only a few teams interested in me coming to play, so there should be no thoughts of me being a professional player."

Outside of the Boilermakers, there were some programs showing interest in Brian and gauging whether they should offer him a scholarship. North Carolina, Virginia, Stanford, and Michigan were among those schools. Stanford's academic portion was too good to look past. Unfortunately for him, Stanford had already gained a commitment from a quarterback in that class. The quarterback who took the scholarship spot was none other than Scott Frost, who would later cross paths again with Brian in college. Frost originally attended Stanford before ultimately finishing his college career at Nebraska.

That didn't deter Brian from attending Stanford football camp, when esteemed head coach Bill Walsh was leading the program. He thought there might still be an opportunity if he could show Walsh what he was capable of, so he went to the camp the summer before his senior season in 1992. "I went out there to learn from Bill Walsh and I had a really good experience," Brian said. "I played well at the camp, and that's really when they started recruiting me."

There was still no scholarship offer because of Frost, but he had the invite from Walsh to come as a walk-on. Wanting to continue exploring what other schools were interested, Brian didn't make any decisions or tell the staff how he felt about that option. He felt as though Stanford would be a good opportunity academically, but after doing a bit of research, he found that Michigan was the best combination of academics and athletics that he sought. He wanted to go into political science, and Michigan was an excellent option for that major. The football team had gone to five straight Rose Bowls, so the athletic side was just as revered as the education, but Michigan had not extended an offer. They, too, were chasing another quarterback in that class, Scot Loeffler. The coaching staff already had already identified Loeffler as the quarterback they wanted in the class, and Loeffler committed to the Wolverines, so the scholarship at the position was already taken.

Brian had faced an uphill battle with his recruitment. Michigan hadn't even seen him throw, and the opportunity to get the Michigan coaches—or any coaches—down to see him play was delayed his senior season as Hurricane Andrew rolled through south Florida in August of 1992. "Half our season was eliminated because of the hurricane. It came right through Miami, and a bunch of our coaches lost their homes," Brian said. "Half our season was truncated, so there wasn't a lot of film either."

The hurricane tore apart much of south Florida and potentially impacted Brian's shot at any other schools showing interest. Without much senior film and with other quarterbacks making their commitments and taking up scholarship offers, the opportunities were few and far between. Because of the situation he was in and with his father being able to afford college without a scholarship, Brian figured that his best bet was to choose between some of the schools that had offered him an opportunity to walk on. Once his senior season was complete, Brian did entertain a few other schools but knew that Michigan and Stanford would be the schools in the final running. "I had two older brothers, so I went selfishly, I went to visit them at their schools. One was at Virginia, and one was at North Carolina," Brian said. "I sat down with George Welsh, the coach at Virginia, and he told me that he wanted me to run the option. I looked over my shoulder to see if there was someone else in the room to see who he was talking to. I said, 'Thanks, Coach. I'll go ahead with my nice meal at the steakhouse and visit my brother and I'll be out of your hair.'"

Brian also met with North Carolina coach Mack Brown on his visit to see the Tar Heels, but again it came back to Michigan and Stanford. He was going back and forth between the two, so he decided to take a visit after his senior year to see up close and personal what Michigan had to offer. "I was just waiting for someone to offer me. If somebody would've offered me a scholarship, I would've gone to Stanford, but they didn't offer me," Brian said. "On the Michigan visit, to me what was more important was seeing the academics, seeing how the university life worked there, and whether I would fit in there from an academic standpoint."

After his Michigan visit was over, Brian still felt as though he could compete and deserved a scholarship from somewhere, but with a lack of film and time running out, it looked as though walking on to a program would be his final option. There were no new programs showing any interest—none at least that could stack up to Michigan and Stanford.

So after his senior season—because of the combination of athletics and academics—Brian decided he should walk on at the University of Michigan. Coaches Cam Cameron and Gary Moeller came down from Michigan to his home in Florida to visit him and talk to him about the opportunity, essentially telling him that he would be a preferred walk-on. That meant that he lacked a scholarship offer, but he didn't have to try out for the team either. His place as a walk-on would be secured. The coaches also told him that if a scholarship opened up once he got to campus he would be in line to receive that financial aid. "You know what coaches say: get on campus. If things work out, then yeah, if there's a scholarship that opens up, we'll talk to you about it," Brian said. "But you have to show up and do it. They did that through the first camp at Michigan and saw that I could play. That was their first time seeing me play in person was at practice at Michigan."

Brian told his father that Michigan was where he wanted to go, and they told the coaches that he was coming to Ann Arbor. It was unceremonious—much like his recruitment—because there was no real paperwork to sign without a scholarship. He made sure he told Babers, a coach he admired in the recruiting process, that he was choosing the Wolverines and thanked him for recruiting him. "I was under the impression because Michigan hadn't offered him [that] he was going to come to Purdue. I can still remember him calling me on the phone and waiting for him to say, 'Hey, Coach Babers, I'm coming to Purdue,'" Babers said. "What he actually said was: 'Coach, thanks for recruiting me, but I'm going to walk on at Michigan.' I was like, 'Are you kidding me? I just got beat by Casper, the Friendly Ghost? Michigan doesn't even have a scholarship, and you're going to go to Michigan?' He said, 'Coach, I just don't want to play at the same place my dad played. I want to blaze my own path.'"

Brian wanted to blaze that path at Michigan despite the fact he didn't have a scholarship offer. Financial aid or not, his mentality about his ability and his value to the team remained steadfast. Brian wasn't going to Michigan just to sit on the bench, to be a scout player. The Wolverines had been to five straight Rose Bowls prior to his joining the Michigan team in 1993, and Brian wanted to help continue that excellence.

He enrolled at Michigan and went to work, trying to show the coaches he was worth the scholarship and that he was there to play. As it just so happened, Brain held up his end of the bargain by performing at a high level, and the Wolverines had a defensive lineman quit during Brian's freshman season. True to the their word, the coaches put Brian on scholarship and gave him a full ride. "I was appreciative, but honestly I felt like I deserved a scholarship from the get-go. It was nice to call home and tell my dad he didn't have to pay for school anymore," Brian said. "I felt like I belonged and I fit from a competition stand-point from the start. And after I got that scholarship, it was right back to the scout team and getting the crap kicked out of me."

Brian was low man on the totem pole, so he was live in practice, meaning the defense could hit him. He was the quarterback throwing in third-down drills when the defense is practicing its pass rush. So it was right back to being humble again. The only difference now was that he was on scholarship. He took a redshirt that year, and his big break came the following season, his redshirt freshman year, when he was given the holder job. He was the holder for extra points for kicker Remy Hamilton, and it meant that he was actually on the field in games. "That was my whole year of just holding," Brian said. "But after that year, they signed the No. 1 quarterback recruit in the country in Scott Dreisbach. I went through my grunt year, went through the year of holding, and I'm ready to do something, and sure enough, they bring in the No. 1 guy in the country, which is how it goes at Michigan."

For the 1995 season, the Michigan coaches started Scott Dreisbach as a true freshman over the now redshirt sophomore. After putting in his time and competing with the list of quarterbacks on the depth chart, Brian was now behind a quarterback who would have four years of eligibility. Todd Collins had graduated, Jay Riemersma was moved to tight end, and Scot Loeffler, the other quarterback in Brian's recruiting class, eventually suffered a career-ending shoulder injury. But coaches handed the ball to the true freshman for the first game against Virginia.

On fourth and 10 with four seconds left in the game and Michigan down 17–12 to Virginia, Dreisbach connected on a pass to wide receiver Mercury Hayes in the back of the end zone to come back from a 17-point deficit and win the game. That performance sealed Dreisbach's position as the starter and put Brian back on the bench for now. "If there was ever a time to say, 'Man, I'm out of here,' it was that time. But again it came back to why did I go there in the first place?" Brian said. "I had to suck it up, and then Scott got hurt midway through the season, and I came in and played five games. So that was the first time I got on the field as a quarterback was in 1995."

Brian came in and posted a 4–4 record, which included a 31–23 takedown of No. 2 ranked Ohio State. Running back Tim Biakabutuka rushed for 317 yards in that game to help push the Wolverines past the Buckeyes. Brian completed nine of his 18 passes for 103 yards with one touchdown and three interceptions in the game.

His performance in the second half of the 1995 season, though, wasn't enough to push him past a now healthy Dreisbach for the 1996 season. Dreisbach was once again named the starter, and Brian was back to the bench. Dreisbach started the whole season, and Brian began to grow anxious. "We lost four games, didn't have a great year, and I was frustrated. I was graduating school and I was frustrated," Brian said. "I'm not going to play professionally now because I can't even start on my college team. So I remember we went to Columbus, and they were ranked second in the country, and we had lost four games. We started the game, and Scott got hurt at the end of the second quarter with us down 9–0 at the half. I remember sitting in the locker room at halftime and I was like, *Well, I have 30 minutes. The last 30 minutes to play football, this is it. Let it hang out and see what happens.*"

At that point in the season, Brian had made up his mind that he would not return to Michigan for his fifth year just to sit behind Dreisbach again because he had already graduated and now had a scholarship offer to pursue a graduate degree at George Washington University through the Maxwell Award Foundation. In his mind this would be the last game he would play as a Wolverine, so he had nothing to lose.

On second and 9 from the Michigan 32-yard line to open the third quarter, Brian dropped back. Tai Streets ran a slant and saw Ohio State cornerback Shawn Springs slip on the play. Brian hit Streets in stride, and the receiver took care of the rest, scoring on a 68-yard pass to pull Michigan within striking distance. The Wolverines would go on to add two field goals, including a 39-yarder from Hamilton with one minute and 19 seconds left in the game, sealing the victory against Ohio State. "Probably the most disappointing loss we had. We were beating them pretty good at halftime, but the score was only 9–0," then-Buckeyes head coach John Cooper said. "One of the best cornerbacks to ever play football at Ohio State slipped, and they catch the ball and run for a touchdown. That was probably the most disappointing loss because we probably had a better team than they had and probably should've won the game, but we didn't."

Michigan won and moved on to the bowl game. Dreisbach wasn't healthy enough to play, so Brian started the final game of the season. Michigan lost 17–14 to Alabama in the Outback Bowl, and Brian thought his Michigan playing career was over. He had a nice run, but this would be it as he wasn't interested in sitting behind Dreisbach any longer. "I had one year of eligibility left and I had dinner with my brother, who was older than me, and I was telling him that I was going to use my scholarship and go to grad school," Brian said. "He asked how long the scholarship was good for, if it was just one year. I said, 'No, I could use it at any point over five years.' So he told me that I have the rest of my life to get a real job and that I should go back just to see what happens. I said, 'Yeah, but Jeff, I've been sitting on the sidelines, most frustrating year of my life, watching this kid throw picks and us lose games.'"

Brian knew his brother was right, though, so he thought about the decision. There was no assurance from head coach Lloyd Carr that Brian would play if he came back—especially because now the coaching staff had added another quarterback to the mix named Tom Brady in 1995. Now a fifth-year senior, Brian thought about what his brother had said and decided that he would come back for one more year. The quote that kept running through his mind was from Bo Schembechler, who had so famously stated that those who stay will be champions. When Brian was thinking about choosing Michigan out of high school, the Wolverines had won the Big Ten five times in a row and had been to the Rose Bowl each year. For four years his class had not won anything.

At one point Brian looked around the locker room at the other fifth-year players. Only six were left, and they were at risk of being one of the first classes not to go to the Rose Bowl since the 1960s. Brian knew he had more to accomplish and didn't want to end his college career on that note. "So Tom, Scott, and I battle it out, and it was pretty clear that Tommy was better than Scott, so it really came down to Tommy and I," Brian said. "Lloyd didn't name the starter until the week of the first game against Colorado. He named me the starter, and the rest is history."

The rest is history, as Michigan and Brian mowed through their schedule that season in 1997, beating Notre Dame, Iowa, Michigan State, Penn State, Wisconsin, Ohio State, and eventually Washington State to win the national championship. Brian and the Wolverines were named national champs along with Nebraska, who was quarterbacked by none other than Frost, the player who had taken Brian's scholarship spot at Stanford.

Brian's decision to stay at Michigan was a wise one, as he became a champion. He finished that season completing more than 63 percent of his passes while throwing for 2,042 yards and 14 touchdowns. His performance in his senior season led him to something he never thought would be a possibility. After that 1997 season, the Denver Broncos drafted him in the third round with pick No. 91, where he helped succeed John Elway. Brian, who now broadcasts college football games for ESPN, went on to have a 10-year career in the NFL and fulfill the thoughts he had so many years ago that he was worth that scholarship offer when he walked on at the University of Michigan.

University of Michigan Athletic Public Relations
Student-Athlete Information Release

Name   Brian Griese

Note: This form comes under the purview of the Family Educational Rights and Privacy Act of 1974.

Principle Specification of Records: This consent statement authorizes administrative personnel of the University of Michigan Athletic Department and its Athletic Public Relations office to review and to disseminate to third parties information in my personal "educational records," including information contained on this release form and any other education information, bodily injury/health data, or family tragedy facts collected and/or maintained by this institution, for public relations purposes.

Purpose(s) of Disclosure: Information obtained from these records will assist in compilation of personal information for use in official athletic department/athletic public relations publications for dissemination to legitimate news media, for purposes of nominating me for athletic and academic honors programs, awards and scholarships, and for general public relations purposes.

Party or Class of Parties to Whom Disclosure May Be Released: By signing this consent statement, I authorize administrative personnel of the University of Michigan Athletic Department and its Athletic Public Relations office to review and disseminate any information per Principal Specification of Records (above) to third parties for general public relations purposes, including marketing and promotions, and academic award programs.

Brian Griese
Signature (legal name only; no nicknames)

3/30/93
Date (month/date/year)

Football
Sport(s)

1993-94
Commencing Academic Year

149

University of Michigan Athletic Public Relations
Student-Athlete Biographical Information

This biographical information is a permanent record in your athletic public relations file. Please complete the form neatly, accurately and completely. Supplemental information (newspaper articles, etc.) may be included to complete background information.

Date 3/30/93   U-M Sport Football

Personal Information

Legal Name (first, middle, last) Brian David Griese

Preferred Name / Nickname Brian

Date of Birth (month/date/year) 3/18/75   Height 6'3   Weight 215

Home Address (address/city/state/zip) 4412 Santa Maria / Miami, Fl. 33146

U-M Address (address/city/state/zip) ▮▮▮▮▮▮▮▮▮▮▮▮▮▮

Home Phone ▮▮▮▮▮▮▮▮▮▮   U-M Phone ▮▮▮▮▮▮▮▮

Academic Class (fr., so., jr., sr., grad.) fr.   Athletic Eligibility (fr., so., jr., sr., 5th yr.) fr.

U-M School Enrolled In L, S, A   Major undecided

Family Information

Father's Name (first/last) Bob Griese   College Purdue

Father's Address (if same as yours, omit) _____

Mother's Name (first/last) Judy Griese (deceased) College Purdue

Mother's Address (if same as yours, omit) _____

Parent's Marital Status: married _____ divorced _____   Number of: brothers 2 sisters _____

Parent, sibling(s) who are now or have been members of intercollegiate varsity athletic team (indicate school/sport/years)

(BROTHER)	SCOTT	- UNIV VIRGINIA	'89, 90, 91
''	JEFF	'' NORTH CAROLINA	'90
(FATHER)	BOB	PURDUE	'64, '65, '66

Hometown Media Information
Name(s) of Newspaper(s) which regularly cover your high school. Give complete name and location, if possible.

Miami Herald, St. Petersburg Times

150

High School Information

High School (name/city/state) Columbus / Miami, Fl.

Year Graduated 1993   Athletic Conference (spell out) Greater Miami Athletic Conf.

Academic Honors, Clubs (i.e., National Honor Society, Honor Roll, etc.) National Honor Society,
First Honors.

By Year, list sports competed in, honors received, varsity letters earned, season-ending statistical information, team achievements. Be sure to give complete name of each award/honor (i.e., All-West Central Conference Football First-Team; All-Putnam County Girls' Track - selected by Putnam County Banner-Graphic).. List coach's complete name with sport. Use an additional piece of paper if necessary.

Freshman Year, 19___- 19___ (9th grade):

VARSITY GOLF
J.V. BASKETBALL
J.V. FOOTBALL

Sophomore Year, 19___ - 19___ (10 grade):

VARSITY GOLF
J.V. BASKETBALL → M.V.P.
VARSITY FOOTBALL

Junior Year, 19___- 19___ (11TH grade):

VARSITY GOLF - 2ND TEAM All COUNTY
VARSITY BASKETBALL
VARSITY FOOTBALL

Senior Year, 19___- 19___ (12 grade):

VARSITY GOLF
VARSITY BASKETBALL · Co·CAP'T
VARSITY FOOTBALL Co·CAP'T, 2ND TEAM All COUNTY QB
        3RD " All STATE PUNTER

CHAPTER 9

Tim Biakabutuka

Michigan fans often remember Tim Biakabutuka for his performance against Ohio State in 1995 that helped push the Wolverines past the Buckeyes in a 31–23 victory. Biakabutuka ran for 313 yards and one touchdown in a game where he was supposed to be the secondary running back behind Ohio State's eventual Heisman Trophy winner, Eddie George. Biakabutuka's performance spoke for itself, and Michigan shelved George and Ohio State's national championship hopes, breaking up the Buckeyes' undefeated season. That performance is still the second most rushing yards in one game by any Michigan running back behind Ron Johnson, who ran for 347 yards in 1968. After the game Biakabutuka told *The Michigan Daily* that he had never seen running lanes that big, crediting his offensive linemen. He was able to accomplish such a performance after only six seasons playing football, adjusting to a language barrier, and fighting for a chance at a better life.

Born Tshimanga Biakabutuka in Zaire, Africa, he and his family moved from a French region of Zaire, which is now known as Congo, when he was only six years old. His father, Mulenga Wa Biakabutuka, and his mother, Misenga Batuabile Bibi, moved their family from Africa to the South Shores, a suburb of Montreal, Quebec. The area is situated just across the St. Lawrence River from Montreal and is largely a French-speaking region. It was a new environment, but his father found a job as a teacher, and his mother was a clothing designer, and the family settled in to their new home.

Neither Tshimanga nor his parents knew what American football was when they moved to Canada, and even into high school, it was never something he had watched or paid attention to. His parents were more focused on academics than athletics because they had never heard of anyone close to them gaining much from sports. Biakabutuka attended Jean-Jacques Rousseau High in Longueuil in the late 1980s and early 1990s at a time where there was racial tension in the school. With a predominantly French community, the immigrants often faced scrutiny. Because of that tension, the school saw fights and a lack of togetherness from its students.

When he was younger and caught up in his surroundings, Biakabutuka often participated in the fights and got himself into minor trouble at school. He was a good student but wasn't afraid to fight back and hold his own. To help combat against the fighting and tension in the school, the administrators decided to start a football team in 1990. They figured that would be a good way of channeling the energy from the students and help bring them together.

The eventual coach of the high school team approached Biakabutuka on the sidelines during a physical education class and asked him if he had any interest in playing football. "I said, 'Which one, soccer?' He said, 'No, American football,'" Biakabutuka said. "I said, 'The one where they run into each other?' And he said, 'Yes.' I told him I wasn't interested, but his comment was that I would get to hit those guys I was fighting all the time. So I said, 'Okay, I'll be there,' and that's why I got started playing football."

The first practice was difficult—not just for Biakabutuka, who was learning a new sport, but also for everyone else who showed up to participate in the new team. Because of the strenuous nature of the practices, the coaches saw quite a few players quit from the team. "There were only two black kids on the team, and the other guy quit. I said, 'Well, I'm not going to quit, so they see all the black kids quit,'" Biakabutuka said. "I stayed, and luckily the next day got easier. I started playing safety, and then they moved me to running back, where I started to excel and I went from there."

After his first season ever playing football, Biakabutuka thought he had grasped the sport pretty well and started to build a love for the game. He had a successful first season and started to have aspirations of playing on a bigger stage. He asked his coach at the time if he thought he would ever have a shot at playing football in college. Though his coach had never had any of his past players go on to play at the next level, he encouraged Biakabutuka to work even harder and take the sport more seriously so that he could achieve that goal.

The problem for Biakabutuka was that American football wasn't popular in the area he lived and was often taken as a joke. To add to that, his own parents neither understood the sport nor believed it was a path that would offer anything of value. His mother only attended one of his high school games, and his father attended none.

He continued to improve in his second year of high school and started to wonder what it would take to play at the next level. In Montreal the high school only goes up to grade 11, and before heading to university, students are required to attend a CEGEP program. An acronym for *Collège d'Enseignement Général Et Professionnel*, the CEGEP schools are comparable to prep schools or junior colleges in America but were mandatory before any student could attend a university. CEGEP was a two-year pre-university college program that most students finished in three years. Recruiting a prospect from Canada often meant you were recruiting a player who was already two or three years removed from high school.

Jim Herrmann was the linebackers coach at Michigan at the time and recalls going on recruiting trips up to Canada, taking the coaches out for dinner and a drink, and oftentimes the prospects would be there drinking with them because they were legally allowed to drink alcohol in their home country. "If you go back in Michigan history, we had a punter, Eddie Azcona, who was from Montreal, and that's how it all started for us recruiting that area. We developed relationships, and there was one program, Vieux Montreal, and the head coach there was Marc Santerre," Herrmann said. "The recruiting part of it was different because they could go to CEGEP for three years and still come to the United States and have four or five years of eligibility. Trying to go through the transcript in French and trying to translate it to English, there was a little bit of gray area in there that made it really interesting, too."

Santerre had been driving Canadian prospects to Michigan's summer camp for a few years by the time Biakabutuka was ready to leave high school and attend a CEGEP program. Santerre knew that Michigan had one of the biggest summer camps for high school football players in the country, so he wanted to give some of the local players an opportunity to be seen by American coaches. Smaller colleges attended the camp, and coaches from all divisions worked with the prospects, so it wasn't just an opportunity for a scholarship to Michigan but rather many schools in one place.

Santerre had seen Biakabutuka play in a high school championship game and knew that he wanted him to play at Vieux Montreal. He recruited Biakabutuka in 1992 and tried to get him to join his program. Biakabutuka was interested in Vieux Montreal, but another school that was farther away, Vanier, was an English-speaking school. Vieux Montreal was mainly French, and Biakabutuka wanted to attend a school that would teach him more English. He hadn't quite decided yet on which program he would attend, though, and before he did, Santerre asked Biakabutuka if he would like to attend the Michigan summer camp. "Tshimanga hadn't even played at CEGEP at the time, so he wasn't known by any of the American schools. The only guy who knew about him was a guy named Ron Dias, who ran a recruiting company," Santerre said. "Ron had Tshimanga on his recruiting list for schools, but he himself didn't know that much about him. So we go to the camp, and Coach Carr came up to me and said, 'Who is that kid? How come we didn't know about him?' I said because he hasn't even played yet in CEGEP."

Biakabutuka was really only the equivalent of a high school junior at the time, but because Montreal's schooling system was different he wasn't yet identified as a true prospect. Most of the Canadian players went to CEGEP for the full three years—or at least two years—before having a real opportunity at an American scholarship.

Because the Michigan coaches weren't aware of who Biakabutuka was when he got to the camp, they initially put him in a group with the other junior running backs. Biakabutuka looked across the field and saw the seniors and thought they looked bigger and faster than the group he was in. So when running backs coach Fred Jackson walked by, Biakabutuka told Jackson he thought he was in the wrong group. Jackson asked him what year he was, and Biakabutuka wisely told him he was in his last year, which was not false, because he technically was in his last year of Canadian high school.

Jackson told him he was supposed to be with the seniors and moved him over to the older group. The running backs coach stayed there and watched Biakabutuka complete a drill. If Biakabutuka didn't understand the first time, he asked him how to do the drill and then completed it. After the session was over, Jackson told Biakabutuka to stay where he was when all the other campers went to lunch. He wanted Biakabutuka to meet Michigan's head coach, Gary Moeller, to talk about how well he was doing at the camp. "I have never seen in my life a kid with feet that fast. You have 200 or 300 running backs there and you're trying to evaluate talent," Jackson said. "Once I got him in a group where I could zero in on him myself, I saw the speed of his feet and his shiftiness and I had never seen anything like it."

But Michigan didn't offer him a scholarship just yet. Because he hadn't even played at CEGEP, the Michigan coaches figured Biakabutuka still had two more years before he would be cleared by the NCAA and at a level where he would be ready to compete at a place like Michigan. Biakabutuka didn't have a scholarship, but he had the attention of the Michigan coaches. He had a decision to make when he got home, though, as to what CEGEP he would attend.

Santerre continued recruiting him, but Vieux Montreal already had an excellent running back on the roster that Biakabutuka knew about. Bruno Heppell, who would later go on to play at Western Michigan and in the Canadian Football League, was already at Vieux Montreal. With only limited time to get an opportunity in CEGEP and also wanting to learn more English, Biakabutuka ultimately decided to attend the rival school, Vanier.

Unlike Vieux Montreal, however, Vanier hadn't been recruiting the talented running back. Tim Matuzewski was the head coach at Vanier and was quite frank with Biakabutuka about his status with the team. "I walked into camp and asked the coach how I could make the team. I told him I was coming out of high school, and he said, 'Well, look, why don't you watch practice today, and if you still feel like you can play, we'll give you a helmet and pads, and you can try out for the team,'" Biakabutuka said. "So the first day, I stood on the sideline and watched practice, and the coach asked me if I wanted to join the team, and I said yes. They had red helmets and red jerseys and they didn't have a helmet that fit my size, so I was the only one with a black helmet."

Vanier had just won the league championship the year before. But Biakabutuka knew what he was capable of, so he tried out for the team and made it. Just as Santerre had connections with Michigan, the Vanier coaches had connections with Syracuse. So the Orange soon found out about the not-so-well-known back from Montreal and started recruiting him as well. Cincinnati also tried to get in the conversation, but it was really Michigan and Syracuse that had the best inroads and shot at landing him.

It was rare that a player would leave a CEGEP program after his first year, but because of the success Biakabutuka saw after his first season, he felt as though he was ready to take the next step. Santerre eventually got word that Biakabutuka was leaving after his first year and had heard that Michigan still hadn't offered a scholarship. "I called Lloyd Carr and said I don't know if you know that Tim is about to leave for Syracuse, but if I were you, I would give him a call. Lloyd said, 'I didn't know he was going to leave this year. I didn't know he would be a recruit for this year,'" Santerre said. "I told him he was allowed to leave because he had been cleared by the Clearinghouse and the NCAA. So Lloyd called Tshimanga and came up to Montreal."

Santerre picked Carr up from the airport and took him to Biakabutuka's house. The visit took place after the season in 1992. Otherwise Santerre would not have been visiting the home of a rival player. Carr came in and sat with the family, spoke to them about Michigan, and offered Biakabutuka a scholarship. Biakabutuka still had Syracuse and Cincinnati after him, so he wanted to make sure he got a clear view of each program and decided to take official visits to each school.

In Montreal the only teams they saw play American football on television were typically Michigan and Notre Dame. Biakabutuka remembers watching Ricky Powers run the ball in the winged helmet and had an affinity for the Wolverines. Still, he wanted to be sure. "Syracuse was the first visit, and we went there and came back, went to Michigan, and then Cincinnati. When I went on my recruiting visits, Michigan was my worst recruiting visit and Cincinnati, I had a blast," Biakabutuka said. "Michigan put me with a host from Montreal, and he wasn't very social with his teammates, so we didn't do anything. When I went to Cincinnati and Syracuse, they put me with the most entertaining guys, and we barely slept. My priorities weren't really in the right place."

Because he enjoyed himself so much on his Cincinnati visit and the fact that the excitement was still there from being the last visit, Biakabutuka came home and told his parents he was going to pick Cincinnati. His parents didn't care about sports and they certainly did not care about their son enjoying the party scene at an American university. Biakabutuka didn't know, but his father had been conducting his own research without his son knowing. His father has a PhD in psychology, and education was a priority. "Sports even at that time was a pasttime, not a profession to my parents. When he said that he was doing research, I was surprised," Biakabutuka said. "It was never a goal of my parents to have a kid play professional sports. So I came back and told my dad I'm going to Cincinnati, and his response was, 'I've never heard of Cincinnati being a good school. You're going to Michigan.' That was it."

Despite a disappointing recruiting visit and his initial decision to attend Cincinnati, his parents had spoken, and he would eventually see that their thought process led to the right choice for him. He had been wrapped up in the excitement of the Cincinnati visit, but when that feeling wore off, he knew Michigan was where he was supposed to be. Biakabutuka called the Michigan coaches and told them he would be a Wolverine. From the kid who had only gotten into football to have a chance at hitting some of his classmates to having an opportunity to join the University of Michigan, Biakabutuka's rise in football was unchartered territory in Canada and is still viewed as one of the more extraordinary recruiting stories from that area.

His journey to Michigan wasn't a straight path, and once he got to campus it was very similar. He could speak English, but since French was his native language, he still spoke with an accent. That made it difficult initially for his teammates and coaches to understand him and fully take him in as one of the guys. Aside from that, he was also getting used to a smaller field in America. The Canadian fields are wider, giving running backs more room to bounce outside with the ball. "Another thing that he had to deal with was those poor kids from Canada had to pay taxes on their scholarships because they were from out of the country. There were some times where he was hard-pressed for money," Herrmann said. "That transition was not easy for him because of all the extra stuff they had to do with the student visa to the scholarship money getting taxed. We had to talk to people in the state department, immigration. It was a pain in the ass."

There were also a few times early on that Biakabutuka felt homesick as any college student far away from his home would. Santerre still traveled to Michigan's summer camp every year and would meet up with Biakabutuka to check on how he was doing. During that first summer, Jackson told Santerre that Biakabutuka was thinking about going home for the summer and wondered if that was a good idea. Santerre spoke with Biakabutuka about being homesick, assured him that it was normal, and that his best bet was to stay at Michigan for the summer. If he left, he wouldn't have an opportunity to get better and compete with the other backs who were staying in Ann Arbor during the offseason. If he left, it might make him more homesick, and who knows what would happen if he made the trek back to Montreal.

Biakabutuka decided to stay, and the decision paid off. As tough as the transition was personally for Biakabutuka, it all came naturally on the field. Once he adjusted to the size of the field, he showed the coaches exactly what they were hoping to see. His famously fast feet and shiftiness were on display very early in his career at Michigan. After that it was mainly smooth sailing for the Canadian and Nigerian, who was assimilating to Michigan and his teammates. Save for a few pranks here and there, he was getting along just fine. "Tyrone [Wheatley] would tell him the wrong stuff on purpose in practice. Tshimanga would ask Tyrone what the play was, and Tyrone would tell him something totally different," Jackson said. "If you ask Tyrone about it, he would say, 'I was just trying to make him learn.' They were buddies, though, and I had them on the phone talking about this in 2017. I never knew about it until Tshimanga told me about it later on."

During his first season on campus in 1993, Biakabutuka ran the ball 43 times for 209 yards and five touchdowns. He was behind some talented backs that included Wheatley, Ed Davis, and Powers, whom he had watched on television in Canada. In 1994 Biakabutuka saw his carries increase despite backing up Wheatley. He ran the ball 126 times for 783 yards and seven touchdowns. The confidence wasn't lacking even in the 1994 season, when he wasn't the featured back. "I remember when Lou Holtz, who was at Notre Dame at the time, couldn't pronounce his name correctly," Jackson said. "Before the Notre Dame game that year, Tshimanga came up to me and said, 'He'll be able to pronounce my name after this game.'"

Biakabutuka ran for 102 yards and a touchdown in that game and started to make a name for himself. But it wasn't really until his third season in 1995, when Biakabutuka had the chance to be the featured back. He made the most of that opportunity as he ran for 1,818 yards that season, which is still the most rushing yards in a season for any Michigan running back.

And the confidence continued to grow as he gained more and more strength throughout the season. He racked up eight games of 100 yards rushing or more, and while the team's record was only 9–4, Biakabutuka and his Michigan teammates made the most of the end of the season.

The day before the game against Ohio State, Biakabutuka knew that star Ohio State running back George was coming to The Big House. All the attention was on George and the undefeated Buckeyes, but Biakabutuka wouldn't back down. He had fought when he was younger and he would fight again the next day to make sure people knew who he was. The kid from a small town in Quebec, whom no one recruited and had to scrap for every opportunity he got, would make sure that he took the stage away from George on Saturday. "Eddie George was going to wrap up winning a Heisman Trophy," Jackson said. "Tshimanga looked at me and told me Eddie wouldn't be the best back on the field the next day. That was the game Tshimanga rushed for over 300 yards."

He ran for 313 yards, to be exact, and a touchdown for an exclamation point. Bested by Biakabutuka on that day, George finished with 105 yards and one touchdown. That would be Biakabutuka's final season at Michigan in 1995, and he finished his career with 2,810 yards and 24 touchdowns. He left his mark in the Michigan record book and was drafted eighth overall in the 1996 NFL Draft by the Carolina Panthers.

He had a six-year career in the NFL but was hampered by injuries, eventually ending his career with a foot injury in 2001. Biakabutuka, however, showed how far someone can come from such humble beginnings. He showed his parents that football wasn't just a hobby and because of his persistence and determination he'll be forever remembered as one of Michigan's best running backs to wear the winged helmet.

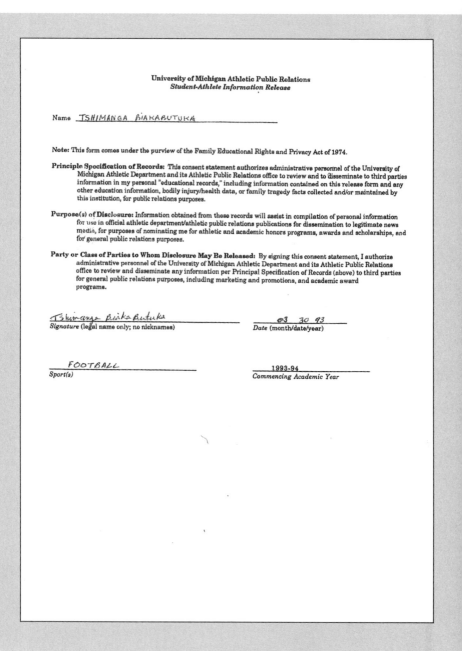

University of Michigan Athletic Public Relations
Student-Athlete Information Release

Name   _TSHIMANGA BIAKABUTUKA_

Note: This form comes under the purview of the Family Educational Rights and Privacy Act of 1974.

Principle Specification of Records: This consent statement authorizes administrative personnel of the University of Michigan Athletic Department and its Athletic Public Relations office to review and to disseminate to third parties information in my personal "educational records," including information contained on this release form and any other education information, bodily injury/health data, or family tragedy facts collected and/or maintained by this institution, for public relations purposes.

Purpose(s) of Disclosure: Information obtained from these records will assist in compilation of personal information for use in official athletic department/athletic public relations publications for dissemination to legitimate news media, for purposes of nominating me for athletic and academic honors programs, awards and scholarships, and for general public relations purposes.

Party or Class of Parties to Whom Disclosure May Be Released: By signing this consent statement, I authorize administrative personnel of the University of Michigan Athletic Department and its Athletic Public Relations office to review and disseminate any information per Principal Specification of Records (above) to third parties for general public relations purposes, including marketing and promotions, and academic award programs.

Tshimanga Biaka Butuka
Signature (legal name only; no nicknames)

_03 30 93_
Date (month/date/year)

FOOTBALL
Sport(s)

_1993-94_
Commencing Academic Year

166

Tim Biakabutuka

University of Michigan Athletic Public Relations
Student-Athlete Biographical Information

This biographical information is a permanent record in your athletic public relations file. Please complete the form neatly, accurately and completely. Supplemental information (newspaper articles, etc.) may be included to complete background information.

Date _03 - 30 - 93_   U-M Sport _FOOTBALL_

Personal Information

Legal Name (first, middle, last) _TSHIMANGA   BIAKABUTUKA_

Preferred Name / Nickname _TSHIMANGA_

Date of Birth (month/date/year) _01 - 24 (?) 74_   Height _6'0_   Weight _201_

Home Address (address/city/state/zip) ▮▮▮▮▮▮▮▮▮▮

U-M Address (address/city/state/zip) _____

Home Phone ▮▮▮▮▮▮   U-M Phone ▮▮▮▮▮▮

Academic Class (fr., so., jr., sr., grad.) _fr._   Athletic Eligibility (fr., so., jr., sr., 5th yr.) _fr._

U-M School Enrolled In _____   Major _ENGINEERING_

Family Information

Father's Name (first/last) _MULENGA-WA BIAKABUTUKA_   College _____

Father's Address (if same as yours, omit) _____

Mother's Name (first/last) _MISENGA BATUAMBILE - BIBI_   College _____

Mother's Address (if same as yours, omit) _____

Parent's Marital Status: married _X_ divorced _____   Number of: brothers _4_   sisters _5_

Parent, sibling(s) who are now or have been members of intercollegiate varsity athletic team (indicate school/sport/years)

_____

Hometown Media Information
Name(s) of Newspaper(s) which regularly cover your high school. Give complete name and location, if possible.

(News) THE GAZETTE (WEST ISLAND)

167

CHAPTER 10

Tom Brady

It's common belief that Tom Brady had a chip on his shoulder from being drafted in the sixth round of the NFL draft. He was passed over, seeing six quarterbacks drafted ahead of him in 2000, wondering if his NFL dream would ever come true. Although that added to the size of the chip, the truth is teams had looked past Brady his whole football career. Before he was waiting for his name to be called by an NFL team and before he was battling with quarterback Drew Henson for playing time at Michigan, Brady was waiting and hoping that the Wolverines would even offer him a scholarship.

His recruiting story is somewhat similar to his draft story. He wasn't the first quarterback Michigan went after in that 1995 recruiting class and Brady was forced to sweat it out all the way to the end. Brady's sophomore season in high school was when his quarterback journey really began. He started to flourish as a passer under Junipero Serra High's junior varsity coach, Bob Viñal. "Tom played basketball for us and he was a hell of a baseball player, too," Viñal said. "He was a very intelligent and very intense kid. He would do anything and he really started to understand that he was actually pretty good after that sophomore year."

Brady spent time with his receivers during the summer before his sophomore season, building timing and chemistry through the tutelage of Viñal and quarterback coach Tom Martinez. John Kirby was one of those receivers who spent extra time—two hours a day— on the field with Brady. Kirby remembers that sophomore year as the time everyone started to take notice of what Brady was capable of. "Freshman year we went 0–8, Tommy was the second-string quarterback, and I was the second-string receiver," Kirby said. "His sophomore year is when he really started to get good because we were getting individual time. We ended up playing Bellarmine Prep in the championship game our sophomore year, and Tommy was on fire that game."

Brady found his team down late in that championship game, looking for a game-winning drive. Kirby recalled Junipero Serra driving with two minutes left in the game when the sprinklers unexpectedly turned on in the middle of the field. After a 20-minute delay, Brady ran a few plays, but the sprinklers turned back on for a second time. Viñal was shouting that the game was fixed and that his team was being set up with the sprinklers. The first play after the sprinklers went off the second time, Brady threw a swing pass behind the line of scrimmage. The ball was wet because of the sprinklers, and Brady's receiver fumbled the ball. A Bellarmine player grabbed the ball and took it into the end zone to seal the championship. Despite the loss Kirby noted that game was one of the first signs that his teammate was going to be something special.

Throughout that season Brady and his receivers improved their chemistry and used Brady's work ethic to their advantage. His film sessions and knowledge of the game gave Viñal a lot of trust in his quarterback. Brady even developed a code system with his receivers to call audibles in their games. "If we called a hitch and someone was in press coverage against me, Tommy would look at me, look left, then he'd stare at me for four or five seconds, and quickly pull his facemask," Kirby said. "That would change the route from a hitch to a fade. That's where he kind of learned how to take control of the game and call his own. He would pull his facemask, and for me to acknowledge that I got it, I would pull up my sock."

Brady spent even more time working to improve his skills throughout that season. His coach had what he called a five dot drill. In the drill, cones were situated the same way the dots are for the No. 5 on a set of playing dice. The drill was set up to help with quickness and agility. You navigated it by starting at the middle cone, moving your foot to the top left, then right, and so on, working through a preset routine.

Brady decided to set up his own five dot drill in his garage to work on his quickness individually. "A lot of kids were giving him a hard time that he couldn't outrun a sack, so we would go to practice and seven-on-seven stuff, and then he would go do the five dot drill at night to get faster," Kirby said. "He would do that on his own and he told me he was working on it in his garage. People said he was too slow, so he put in a ton of hard work to prove people wrong."

That work ethic was engrained in Brady and it was always above and beyond that of his peers. On Sundays Kirby would head over to Brady's house to watch film at Brady's request. Tom's mom would make sandwiches for lunch, and the two would diagnose what they saw on film. "He'd be like, 'Hey Kirb, when you ran this post, what were you thinking because of where the defensive back was?'" Kirby said. "He'd say, 'Okay good, I'll know next time when I look out there. I'll know what you're going to do.' Watching film—it used to be you'd watch it with your coach and team, and you'd be done, but he would watch it with the coach, and then we'd do our own thing, too."

Brady moved up to varsity for his junior season in 1993. Since the team had a subpar running game and defense, the Junipero coaches decided they would throw the ball as much as possible. That boded well for Brady, who was trying his best to get better at his position and get noticed by college coaches. His high school coach, Tom MacKenzie, did what he could as far as recruiting goes but didn't reach out to a lot of schools on Brady's behalf. So after his junior season, Brady and his father, Tom Brady Sr., decided to put together a highlight film to distribute to college coaches. "We sat down, and I ordered the NCAA book of universities. And once I had the tape professionally edited, we went through the book," Brady Sr. said. "He made the selection of would he consider going to UCLA. *He said yes.* Would you consider Alabama? *No.* Louisville? *No.* So at the end of it, there were like 53 schools that were on his hit list that he said he would consider."

Brady Sr. sent the highlight tape out to those 53 schools that his son said he would have interest in. Three of the schools, which included Nebraska and Hawaii, came back right away and said they weren't interested. Neither ran a pro-style system, so Brady didn't fit what they were looking for at quarterback.

One of the first schools that courted Brady heavily happened to be a program situated very close to home. Cal had heard about Brady because of his proximity to the Berkeley campus and started to take notice. Keith Gilbertson was the head coach at Cal at that time and knew that he would be something special the moment he saw Brady throw. "We fell in love with him at our camp," Gilbertson said. "A great young guy, had the most beautiful throwing motion, great arm, and a classic thrower. I saw him and just thought, *Man, here's the guy; here's the next guy.*"

Gilbertson had an eye for quarterbacks and had seen something similar when the then-head coach of the University of Idaho coached quarterback John Friesz, who went on to win the Walter Payton Award, passed for more than 10,000 yards, and earned induction into the College Football Hall of Fame in 2006. (Friesz and Brady would end up teammates on the New England Patriots, as Friesz neared the end of his NFL career and Brady began his.) The throwing motion and mechanics displayed by Friesz were comparable to Brady's as Gilbertson evaluated the signal-caller. So Gilbertson and his staff made Brady, the local kid, a priority. "We were recruiting several other players," Gilbertson said. "But I do believe I told him that if you commit to Cal I will only take one quarterback in this class, and you'll be it."

Brady's recruitment was off and running, but there were still other schools on his list that he hadn't heard from. So once camp season started the following summer, Brady made sure the coaches saw what he could do. A Reebok camp came to town at nearby St. Mary's College, and since the Brady family had sent out his recruiting tape, college coaches said they would be at the camp to see the 6'3" quarterback in person. The coaches saw everything they needed to see, and after the camp, Brady was inundated with recruiting letters from schools all over the country. There were as many as 50 schools coming after him at one point, so Brady and his father decided to cut his list down to five schools that he wanted to seriously consider. "When we pared it down to five schools, we had each school make their recruiting pitch," Brady Sr. said. "We had criteria that the schools had to be very strong academically. We wanted them to be very competitive on the field. We had a list of questions, but from that point on, I stepped back to a relative degree because we wanted Tommy to be able to make his own decision."

The five schools that made the cut were Cal, USC, UCLA, Illinois, and Michigan. Those five schools met the criteria that Brady felt would make him a successful quarterback and ultimately get him to the next level. The senior-to-be started doing more research and started to build better relationships with those schools. Two of the schools on the list threw a wrench into the process, though, as both USC and UCLA pulled themselves from the running for different reasons. USC's offensive coordinator at the time was Mike Riley, who had expressed early interest in Brady. He came up to a game and watched Brady play, went back, spoke with Trojans head coach John Robinson, and decided that since they already had two quarterbacks committed in the class that they would pass on recruiting Brady any further.

UCLA told Brady early on that he was their main target and that they wouldn't recruit any other quarterbacks until Brady made his decision. The family was initially intrigued by that but soon found out the dark side of recruiting. "UCLA was pushing us to make a decision, and we didn't want Tommy to make a decision until he took recruiting visits," Brady Sr. said. "The offensive coordinator for UCLA, Bob Toledo, came through and said, 'We want you as our quarterback and we will not take a commitment to another player until we're sure that you're not coming to UCLA.' Toledo checked in during the season, then went up to Oregon, and the next day signed Cade McNown."

The Bruins and Trojans were out. The Cal coaches thought they were right in the mix and that they had an excellent chance at landing Brady. He was Gilbertson's top quarterback on their board in that class by a wide margin, and Gilbertson's staff was doing everything they could to convince Brady to stay home.

What Gilbertson didn't know, though, was that Brady had become enamored and intrigued by what Michigan could offer him. The Wolverines had everything he wanted, and the California kid was hoping the coaches would come calling with an offer. "When he had gone through the school books—and I can remember it as if it were yesterday—Michigan always caught our eye," Brady Sr. said. "When we were going through this book and all the colleges, the first one that really ever caught his eye was Michigan. He said, 'Could you believe if I ever played at Michigan?'" Almost incredulously, Brady said, "How 'bout Michigan? That would be awesome."

The elder Brady shared in his son's excitement for what the Wolverines could offer, but in the back of his mind, he was fearful. Brady Sr. loved the time he spent with his son and how close their relationship was. The two enjoyed playing golf together on Sundays, and Brady Sr. thought if his son were to pick Cal, they could continue those golf outings as they had before.

Ann Arbor was much too far for that, and Brady Sr. knew that would change their relationship. He never expressed those concerns audibly, though, as he still wanted his son to make the best choice for himself without any outside factors taken into consideration.

Luckily for Brady, his highlight tape had made it to the desk of Michigan assistant coach Billy Harris, who had the state of California as his recruiting area. Harris watched the tape by himself in his office and was impressed by what he saw. The tape included all types of passes and even a few incompletions, which was abnormal for a highlight tape that was meant to showcase the player. Harris put the video in front of Michigan's quarterback coach, Kit Cartwright, to gauge his opinion. Cartwright felt the same as Harris and sent the film on to then-head coach Gary Moeller, who needed to give his final approval that Brady would be added to their target board. Moeller liked the film, and Brady was added to Michigan's board. But unlike Cal, who had Brady as the top quarterback target on its board, Michigan had a different prospect at No. 1.

Bobby Sabelhaus was regarded as the top prospect in that recruiting class, and Michigan agreed with that assessment. Coming out of Maryland, Sabelhaus passed the eye test at 6'5", 225 pounds and wowed coaches with his arm. "Coming out of my junior year, I started to get some national recognition from Tom Lemming, *Blue Chip*, those kind of publications back then," Sabelhaus said. "I went through *Blue Chip* or *SuperPrep* and there I was on the first page, the No. 1 preseason quarterback in the country. I'm from a small prep school in suburban Baltimore and had no clue."

Sabelhaus attended the McDonogh School in Baltimore but originally grew up in Ohio, where it was blasphemy to even consider Michigan. The Wolverines were always a team he loved to follow as a kid, though, and luckily for him, the coaching staff wanted him to be a Michigan Man. Wolverines recruiting coordinator Bobby Morrison reached out to Sabelhaus and quickly built an excellent relationship with the talented prospect and his family. Despite being from Ohio, Sabelhaus and his family all took to the Michigan coaches, especially Morrison. "He was a great guy and he came to my house, which was great," Sabelhaus said. "My mom is a football fan because of me, but she would play the Michigan fight song in our house, and I would wake up to that on the weekends. She loved Coach Morrison, the great education. She's from the Midwest and she just had a good feeling about Michigan."

The Wolverines were so serious about courting Sabelhaus that Moeller made a visit to Baltimore to see him. The two had a frank conversation that started with Moeller putting his hand on Sabelhaus' knee and telling him he wanted Sabelhaus to come play quarterback at Michigan. The words coming from the head coach were powerful, but Sabelhaus replied back that if he were to do that Michigan would need to throw the ball more. The Wolverines were more of a running team at the time but were looking to change that style and start that evolution with Sabelhaus.

After his senior season was over, the Baltimore quarterback took his visit to Michigan with his mother and father. The three took in a hockey game and spent some time with Michigan's then-athletic director, Bo Schembechler, which was the highlight of the visit for Sabelhaus' father. The visit couldn't have gone any better, but Michigan wasn't the only school in the picture for Sabelhaus. His final two schools came down to Michigan and Florida. Because he was so highly regarded, Sabelhaus wanted to make a commitment in early January so he could start recruiting other prospects to the school he would be attending. It came time for him to make a decision in early 1995.

While Sabelhaus was weighing his decision, Brady was still maneuvering his recruiting process and taking visits to the remaining schools on his list. Brady took a visit to Illinois, but it was the dead of winter, and the visit did not impress the California prospect. "That wasn't a pleasant experience," Brady Sr. said. "It was a driving rain in the middle of December, and he thought that was not the right place for him. It was just too far from everything."

With Illinois, USC, and UCLA eliminated from Brady's top five, it came down to Cal and Michigan. The only problem was that Brady still didn't have an offer from the Wolverines and was still waiting to hear whether one would be extended. The Michigan coaches were waiting to hear from Sabelhaus before they were willing to extend any new offers to quarterbacks. Fearful that it would push the No. 1 target to Florida, Michigan stayed put, hunkered down, and waited for Sabelhaus to make his commitment.

Sabelhaus and his father sat down in early January and drew up a chart to weigh the positives and negatives for both Michigan and Florida. Michigan had a lot of positives in its favor because of its tradition and strength as a program. But the Wolverines were also loaded at quarterback, while there were nearly three years of separation from Sabelhaus and Danny Wuerffel, the current quarterback at Florida, who would go on to win the Heisman Trophy. The Gators coach Steve Spurrier deployed a pro-style offense, throwing the ball 35 times a game, which appealed heavily to the big-time quarterback recruit. "It felt very crowded at Michigan, and I have no problem with competition, but I liked the idea of having three years to myself to be the Florida quarterback," Sabelhaus said. "Cut to the hardest decision of my life, and it was a heart-to-heart with my family. The irony is that I didn't really care for Spurrier; he was going to use me, and I'm going to use him to a degree, but I convinced myself that I would be successful down there."

A difficult phone call was ahead, and in early January of 1995, Bobby Sabelhaus made a decision that would impact the future of Michigan football forever. He called Coach Morrison and reluctantly told him that he was choosing Florida. Sabelhaus' mother got on the phone at one point during the conversation and was crying, talking to Morrison about how her son wouldn't be going to Michigan. The family really came to like the Michigan coaches and believed it would be a great opportunity for their son, but the young quarterback felt the future was brighter at Florida. "I said to him, 'Listen, you guys are going to be fine. I'm sure you have a slew of quarterbacks you're recruiting,'" Sabelhaus said. "And he said, 'Well, we want you.' I said I can't do it, then asked him who they are going to go after, and he said, 'We have this kid out in California named Tom Brady.'"

Michigan quickly went to work and set up a trip for Brady to come out to Ann Arbor to see the campus for himself. Harris was his main recruiter, so it was his job to coordinate the whole trip and make sure everything went smoothly. So that he could give Brady the right amount of attention, he wanted to make sure it was a weekend that Michigan didn't have many other prospects he was responsible for on campus.

It was January, and, like Brady's visit to Illinois, the weather was terrible. This time he was willing to overlook it, though, and it didn't factor in. It might have been because of a talk Harris had with Brady—or any California kid he recruited. Knowing that weather would be an objection, Harris tried to get ahead of the curve and spin it into a positive for the Wolverines. "The thing that I tried to say on my recruiting talk was we're spending a lot of money, energy, and time and we believe that your stop won't be just here at Michigan, but that you'll go on to the pros," Harris said. "You don't know where you'll play in the pros and you might not play in sunny California. This Michigan weather, you're going to play in snow, rain, and even some hot days, but wherever you end up in the NFL, the weather won't be a deterrent for you."

It might have been that talk or it might have been the mystique of The Big House when Brady walked into the stadium he had only seen in books. Brady got the chance to walk on the field, which was covered in snow, that so many great players before him had walked on, and that left a lasting impression. The visit went as well as it could for both sides, and Michigan finally expressed to Brady that they were serious about his recruitment. He was now the No. 1 quarterback on their board.

Brady went home, and at this point, it was getting late in the process, so his parents decided it was time for their son to make a decision. It would either be Cal, the option that was 30 miles from home and meant a continuation of the close father-son relationship that included golf on Sundays, or it was Michigan, a dream that nearly didn't come true. "He and I sat down on the floor...It killed me when he said, 'I'm going to Michigan,'" Brady Sr. said. "I hate to say it, but I cried for 48 hours because he's my best friend. I said this is going to change our relationship, and he said, 'I know, Dad. It has to.'"

Brady Sr. was heartbroken for himself but ecstatic for his son and acknowledges that it was the best decision he could have made and was definitely something his son needed to do at the time. Once the decision was made, Brady Sr. called Coach Harris at Michigan on a Friday and asked him how sincere Michigan was in their interest in his son. Believing it was one of the most important parts of the process—that the head coach wants you—Brady Sr. wanted to know where they stood with the Wolverines and with Moeller. Only the head coach could make the final decision on scholarship offers and commitments at the time, so Harris told Brady he would get back to him. Two hours later after speaking with Moeller and selling Brady as the guy who could lead the Wolverines offense in the future, Harris informed the family that Moeller would be at their house on Monday at 8:00 AM.

Moeller made the trip out to California to meet with the Brady family one last time and reassured the family of Michigan's interest and intentions. He said the Wolverines would be changing their system and that Brady was the perfect guy for it. "I said, 'If that's the case, then we're coming to Michigan,'" Brady Sr. said.

Mere days before Signing Day in February of 1995, Brady committed to Michigan over Cal. Brady had fond feelings toward the staff at Cal, though, so he called the coaching staff to inform them of his decision. "I do remember he called me at home to tell me," Gilbertson said. "I wished him well, told him he was a great player. I was sorry he wasn't coming to Cal, and then you have to move on. I don't even know if we signed a quarterback in that class."

It took a winding path with twists and turns impacted by the decisions of Cade McNown at UCLA and Bobby Sabelhaus at Florida, but Brady's thoughts of potentially playing in The Big House would now become a reality. Sabelhaus ended up transferring from Florida after clashing with Spurrier and never fulfilled his goal of becoming a star on the football field. He wound up at the University of Maryland, where he eventually stopped playing football and is now a producer in the movie industry.

When Brady enrolled at Michigan, he joined a loaded quarterback roster that included Brian Griese, Scott Dreisbach, Jason Carr, and Scot Loeffler. Much like the situation when he joined the Patriots, Brady was far down the depth chart and would have to wait to see the field. Dreisbach and Griese were the first and second-string quarterbacks. It was much of the same in 1996, as Dreisbach and Griese received the majority of the reps, and Brady only attempted five passes that season. He had to sit and wait, hoping to get his opportunity. But that season he was at least beginning to make an impression.

He was still No. 3 on the depth chart, but Brady was starting to push Dreisbach for that backup role and was starting to move up in the eyes of the coaches. In 1997 Brady had asserted himself as the better quarterback over Dreisbach, but Griese had decided to come back for his fifth season in hopes of taking over the starting role himself. The two competed in practice, and eventually Griese won the job. Brady was frustrated and contemplated transferring closer to home to Cal but was talked out of it by then-head coach Lloyd Carr and counselor Greg Harden. Unfortunately for Brady, he dealt with appendicitis in the fall that would require an appendectomy and impede his efforts to see the field. After meeting with Harden, speaking about believing in himself and what it would take mentally to be the starting quarterback at the University of Michigan, and recovering from his surgery, Brady dedicated himself to earning that starting spot with two years of eligibility remaining.

In 1998 Griese was now off to the pros, but a new kid was added by the name of Drew Henson. He was a flashy recruit, who possessed a ton of ability and athleticism and would push Brady immediately for playing time. Brady competed, though, and earned the starting spot in his redshirt junior season. "Tom Brady has paid his dues," Carr said at a press conference in 1998, according to MGoBlue.com. "He has worked extremely hard. He's a bright guy, he has a good arm, and he has the respect of his teammates. I'm anxious to see Tom play. He's got all the right stuff."

Henson was right there, though, and the fans were very excited about his potential and what he could bring to that offense. He progressed early in his career and had no intentions of sitting as long as Brady did, which fueled a competition between the two. "Drew has made excellent progress," Carr said at the time. "He's picked up the offense well. He is without question the most talented quarterback I've been around. It's just a matter of continuing to compete and continuing to prepare. He's going to play some this year because he's not just another guy. He's got everything you want. He is a guy who really adds a lot of mobility to that position."

Brady started the season with a loss to Notre Dame and saw Henson come in and replace him against Syracuse. That didn't deter Brady, though, as Henson and the Wolverines lost against Syracuse as well. Brady took over from there and held on to his starting spot, completing 200 passes for 2,427 yards and 14 touchdowns. In the 1999 season, Henson would see his role increase as Carr split quarters and snaps between the young quarterback and Brady. The head coach then said he would go with the hot hand after seeing the two perform in the first half of each game. Once again, Brady eventually took over, completing 180 passes for 2,217 yards and 16 touchdowns. He capped off his final game of his Michigan career with a 35–34 overtime win against Alabama in the Orange Bowl. Brady threw for 369 yards and four touchdowns in an incredible finale to his tumultuous career at Michigan.

It was a perfect way to end his college career and led to a transcendent NFL career with the Patriots. Brady is a three-time NFL MVP, five-time Super Bowl champion, and one of the best to ever play the game.

CHAPTER 11

Braylon Edwards

Braylon Edwards, the 6'3" receiver from Detroit, Michigan, had a rare combination of size and speed—part of which came via DNA, and part of which came via hard work and training with his father, Stan. The elder Edwards is a former Michigan back who played for the Wolverines from 1977 to 1981. Stan had a great career for Michigan in his own right and shared time in the backfield with former All-American Butch Woolfolk. He enjoyed a six-year career in the NFL after being drafted in the third round of the NFL draft by the Houston Oilers and has spent time training athletes in various sports, including football.

Stan saw some success on the field, but he always felt as though there was more he could have done and that he could have been even better than he was. "I've always been self-critical and honest with myself with what I didn't do, why I didn't accomplish certain things, and things I know now that I would've done differently to be a better player than I was," Stan said. "I knew that if I had a son, he would get all of those things, and if that's what he wanted to do, he would achieve those things. I knew I could make Braylon a collegiate-type athlete."

Through Stan's experience, Braylon came to understand that running is a learned skill. Genes play a major role, of course, but an athlete also can get better at running by increasing his speed and technique. So to help mold Braylon's future, Stan monitored his footsteps as a small child, how he walked up the stairs, and what he ate. "What was conjured up in everyone's mind was this is Todd Marinovich's dad. The difference between Braylon and Todd Marinovich's dad was that Braylon wanted this," Stan said. "He wanted it more than I was ready to give. There were too many times where I'm in the house and I'm asleep or busy, he'd tap me and say, 'Hey, Dad, can we go do this?' And I never told him no. I fed that monster."

Todd Marinovich is famous for having a father, Marv, who trained his son to be a quarterback and pushed it to the limits, eventually driving his son Todd, who would go on to struggle with drug addiction, into the national spotlight with unhealthy expectations and notoriety. Stan Edwards was no Marv Marinovich, but he did want his son to excel in whatever he did, including football. Braylon came to Stan for his training, whether it was for track or football, and the pair set out to turn Braylon into a Division I college football player.

It wasn't just football that Braylon had success in, though. It was also baseball, especially at a young age. And there was, of course, that speed, which was a result of his DNA and training. "At the age of 10, he was a national finalist in the 100-meter dash in the Junior Olympics. When they walked him out for the bantam boys 100 meter in the USATF Junior Olympics, Braylon was one of the tallest boys on the blocks," Stan said. "That's when I thought there might be something there. Then by the time he was 12 or 13 and he finally started playing football, I knew he was good."

Braylon always had an eagerness to get better and always had the competitive drive to push forward and continue working on his game. At a Little League game when Braylon was just 13 years old, Stan watched his son go up and high point a football and catch it over a defender's head for the game-winning touchdown. It wasn't surprising for his father to see him do that because the two had already practiced that move hundreds of times at home. Braylon's desire to be great and Stan's desire for him to be great matched perfectly, which would eventually help create the incredible athlete that would step on the field for the University of Michigan.

Once Braylon started to really show potential on the football field, Stan knew it was time to get more serious about his son's training. It needed to be a specific regimen that would help him grow and help him learn the game. "There were two things we focused on. The third happened by accident. Because of his height, he was already going to be my height or taller, so we worked on hands and speed," Stan said. "That's all we worked on. His footwork came naturally because he was a knockout, smash-out baseball player. He was okay in basketball, but he understood basketball enough [to know] how to start, stop, and change direction. We played a lot of sports, and that really worked on his eye tracking, too."

At around the age of 14, it was time for Braylon to start making the jump from Little League standout to someone who could earn a college scholarship. That transformation would take time, though, and because Stan had played at Michigan, he understood what type of athlete and what type of person could have success in the winged helmet. Although Braylon was never violent, Stan described his son as a "rascal" in middle school and knew that his son would need to mature before he would ever be ready for a school like Michigan or any college program. "I got this from [former Michigan strength coach] Mike Gittleson. Boys between the age of 13 and 16 are the dumbest people on the face of the Earth. Braylon was between those ages and was an absolute handful," Stan said. "Before he got to high school, he got asked to leave from maybe six different schools. Braylon could talk, and you'd tell him not to talk, and he would. You'd tell him to sit down, he'd sit down for a minute, then get up. He always got good grades, but he needed something to do."

As Braylon got more and more serious about football, heading into his freshman year, Stan punished his son for acting out by not allowing him to go to any football camps. Stan thought his son was still a little too immature for what it took to be a high-level athlete and wanted Braylon to understand that he needed to shape up and take every aspect of school and football seriously. The training continued, and the two did some unconventional things to try to get him better and help him succeed on the field. Whatever it took, Braylon wanted to do it, always asking his dad to help because he needed someone to throw him the ball. "In the snow we would go out there and make a snow dune, and he would say, 'Okay, Dad, throw it right there, so I can dive on that and catch it,'" Stan said. "We'd put a mattress out there, so he could dive for the ball. He asked, so I had to feed the monster."

By this time Stan knew that his son had the potential to be a Division I athlete, which was why he was trying to teach Braylon these lessons at a young age. Braylon was now technically a little behind by not attending camps—but not so much that it would impact his recruitment. "He went to Martin Luther King Jr. High School his freshman year. I wasn't going to send him to King, but a lot of guys I knew for a while were the coaches there," Stan said.

"They heard about Braylon doing well in the Little League circuit, and I said, 'Guys, my son is a wide receiver. You don't throw the ball.' They averaged throwing the ball 10 times a game, and I'm trying to not have to pay for college here."

The King coaches told Stan if they sent his son to their school they would throw the ball and make him a big part of the offense, so Braylon headed to King to start his high school career. That first season, though, Braylon wasn't a big part of the offense and didn't see the ball thrown any more than he had before, which frustrated both Stan and Braylon. During his freshman year, he also was still acting as a rascal, according to Stan. Braylon wasn't violent and still got good grades, but he had some issues with authority at the school. After his freshman year, that meant Stan still would not permit him to go to football camps. Braylon would need to start getting more mature, but Stan didn't panic and began seeing signs that his son was catching on. But because of his lack of production for his high school team and his absence at any football camps, Braylon wasn't on the radar of any college coaches his freshman year.

His sophomore season was much of the same. There was little production on the field because the offense wasn't passing the ball. Braylon played defense as well, but it wasn't his natural position. So he didn't stand out on that side of the ball. After his son's sophomore season, Stan still felt as though Braylon wasn't ready to attend any camps, so he held him out again. This next season would be crucial to his success and vital to getting recruited by a major program. "I got letters as a sophomore, but it was more so just letters," Braylon said. "I hadn't really done anything on the football field. So it was just surveys and questionnaires."

Once Braylon finished his sophomore season, Stan thought this might be the first time that his son was ready. It just might be time for him to get out and attend a football camp to show what he had been working toward and show what had been hiding on the practice fields at King High. Unfortunately, Braylon popped a bone away from his kneecap before camp season started. The injury required surgery, which took place in April of his sophomore year. The recovery went into summer, and another year would go by without Braylon stepping onto any college campuses to show the coaches what he could do.

Part of that lack of attention was on Braylon, part of it was because of his injury, but part of it, Stan felt, was due to the King offense not throwing the ball enough. It was to the point where Stan knew if he didn't make a change, it could dramatically impact his son's chances at playing college football. He saw his son continue to improve through their training, but he was starting to worry that it would never show up on film because Braylon's lack of pass-catching opportunities at King. It wasn't too late just yet, but if they waited too much longer, his chance could pass him by. Braylon played his junior season at King. He wasn't 100 percent recovered, but he toughed it out and played through pain. Once again, the offense didn't feature him, and it was another season that was wasted in the mind of Braylon and his father.

Once his junior season was finished, Braylon and Stan made the decision that it was time to transfer high schools. "I took him out of King High School that January of his junior year and enrolled him at Harper Woods Bishop Gallagher," Stan said. "Because when you move, you have to sit out a semester, and that next semester he sat out track, but he was still training with me, so he got his training in. So going into that summer, he was older, mature, and I said, 'Hey, this is it, time for you to go to camp.'"

Going into that summer before his senior year is when Braylon would finally get out to a football camp and try to get himself on the radar of college coaches. Many people are aware that he was only ranked as a two-star or three-star prospect out of high school. It's a good story to think that a two-star prospect turned into an All-American receiver, but a big reason for his low ranking was because of how his high school career played out.

Heading into his senior season, Braylon only had one receiving touchdown in his high school career. There was nothing on film that showed what Stan believed to be there, so it would be up to Braylon's performance in these camps as to how he would be recruited and who he would be recruited by. In the spring of 2000, the first camp he attended was at Wayne State University in Detroit. His performance there yielded an offer from Akron and caught the attention of a few other MAC schools. "I thought I did well, ran well, caught well," Braylon said. "I started to get letters from other schools wanting me to come up and visit and go to their camp."

The Edwards family could feel a buildup for Braylon, that he had a big opportunity ahead of him. The Michigan camp was looming, and because Stan played for the Wolverines, he still had some friends within the program and knew quite a few of the coaches. Stan had told defensive coordinator Jim Herrmann, a former teammate of his, that he had a son who is going to be good one day. Herrmann had always asked Stan when he was going to bring his son in for a camp, and the time had never been right. Whether it was Braylon acting out or dealing with an injury, Stan had never been able to bring his son in for what would have been a worthwhile experience for both sides.

That year, however, was the right time. "I always grew up wanting to go to Michigan. My dad went to Michigan, and everything I had was Michigan," Braylon said. "I loved Michigan, Charles Woodson, Desmond Howard, being on the sideline with Ricky Powers back in the day."

The Wayne State camp was fine, but the Michigan camp was where Braylon really wanted to impress. This was his shot to show the Michigan coaches that they should be recruiting him and that he's not just Stan's son or someone who got lost on film. "Back in those days, people would remember me playing more than they do now," Stan said. "I said, 'I don't want any pressure on him, so I'll watch camp, but I'm going to let him go up there the first day without me.'"

Braylon went up to the Michigan camp by himself, and Stan waited to hear back from his son or his coaching friends. He started to receive phone calls about the day and how Braylon performed at the camp. He received word from wide receivers coach Erik Campbell, Herrmann, and even head coach Lloyd Carr. All told Stan that they had no idea his son was this good. They hadn't seen any production on film and didn't see much in terms of toughness, so this was all new to the Michigan coaches. "The fourth call I got was Braylon, and he said, 'I'm killing these guys.' I said, 'Yeah, I'm sure you are,'" Stan said. "I remember the second day when I went up there. Jim Herrmann grabbed me in the hallway and put his forearm into my chest and slammed me into the wall and said, 'Goddammit, why haven't you had him up here?' He had no idea he was this good."

Stan explained to his old teammate that Braylon hadn't been ready for this type of atmosphere and event. He explained to Herrmann that he is Michigan through and through and that he believes it takes a certain kind of player to be able to play at Michigan. The elder Edwards came to watch his son perform for the second day of the camp and see what the coaches and his son had been talking about. As he looked on, Stan quickly realized that they were telling the truth and that his son was putting on a show. It didn't matter what defensive back they put on him, Braylon was performing far better than anything the coaches had seen on film. There were some of the best defensive backs in the country in attendance, and Braylon was holding his own against each and every one. The quarterbacks throwing to the receivers were trying to line up for one-on-ones to get a chance to throw with Braylon because he was having so much success.

Stan, of course, wasn't surprised by what his son was doing on the field because the two had trained relentlessly to get to this point. Braylon had matured and was now for the first time really putting everything together, and it was paying off. Or so they thought. "I went to the Michigan camp, performed at the top of everything I did. Afterward there was so much hype that a lot of other schools reached out to me based on what I was doing," Braylon said. "I was talking to Central Michigan, Michigan State every day. I was talking to Vanderbilt. I was talking to seven quality schools on a daily basis after that Michigan camp—except for Michigan."

Despite what happened on the field, Braylon left the Michigan camp without a scholarship offer. The coaches were impressed by what he did in the drills, his size and speed, but there were still a lot of doubts because it didn't match what they saw on the film. At the time Herrmann was the main recruiter for Braylon while receivers coach Erik Campbell watched from a short distance. Since it was his position group, Campbell was a part of the decision to not offer Edwards after the camp and monitor his progress from there. "He did have a good camp, great size at the time and he was actually about 6'2", so he grew a little bit in college. His film really hurt him, though. He didn't get an offer because on film he didn't have that kind of production," Campbell said. "He wasn't getting balls on offense. I watched him play defense to see his toughness because we didn't know how tough he was. We saw good size, good structure, and good physique, and all that, but we didn't see the playmaker yet."

That decision didn't make Braylon or his father too happy, but they understood to a degree that he needed to produce in a game. To them, though, his circumstance was different than not being able to do it; they felt he just wasn't given the right opportunity yet. They were hoping that would change with the transfer to Bishop Gallagher because the school had a returning quarterback, Sam Martinisi, who just had an outstanding junior season. Braylon was hoping that would help with his film and would increase his production on the field.

The week after Braylon was at Michigan's camp, he attended the Michigan State football camp where head coach Bobby Williams and assistant Bill Sheridan were recruiting him. He had heard from Sheridan and Williams, but he did not have an offer from the Spartans up to this point. "Bobby Williams offered me after a few drills after the first session. He said to come up to his office and told me I was offered," Braylon said. "That had been after being there for an hour, so that was my first big offer, Michigan State."

After those two camps were done, Braylon decided to start putting in some more training for his upcoming season and worked with his new quarterback, Martinisi, before the season started. The two were developing a good chemistry, and it looked as though his film would be full of big catches. That is until about three weeks before Braylon's senior season. Martinisi got into a motorcycle accident, injured his back in the process, and was now out for the forseeable future. The backup quarterback, Brian Seery, wasn't nearly as talented as the starter, so the Bishop Gallagher coach, George Sahadi, played Edwards at wide receiver, running back, and even a little quarterback to try to help the offense. It seemed as though Braylon's luck just wouldn't be there, and he would have to figure out a way to earn his scholarship to Michigan.

His luck turned, though, as midway through the season, Martinisi returned from his injury, and the two picked up where they left off in the summer. In the first game back with the starting quarterback, Braylon caught eight passes for 210 yards and three touchdowns. His film was instantly bulked up by that game alone. The very next game, Braylon had two touchdowns in the first half, but in his second game back from injury, Martinisi blew out his knee and was out for the remainder of the season.

Braylon became discouraged, and with the lack of communication from Herrmann, his main recruiter at Michigan, he was about ready to commit to Michigan State. He had an offer in hand from the Spartans and wouldn't have sufficient film to send to Michigan, so it seemed as though his path might lead to East Lansing, Michigan. "Herrmann would never call Braylon, and Jim wouldn't even call me back, so I was getting a little angry. Braylon said, 'Dad, if Michigan doesn't want me to come, I'm going to commit to State,'" Stan said. "Michigan hadn't offered. And now I know why: because they thought Reggie Williams was better and were waiting on Reggie."

Campbell contends that as the wide receivers coach he would have taken both Williams and Edwards in the class but acknowledged that Williams was likely ahead of Edwards on their board. Williams was a big, tall receiver who played high school in Washington state. "He was from the West Coast, and I liked those big receivers, but we had Braylon right here. He was homegrown, and I wanted homegrown," Campbell said. "Reggie was higher ranked and had more production on film than Braylon, so we were definitely going after him. Reggie probably was the first choice because of the production, but I would've taken both of them."

Campbell wasn't sure where Williams was going to go and he got word that the Edwards were unhappy with how Herrmann was recruiting Braylon. He took matters into his own hands and decided that he would now be the main recruiter for Braylon and started building the relationship back up. "I said, 'I got it. Everybody step back.' And Lloyd Carr said, 'If you want him, go get him.' We hadn't offered him yet, but there was no way I was going to let him go to Michigan State," Campbell said. "He was too talented of a young man, so I started recruiting him. I started going down to see him, spending time at the school and with the family."

Campbell told Braylon to wait on any decision he was about to make and not commit to Michigan State. Campbell saw the talent; he just needed Carr to see it on film, so that he could extend the offer. Braylon waited and got his truncated highlights to Campbell, who finally got the chance to show them to Carr. The coaches saw the toughness they were looking for and, even though it was only a few games, they saw hints of that playmaker who was in their camp that spring and summer. They also started to feel the pressure that Michigan State had already offered, and the coaches in East Lansing were hoping to land the tall, in-state receiver. "I knew after the camp, and then once I got the film, it was like, okay he is tough. He can make the plays, he can do this and that, and Coach Carr gave me the greenlight," Campbell said. "I finally got the chance to show Coach Carr the film and I said I can work with this. Coach Carr put it on me and said go get him."

Campbell and Carr invited Braylon up to the Michigan game that weekend, and after Michigan won the game, Carr told the receiver to come in the locker room. After Braylon went down to the locker room, the head coach told him he had a scholarship offer from the University of Michigan. Braylon didn't have to accept the offer right then, but Carr told him that they had an outstanding recruiting class coming in. So if it started to fill up and scholarship offers got low, Carr would let him know that he needed to decide soon. Michigan was able to pull in some big names in that class, including Pierre Woods, Ernest Shazor, and Marlin Jackson, among others. So the spots were filled with playmakers and were starting to dwindle. "About a week later, Erik Campbell called me and said, 'What are you waiting on?' I said I was just weighing my options. A few schools like Cal came on late," Braylon said. "How crazy would that have been to play with Aaron Rodgers? It was like, 'Let me just wait and make a decision.'"

It was starting to get late now—November of Braylon's season—and true to his word, Carr called Braylon to let him know that there were only roughly three scholarship spots open. He didn't want to force him into a decision, but he told him that spots would fill up and he would give him the opportunity to take one. "I called Erik shortly after that and told him I was committing. Lloyd called me the next day at school because Lloyd was good friends with my coach," Braylon said. "I think it all hit me when I told my friends because I always knew where I wanted to go and I was hopeful for it, but to tell my friends, that was when it hit me. My neighborhood friends and teammates were all more excited than I was, and that's when I kind of saw how big it was."

Even more excited than his friends and teammates was his father. Stan had been there for the whole story and saw an insubordinate, immature kid grow into someone who was ready to become a Michigan Man. His son had put in the work, diving onto mattresses and snow banks, and it was all paying off. Stan took a step back after Braylon's commitment and thought about what this really meant. His son would be able to wear the same winged helmet that he wore earlier in his life, and the two would share a bond that few father-son duos get to share. "It was absolutely a dream come true. I couldn't believe that I had an opportunity, a poor boy from the east side of Detroit, to play at Michigan, and now my son is getting ready to play," Stan said. "I knew a couple other father-son combinations there, but it was absolutely a dream come true to say that both of us were able to touch the banner. It was pretty emotional for me when he accepted the offer."

Braylon finished his senior season at Bishop Gallagher in 2001 and was set to join the Wolverines. Before he did so, though, he was asked to play in a high school All-Star Game that summer. Braylon wasn't a first choice for the game because Bishop Gallagher was a smaller school, and the starting quarterback had been injured most of the year, so Braylon's stats still weren't through the roof. Mike Marsh, a coach at Henry Ford High in Detroit, had lobbied for him to get a spot in the game, but he was shot down. As it got closer and closer to the game, a few kids, who were selected to play in the game, decided against participating, which left a spot open for Braylon. He accepted the invitation and once again took advantage of an opportunity put in front of him. "So Braylon gets chosen at the last minute. In that

All-Star Game, Braylon had seven catches for 139 yards and three touchdowns," Stan said. "And he never played in the second half. He did all of that in the first half. At that point I said, 'Barring injury, he will play beyond college.'"

Braylon had gained some confidence on the field now. He enrolled at Michigan and, according to Stan, was again a bit of a "rascal" his freshman year. It can often be difficult for talented high school recruits to adjust to their first year of college and not being treated like they're the man. Braylon went up to Michigan, thinking he was the man and had to face a little bit of "derecruiting," where a coach reminds a freshman that he is part of a team of talented players and that he's not the only one. "Braylon was a freshman, thinking he was better than he is, and he had to develop first—not just go throw him to the wolves and learn that way," Campbell said. "I had to make sure he paid his dues and developed because I knew he had talent. One day he will be a great player, but he had to pay his dues first, and I think it really paid off for him later in his career."

That freshman season he only caught three passes for 38 yards in six games. Similar to how his father pushed him to be great as a freshman in high school, Campbell was now doing the same at Michigan. Both knew how great he could be, but they needed to pull it out of him and let him see it as well. This time, though, Braylon caught on sooner and grasped what Campbell was trying to teach him.

In his sophomore season, he appeared in all 13 games and caught 67 passes for 1,035 yards and 10 touchdowns. He had 100 yards receiving that season against Utah, Illinois, and Ohio State, who beat Michigan 14–9. Braylon led all receivers in that Ohio State game with 107 yards on 10 catches. He led all receivers in the next game as well, the Outback Bowl against Florida, with 110 yards on four receptions.

Naturally there was a lot of hype surrounding Braylon, who wore No. 80 his freshman and sophomore seasons. After his pupil's 1,000-yard receiving season as a sophomore, Campbell still saw a little bit of Braylon's troublemaker side surface. "I made him swallow his pride sometimes and I was hard on him. He was probably the only receiver I threw out of practice," Campbell said. "He wanted to do something his way, wouldn't listen, so I tried to throw him out of practice. He thought he was a big-time, 1,000-yard receiver, but Coach Carr said, 'You can't throw him out. Only I can do that.' So I didn't give him another rep in practice."

Campbell was tough on Braylon. He even said, "he wouldn't let him breathe" because he knew how great he could be if he stayed grounded and stayed focused. But Campbell picked up where Stan left off and pushed Braylon to be great. Coming off of his successful sophomore campaign, Braylon changed jersey numbers, going from 80 to No. 1, joining a prestigious list of past Michigan receivers to don the No. 1 in maize and blue. Anthony Carter was the first followed by Greg McMurtry, Derrick Alexander, Tyrone Butterfield, David Terrell, and now Braylon Edwards. That junior campaign he would improve on his sophomore stats, catching 85 passes for 1,138 yards and 14 touchdowns. He had 100-yard receiving games against Oregon, Iowa, Michigan State, Northwestern, Ohio State, and USC and finished the season ranked No. 19 in total receiving yards for any Division I player. Larry Fitzgerald out of Pitt led the way with 1,672 yards, but Braylon topped Reggie Williams, the former recruit that Michigan had targeted over Braylon in 2001.

Braylon's senior campaign was his best yet. He earned All-American honors and finished the season with 1,330 receiving yards and 15 touchdowns through the air. Those numbers placed him fourth in receiving yards for any player—behind only Roddy White at UAB, Dante Ridgeway at Ball State, and Mike Hass at Oregon State. Braylon had seven games with 100 receiving yards or more, which included his career day against Michigan State when he had 189 yards and three touchdowns. His third touchdown came on a post route. He caught the ball at the 10-yard line and ran it in for the go-ahead and final score, leading Michigan to a 45–37 victory against its in-state rival.

The final game of his career came in the Granddaddy of them all, the Rose Bowl, and he tallied three touchdowns on 10 receptions for 109 yards. He received the Biletnikoff Award as the nation's best receiver and earned first-team All-American honors. One of the best receivers to wear the winged helmet, he had an illustrious career with the Wolverines from 2001 to 2004, and many of his receiving records still stand to this day. He holds the record for most 100-yard receiving games with 17, ahead of Carter's 14. He has the most receptions in a season and for a career, the most career receiving yards with 3,541 yards, and the most career touchdown receptions with 39. After the 2004 season, the Cleveland Browns selected Braylon third overall in the 2005 NFL Draft, and he spent nine years in the NFL.

University of Michigan Athletic Media Relations
Student-Athlete Information Release

Name: *BRAYLON JAMEL EDWARDS*

Note: This form comes under the purview of the Family Educational Rights and Privacy Act of 1974.

Principle Specification of Records: This consent statement authorizes administrative personnel of the University of Michigan Athletic Department and its Athletic Media Relations Office to review and disseminate to third parties information in my personal "educational records," including information contained on this release form and any other education information, bodily injury/health data, or family tragedy facts collected and/or maintained by this institution, for public relations purposes.

Purpose(s) of Disclosure: Information obtained from these records will assist in compilation of personal information for use in official University of Michigan Athletic Department/Athletic Media Relations materials for dissemination to legitimate news media, for purposes of nominating me for athletic and academic honors programs, awards and scholarships, and for general public relations purposes.

Party of Class of Parties to Whom Disclosure May Be Released: By signing this consent statement, I authorize administrative personnel of the University of Michigan Athletic Department and its Athletic Media Relations Office to review and disseminate any information per Principal Specification of Records (above) to third parties for general public relations purposes, including marketing and promotions, and academic/athletic awards programs.

Braylon Jamel Edwards
Signature (legal name only; no nicknames)

2/27/01
Date (month/date/year)

FOOTBALL, TRACK, BASKETBALL
Sport(s)

University of Michigan Athletic Media Relations
Student-Athlete Biographical Information

This biographical information is a permanent record in your athletic media relations file. Please complete the form neatly, accurately and completely. Supplemental information (newspapers articles, etc.) may be included to complete background information.

Date __2/27/01__   U-M Sport __FOOTBALL__

Personal Information

Legal Name (first, middle, last) __BRAYLON JAMEL EDWARDS__
Preferred Name / Nickname __"B"__
Date of Birth (month/date/year) __2/21/83__   Height __6'4"__   Weight __200__
Home Address (address/city/state/zip) ▮▮▮▮▮▮▮▮▮▮▮▮▮▮
U-M Address (address/city/state/zip) _____
Home Phone (▮▮▮▮▮▮▮▮   U-M Phone (▮▮▮▮▮▮▮▮
Academic Class (Fr., So., Jr., Sr., Grad.) __SENIOR__   Athletic Eligibility (Fr., So., Jr., Sr., 5th year) _____
U-M School Enrolled In __KINESIOLOGY__   Declared Major __KINESIOLOGY__
__BUISNESS__

Family Information

Father's Name (first/last) __STANLEY EDWARDS__   College __U OF M__
Father's Address (if same as yours, omit) __20162 STRATFORD DETROIT MI 48221__
Mother's Name (first/last) __MALESA PLATER__   College __OAKLAND__
Mother's Address (if same as yours, omit)
Parent's Maritial Status: married _____ divorced __✓__   Number of: brothers __2__   sisters __2__
Parent(s), sibling(s) who are now or have been members of intercollegiate varsity athletic team (indicate school/sport/years):
__MY FATHER, STAN EDWARDS, PLAYED 5 YEARS OF FOOTBALL__
__FOR THE MICHIGAN WOLVERINES FROM 77 TO 81__

Hometown Media Information

Name(s) and Addresses of Newspaper(s) that regularly cover your high school.

High School Information

High School (name/city/state) BISHOP GALLAGHER   HARPER WOODS   MI

Year Graduated 2001   Athletic Conference (spell out) CLASS D

Academic Honors, Clubs (i.e., National Honor Society, Honor Roll, Etc.) HONOR ROLL ALL THROUGH

10TH, AND 1 SEMESTER OF ELEVENTH.

By Year, list sports competed in, honors received, varsity letters earned, season-ending statistical information, team achievements. Be sure to give complete name of each award/honor (i.e., All-West Central Conference Football First-Team; All-Putnam County Girls' Track - selected by Putnam County Banner-Graphic). List coach's complete name with sport you will compete in for U-M. Use an additional piece of paper if necessary.

Freshman: Year 1997-98 (9 grade):

I PLAYED VARSITY FOOTBALL. RAN AAU TRACK AND TOOK
THIRD IN THE 200 METERS AT THE JUNIOR OLYMPIC MEET
IN DES MUISNLES IOWA.

Sophomore: Year 98-99 (10 grade):

STARTED AT WIDE RECEIVER, AND HAD 15 CATCHES FOR
215 YARDS AND 2 TOUCH DOWNS. RAN TRACK, PLAYED
JV BASKETBALL

Junior: Year 99-00 (11 grade):

STARTED AT WIDE RECEIVER, HAD 28 CATCHES 400 YARDS
AND 5 TD's. MADE 2ND TEAM ALL CITY ACCORDING TO THE
DETROIT NEWS. TRANSFERRED TO BISHOP GALLAGHER
FROM MARTIN LUTHER KING.

Senior: Year 00-01 (12 grade):

STARTED AT WIDE RECEIVER, QUARTERBACK, SAFETY, LINEBACKER,
DEFENSIVE END, KICK RENTURN, KICKOFF, PUNT RETURNER, LONG
SNAPPER. I HAD 38 CATCHES, 479 YARDS, 6 TD's 7 SACKS,
78 TACKLES, 42 SOLOS, 3 BLOCKED KICKS, 3 FUMBLE
RECOVERIES, 5 INTERCEPTIONS, RETURNED 9 KICKS FOR
279 YARDS, AND WAS 10-17 FOR 213 YARDS, 1 TOUCHDOWN,
AND ONE INTERCEPTION.

College/University Information
To be completed by returning upperclassmen and transfer student-athletes

Name(s) of colleges and/or universities (other than Michigan) attended. Give dates of attendance, complete name.

_____

_____

_____

Michigan Academic Honors (i.e., Dean's List, Rhodes Scholar finalist, note year received):

_____

_____

Michigan Activities (clubs, frat/sorority, Big Brothers/Sisters, etc.):

_____

_____

Use space below for additional information, comments:

MY SENIOR YEAR I MADE ALL LEAGUE, ALL CATHOLIC, FIRST TEAM ALL EAST, FIRST TEAM ALL METRO, FIRST TEAM ALL STATE ACCORDING TO THE DETROIT NEWS. I MADE PREPSTAR MAGAZINES TOP SEVEN RECEIVER FOR THE MIDWEST.

CHAPTER 12

Chad Henne

The head football coach of the varsity team at Wilson High School in Pennsylvania, Jim Cantafio, had made a habit of watching all of the ninth grade football games. Chad Henne was only in the eighth grade but was playing with the team a year ahead as a running back and linebacker. Cantafio observed the ninth grade offense call a trick play, a halfback pass, where the ball was pitched to Henne at running back, and he then threw a pass to a receiver. The varsity coach immediately saw something in the way Henne threw the ball, delivering it on its mark, and felt as though he needed to take action to cultivate that talent. "Not too soon after I saw him throw the ball, I called him and his father in to see me. I told his dad, 'I know quarterbacking and I know a great arm when I see it,'" Cantafio said. "'Your son is a natural, and I want to make him a quarterback.' His dad looked at me and said, 'Well, I always knew he could throw a football.' So I said I wanted to make him a quarterback, and we did."

After that conversation Henne and Cantafio worked relentlessly on quarterback fundamentals leading into his freshman year. Four days a week, the two would practice before school at 7:00 AM to teach Henne the basics of being a quarterback. They started it that year and continued it for the next four years until Henne graduated. Their work had started to pay off as Henne was catching on quickly and taking to the coaching he was receiving. It was great timing for Cantafio as he had just lost his All-State quarterback from the previous season to graduation and didn't have an immediate replacement. One option was to move wide receiver Ian Firestone to quarterback, but Firestone was one of the best receivers in the league, so Cantafio would not only be starting a new quarterback in that scenario, but he also would have lost his top receiver in the process.

Cantafio decided in summer camp that Henne would take all the snaps at quarterback for one day and that Firestone would remain at receiver. The quarterback-wide receiver duo spent the whole day working together to gain a rhythm. "That night I had a meeting with my staff and I said, 'It's quite apparent that we're a better football team with Chad at quarterback and Ian at receiver.' I said, 'He's young, he's going to make mistakes, and it's going to be a growing process,'" Cantafio said. "But my gut told me this is the right move, that we need to go with Chad as the starting quarterback as a true freshman. It was so apparent that we were better with Chad at quarterback, and his freshman year, he led us to the league championship, and we won it."

Henne's team was down 26–7 heading into the fourth quarter of that league championship game, and the freshman quarterback helped lead his team back from a 19-point deficit to win the game in the last stanza. No one at Wilson High knew it, but Henne was about to become a national name because of that freshman season. The way he stepped in and guided his team impressed some of the biggest college coaches in the country.

At the beginning of the millennium, it was still very unusual for underclassmen to gain national attention and receive scholarship offers that early in their career, but Henne's potential and talent would put him in that rare air. Cantafio was big on promoting his players to college coaches. Knowing that Henne was special, Cantafio distributed his star freshman's film to college coaches across the country. Because of Henne's work ethic, size, and arm, the coach felt as though Henne was a major Division I prospect, but he never expected the response they got after that freshman season.

Shortly after Cantafio sent out Henne's film, the budding quarterback was offered by LSU offensive coordinator (and current Texas A&M head coach) Jimbo Fisher. Henne's name started circulating among high-profile coaches, and then the young quarterback attended a camp that pushed him even further up the recruiting boards at colleges all over. "It was an elite quarterback camp at Purdue. They were one of the first offenses in the Big Ten with the spread offense, so I went there," Henne said. "I was the MVP of that camp, and then pretty much all the Big Ten schools jumped on board. I got offers from pretty much every Big Ten team after that."

Joe Tiller was the head coach at Purdue at the time. Tiller brought Henne and Cantafio into his office midway through the camp and offered the soon-to-be-sophomore a scholarship without hesitation. His coach started getting phone calls from then-LSU head coach Nick Saban, Tennessee's Phil Fulmer, and coaches from Penn State, Michigan, and Maryland. Once word got out that Henne was the real deal, the floodgates opened, and his recruiting process took off after that freshman year. Cantafio knew that his courtship would be big, but he didn't know just how big it would get, and neither did Henne. "Coming from the north and hearing a hillbilly like Jimbo

Fisher talk to me was kind of funny," Henne said. "I said, 'Mom, this guy from LSU just called and said he wants to offer me.' And I had no idea who he was or how good they were. I wasn't really into the college football rankings and who was good or who wasn't."

Growing up in Pennsylvania, Henne admittedly was a fan of Penn State. He also had an affinity for the University of Miami because of the success they had during that time period. Receiving that first offer from LSU was exciting, but he wasn't familiar with the program or many of the other schools coming after him. He attended Penn State games as a fan growing up, and his older sister attended the university as a student. Because it was close to home, Henne was afforded the opportunity to take several recruiting trips to Penn State throughout the process to see everything up close and personal. "Early on I really wanted to stay at home and go to Penn State," Henne said. "I really liked it up there. I had some other family members that went there, some friends that went there, and it was close to home, so I always wanted to go there."

The Nittany Lions offered early, and assistant coaches Bill Kenney and Jay Paterno were tasked with recruiting the in-state quarterback. Because he was getting so much attention from schools all over the country now, including Florida State and Miami, Henne felt as though he needed to get his process under control and didn't want to lead on any of the coaches who were recruiting him. He also wanted to make his recruitment easier on himself. So the summer after his sophomore season, he narrowed his list down to Penn State, Michigan, Miami, Georgia, and Tennessee. "Everything came so heavily," Henne said. "You get all the mail, all the phone calls. So we said let's limit it to these five teams, break it down, and deal with them. If anyone else calls, we say: this is my top five, and you're not in it."

Michigan was in it, but—along with the other schools on his top list—the Wolverines were behind Penn State. That didn't matter to Michigan quarterbacks coach Scot Loeffler, though, who found Henne very early in the process. Loeffler was watching film in his office of a few prospects and came upon Henne's. He set the tape aside as someone he wanted to review again and figured it was a junior or senior-to-be. It was actually Henne's freshman film, and once Loeffler figured out how young the quarterback on that tape was, he knew right away that Henne needed to be a priority for Michigan. "From that point forward, we treated Chad as if he was a senior-to-be in high school. We recruited him every possible week we could go out to high schools during the evaluation and contact periods," Loeffler said. "We treated him like he was an older guy and went to his high school and developed relationships with people in his school. Chad Henne is probably the hardest I've recruited a guy without a doubt because you knew right then and there that Chad was going to be a special football player."

Loeffler wasn't exaggerating. He was out to see Henne as much as the NCAA rules would allow. Since it was a prospect in the state of Pennsylvania, where then-Penn State head coach Joe Paterno had typically owned recruiting, Loeffler knew that it would take quite a bit to pull Henne from his home state. That meant building a relationship with Cantafio, Henne's family, and anyone who was close to him to make sure they were all comfortable with Loeffler and knew what Michigan had to offer. "To be honest with you, Scot Loeffler was in my office so much for four years it was like we were relatives. It was like having a brother around," Cantafio said. "Honest to God, his recruiting of Chad was unbelievable. At the time Scot was considered one of the top quarterback coaches in the country, and it was so obvious how important Chad was to him."

But it still didn't help Michigan overcome the fact that Penn State was close to home and it was the school that Henne was most familiar and most comfortable with. Loeffler was in the process of building a close bond, but the Nittany Lions were right there and in Henne's ear as much as the next school. On top of that, Cantafio was a fan of Penn State himself and was also the president of the Pennsylvania Scholastic Football Coaches Association. To have his star pupil play in Beaver Stadium was a dream come true and something Cantafio hoped would happen. Though that was his hope, he never pushed Henne toward a decision one way or the other and still knew it had to be Henne's choice.

Cantafio did have a personal relationship with Joe Paterno, though, having spent quite a bit of time around the head coach and even having dinner with him several times. The odds were still in Penn State's favor, but Michigan was starting to build some momentum. The main problem for the Wolverines was that Henne, as he had stated, was not educated on the tradition, history, or clout of every program in the country, and that included Michigan. He wasn't aware of the success of past Michigan quarterbacks and its winning program throughout the years.

None of that factored in for him initially, and all he had to go on was the relationship he was building with Loeffler. As Henne made his way through high school, he continued having success and continued to see the coaches from his list pursue him as hard as they could. He had been identified as one of the top quarterbacks in the country, and once his junior season had ended, he and his coach knew it was nearing time to end his recruitment.

Henne went to his coach in the spring of his junior year in high school and told him he thought he was ready to make a commitment. He didn't want it to be announced publicly, though, as he still wanted to take a few unofficial visits and make sure it was the right choice before he would make his decision known at a press conference that would take place in August before his senior season. "I committed to Penn State," Henne said. "It wasn't public, so it was all kind of under the radar."

He and Cantafio called Joe Paterno and told the Penn State head coach that the top quarterback in the state would stay home. Cantafio didn't tell a single person, and neither did Henne—outside of his parents and family. Cantafio was thrilled that his high school quarterback would one day play in Beaver Stadium and he would be right there to see it all happen. There had been some questions at the time whether Joe Paterno could still keep the top in-state prospects home, and announcing Henne's commitment publicly would do a lot to quiet those whispers. It would also give the Nittany Lions a tremendous talent at quarterback and someone who could realistically lead the team for three or four years.

Because Henne had made his decision and the recruiting process had started to get to be too much for Henne and his coach, Cantafio decided to create a recruiting dead period for his pupil. "We got to the end of May, and it was like, *Oh my God*. I called a truce and I told all the coaches, 'I don't want anybody calling him,'" Cantafio said. "'You can call me all you want but not him.' They all paid attention, and Chad made some unofficial visits, but other than that, they let him relax a little bit."

After he told the Penn State coaches he was committed, one of those visits he took was to Michigan. At this point Henne and Loeffler had established a great relationship, but it obviously wasn't enough to get the Wolverines past the Nittany Lions. Henne went on the trip to Ann Arbor despite not knowing much about Michigan or what the school had to offer. On the visit Henne saw the facilities at Schembechler Hall, spent time with head coach Lloyd Carr, and learned about the quarterback tradition Michigan had built. "It was a great visit. It was kind of like getting a feel for the offense and the tradition," Henne said. "When I heard about all the quarterbacks and all the guys that played in the NFL, I was like, *Oh they actually have something going on here.* I had no clue about it, and that really increased my interest in the school."

That visit, though, still didn't move Henne to back away from his commitment to Penn State. Having spent so much time around him, Loeffler had a good feel for Henne at this point and he knew that Michigan still wasn't the choice. "We showed him all the X's and O's and all the things we were going to do with him and how we were going to develop him," Loeffler said. "We played on: 'You're not only going to come play for a place that you're going to win a Big Ten championship, but you're going to get a great education.' When he left you didn't feel 100 percent that he was coming to Michigan. I knew that he was very intrigued by Michigan."

The Michigan staff had set their sights on Henne and knew that if they were still behind, they needed to do everything they could to land their top target at quarterback. Henne was someone whom Loeffler believed could eventually be an NFL quarterback, and he wanted to land his guy.

Henne didn't do much in his recruitment after that unofficial visit to Michigan in the spring of 2003. He didn't take any other visits and tried to maintain a low profile to keep some normalcy. Once the summer rolled around, though, Cantafio was putting on a quarterback camp for other high school prospects, and Henne was scheduled to perform at the camp for one day. A recent rule change within the NCAA allowed college coaches to work at the camp and work with the prospects on the field. Loeffler got word that Henne would be at the camp and that he would be allowed to work with Henne on the field. So he made sure he was one of the coaches participating in the camp. He fulfilled his obligation at Michigan's summer camp and flew out the next day to work at Cantafio's camp.

Loeffler was able to give Henne a live, in-person look at what it would be like to be coached by him, and it gave the two another chance to grow their bond. "Chad was only supposed to be at the camp for the afternoon and he ended up being there for three days. The ability to work with him for those three days was huge," Loeffler said. "I remember calling Coach Carr, and he said, 'What do you think of him?' I said, 'I think he's going to be a starter and an NFL quarterback without a doubt.'"

From Henne's perspective, he only had three years experience as a quarterback and really only knew what his high school coach had taught him. So to learn from a college quarterbacks coach, someone who had been part of such a rich tradition at the position, was eye opening for Henne. That experience at that camp made Henne start to rethink his commitment to Penn State and turned the tables in Michigan's favor. "At the camp he told me to try a few things and try this, and I was like, *Man this guy really knows what he's talking about.* And that was when I thought things might change to Michigan,"

Henne said. "I felt that there weren't any questions a quarterback could ask him that he wouldn't know. I thought, *Man, this guy is really going to create the knowledge for me to be great at college football but also have the opportunity to move on to the NFL, and I'll be prepared for that, too.*"

Loeffler continued working with Henne at the camp and before leaving he asked if "they were good." He meant was Henne on the same page as Loeffler with where they could go together as coach and pupil? Henne replied that they were good. It wasn't a firm commitment, but it was a good indicator that his recruitment had swung to Michigan's side, and Loeffler, being able to read Henne by now, traveled back to Ann Arbor very confident that the Wolverines were about to land the quarterback target they had spent so much time recruiting.

Loeffler got back to Schembechler Hall, walked into Carr's office, closed the door, and told the head coach that he thought they were about to land Henne. Loeffler did not repeat that to anyone but Carr and waited to get official word. The information that Henne had made a commitment to Penn State and that he was thinking about flipping his decision to Michigan was never made public. No one knew that Henne had already made a commitment and that his press conference scheduled for August was now thrown for a loop.

The reason Henne and his coach had scheduled the press conference for August was so both could focus on Henne's senior football season and put his recruitment officially behind them. It had become a much-anticipated event, and many reporters were planning on covering the commitment. Hearing the Nittany Lions were heavily involved, many of the in-state sportswriters were intrigued to see if Henne would stay home or if he would entertain any of the out-of-state schools. Cantafio wanted to make sure his student was well-prepared for the press conference, so he decided to have Henne practice what he would say and how he would answer certain questions, thinking it would be a routine run-through. "I called him about a week before and I said let's go over the press conference. I made him get up at a podium, instructed him that the press conference needs to be positive," Cantafio said. "He was well-prepped, he was ready to go, and then he said, 'Coach, I need to talk to you.' He said, 'I've changed my mind. I'm going to decommit from Penn State and I'm going to go to Michigan.'"

Cantafio paused, and Henne asked his beloved coach if he was mad at him for changing his mind. Cantafio explained that he wasn't mad. He was just going through his mind how he would deal with the questions he would face if Henne flipped his commitment. The questions from the Penn State coaches, the fans that thought Henne should stay home for the Nittany Lions—they would all come to Cantafio.

He understood, though, that Henne was going with his heart and that the time Loeffler had spent building the relationships with everyone around the star quarterback had been too strong to break. "Was I heartbroken? Sure I was. I was a Penn State die-hard," Cantafio said. "I was happy he was going to Penn State, but he made up his mind because that's where his heart needed to be. Nobody knew he committed to Penn State—other than Chad and I and his mom and dad—but Scot Loeffler was one of the main reasons why he changed his mind, if not the main reason."

A week away from his press conference, Henne finally decided that he would switch his commitment and he would be a Wolverine. A few days before the big event, Henne called Loeffler and made it official that he was coming to Ann Arbor. All of Loeffler's work and the time spent at his school had paid off. Henne wanted to be respectful to Joe Paterno and his staff, so he also called Paterno and notified him that he was switching his commitment. He thanked the coach and told him he was going to Michigan. After the phone calls were made, Cantafio made sure Henne knew what he was doing and that this was the final choice he would make. Back then decommitments were rare and were not thought of in the greatest of light. Before they went to the press conference, Cantafio made sure this was what Henne felt was right. "I told him, 'Am I upset? I'm not upset at you. You're doing what you need to do because you feel this is the best decision for you, and that's all that matters,'" Cantafio said. "I asked him: 'Between you and I, why are you changing your mind?' He said, 'Coach, I want to be coached by Scot Loeffler.' That was the key to him decommitting, and he felt it was the right choice."

That was all Cantafio needed to hear. He knew that Henne's mind was made up, and his decision was set. Michigan had overtaken Penn State at the right time and through the relentless efforts of the Michigan coaching staff. On August 7, 2003, Chad Henne held his press conference and announced to the public that he was heading to the University of Michigan.

With his commitment made, the other programs, including Penn State, backed off and let Henne finish out his senior season. He took his official visit to Michigan that senior year and never wavered in his commitment to the Wolverines.

The star quarterback graduated high school and made his way to Ann Arbor, where he thought he would be in a battle with Matt Gutierrez, who was a junior when Henne hit campus. The Michigan coaches felt Henne would play one way or another that first year, but figured it might be in a backup role. Unexpectedly, though, Gutierrez injured his shoulder in training camp, which required surgery, and vaulted Henne into the spotlight. "We ended up starting Chad, and I think we told Chad he was starting on Wednesday the week of the first game," Loeffler said. "We said to him that we didn't want anyone to know. What's fascinating—I don't think this could happen in today's world, but it wasn't announced, and someone leaked it about five minutes before kickoff."

Just as his high school career had started, his college career would start the same way—an opportunity to lead his team as a true freshman starting quarterback. Knowing they had something special the moment he stepped on campus, the coaches handed Henne the reins of the team in his first season. During that freshman year, Henne completed a little more than 60 percent of his passes for 2,743 yards, 25 touchdowns, and 12 interceptions. The team finished with a 9–3 record, a Big Ten championship, and a No. 14 ranking in the AP poll. "When we found out he was going to be the starting quarterback, it was like, *Are you kidding me?*" Cantafio said. "He's going from Wilson football, a couple thousand people in the bleachers, and now he's going to be the starting quarterback for Michigan as a true freshman with 110,000 people in the stands?"

Henne started all four years at Michigan and still owns the most career passing yards for any Michigan quarterback with 9,715 yards. He is tied for the most touchdown passes in a season with Elvis Grbac at 25 and is alone at the top for the most career touchdown passes at Michigan with 87. In 2006 his two college finalists would intersect when Michigan traveled to Penn State to play against the Nittany Lions. The Wolverines were undefeated coming into that game, and

Henne had thrown 13 touchdowns against four interceptions on the year.

Cantafio finally got to see his quarterback play in Beaver Stadium—just in a different jersey and helmet than he initially imagined it. Cantafio made it to as many home games as he could and knew he wouldn't miss this opportunity to see Henne play at Penn State. "We're there, and I'm all dressed up in my Michigan attire. People are busting my hump because here I am—the president of the Pennsylvania Football Coaches Association—and I'm at the Penn State game wearing Michigan attire," Cantafio said. "I got interviewed by ABC. Then after the game, I went down to the field, jumped over the wall, told the security guard who I was, and went out to midfield. I have a beautiful picture of Chad in his uniform and me at the 50-yard line the night Chad and Michigan beat Penn State."

His final season at Michigan is something Loeffler still remembers for Henne's resilience. It leads him to call Henne one of the toughest players he has ever been around. Henne injured his knee against Oregon in the second game of his senior season. He had surgery and was back in two weeks but suffered another injury later in the season. In an October 20 game against Illinois, Michigan's offensive line messed up the protection on an inside blitz, and a defender threw Henne down on his shoulder. The hit caused a problem with a joint, and his prospects didn't look good to finish the game. "I remember going down at halftime and saying, 'Chad, you're not going to play' because it was ugly. It was gross. I go, 'Chad, you're done. We'll play Ryan [Mallett] the rest of the time,'" Loeffler said. "He goes, 'Scot, you tell these doctors to shoot me up, and I'm going to play in this game.' I told him he couldn't do that, but the fourth quarter rolls around, and Chad picks up the phone. I'm in the press box. He goes, 'I'm going in the game.' I said, 'No, you're not.' He goes, 'I'm telling you right now I'm going in the game' and slams the phone down."

Henne went back in the game and finished with two touchdowns and 201 yards passing on a barely functional shoulder. After that game Henne wasn't able to practice—let alone lift his arm above his shoulder. He took mental reps during practice and eventually got treatment from the team doctors. They determined that Henne couldn't cause any further damage by playing, so—true to form—he told his coaches he would play the next game. At that point Loeffler knew his quarterback very well and knew there was no stopping Henne if that was the choice he made. The team headed into the Michigan State game with two losses on the season (to Appalachian State and Oregon) but without any conference losses. So they still had a shot at winning the Big Ten.

Henne and the Wolverines found themselves down to the Spartans 24–14 in the fourth quarter. With 6:47 left in the quarter, Henne found receiver Greg Matthews for a 14-yard touchdown that put Michigan within three points at 24–21. Then with 2:28 left in the final quarter, Henne showed his teacher, Loeffler, that he had absorbed all of the coaching over the past four years. "It was third down and 12, a waning part of the game, and I called a particular pass play. When he broke the huddle—I know these guys like the back of my hand—and when he broke the huddle, I'm going, 'Something's up,'" Loeffler said. "He completely changed it and put a double move on the pass play that we called and hit it for a touchdown to Mario Manningham to beat Michigan State. I remember picking up the phone saying, 'Chad, What a great throw! And if you ever do that again, I swear to you I'll come down there and kill you.' He just started laughing."

He laughed because he knew that Loeffler was proud of him. There were some bumps and bruises along the way, but Henne, who started all four years of college, finished his career at Michigan atop the record books and as one of the winningest quarterbacks in Michigan history. The Miami Dolphins selected him in the second round of the 2008 NFL Draft. As part of a nearly decade long tenure in the NFL, he now plays for the Kansas City Chiefs.

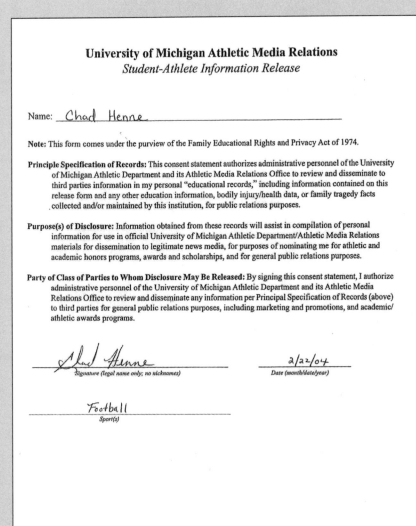

University of Michigan Athletic Media Relations
Student-Athlete Information Release

Name: Chad Henne

Note: This form comes under the purview of the Family Educational Rights and Privacy Act of 1974.

Principle Specification of Records: This consent statement authorizes administrative personnel of the University of Michigan Athletic Department and its Athletic Media Relations Office to review and disseminate to third parties information in my personal "educational records," including information contained on this release form and any other education information, bodily injury/health data, or family tragedy facts collected and/or maintained by this institution, for public relations purposes.

Purpose(s) of Disclosure: Information obtained from these records will assist in compilation of personal information for use in official University of Michigan Athletic Department/Athletic Media Relations materials for dissemination to legitimate news media, for purposes of nominating me for athletic and academic honors programs, awards and scholarships, and for general public relations purposes.

Party of Class of Parties to Whom Disclosure May Be Released: By signing this consent statement, I authorize administrative personnel of the University of Michigan Athletic Department and its Athletic Media Relations Office to review and disseminate any information per Principal Specification of Records (above) to third parties for general public relations purposes, including marketing and promotions, and academic/athletic awards programs.

_____   _____2/22/04_____
Signature (legal name only; no nicknames)   Date (month/date/year)

_____Football_____
Sport(s)

University of Michigan Athletic Media Relations
Student-Athlete Biographical Information

This biographical information is a permanent record in your athletic media relations file. Please complete the form neatly, accurately and completely. Supplemental information (newspapers articles, etc.) may be included to complete background information.

Date 2/22/04   U-M Sport Football

Personal Information

Legal Name (first, middle, last) Chad Steven Henne

Preferred Name / Nickname Chad

Date of Birth (month/date/year) 7/2/85   Height 6'3"   Weight 215

Home Address (address/city/state/zip) ▮▮▮▮▮▮▮▮▮▮▮▮

U-M Address (address/city/state/zip)

Home Phone (▮▮▮▮▮▮▮▮▮)   U-M Phone (▮▮▮▮▮▮▮▮▮)

Academic Class (Fr., So., Jr., Sr., Grad.) Fr.   Athletic Eligibility (Fr., So., Jr., Sr., 5th year) Fr

U-M School Enrolled In   Declared Major Business

Family Information

Father's Name (first/last) Sheldon Henne   College Stephen's Tech.

Father's Address (if same as yours, omit)

Mother's Name (first/last) Sue Henne   College

Mother's Address (if same as yours, omit)

Parent's Maritial Status: married ✓   divorced _____   Number of: brothers _____ sisters 1

Parent(s), sibling(s) who are now or have been members of intercollegiate varsity athletic team (indicate school/sport/years):

Hometown Media Information

Name(s) and Addresses of Newspaper(s) that regularly cover your high school.

Reading Eagle

Lancaster New Era

High School Information

High School (name/city/state) ___Wilson, West Lawn, Pa___

Year Graduated ___2004___   Athletic Conference (spell out) ___Lancaster-Lebanon League___

Academic Honors, Clubs (i.e., National Honor Society, Honor Roll, Etc.) ___Honor throughout High School___

By Year, list sports competed in, honors received, varsity letters earned, season-ending statistical information, team achievements. Be sure to give complete name of each award/honor (i.e., All-West Central Conference Football First-Team; All-Putnam County Girls' Track - selected by Putnam County Banner-Graphic). List coach's complete name with sport you will compete in for U-M. Use an additional piece of paper if necessary.

Freshman: Year ___2000___ (9th grade):

1st Team All Berks County Quarterback
142 comp. / 266 att. / 53.4 pct. / 1835 yds / 16 TD's / 6 ints /

Sophomore: Year ___2001___ (10th grade):

118 comp. / 231 att. / 51.1 pct. / 1405 yds / 16 TD's / 11 ints /

Junior: Year ___2002___ (11th grade):

1st Team All Berks County QB / 1st Team Lancaster Lebanon QB
Berks Player of the Year / All Berks & Lancaster Lebanon Offensive
Back of the Year / 2nd Team All State Pennsylvania QB
156 comp. / 242 att. / 64.4 pct. / 2,088 yds / 23 TD's / 3 ints /

Senior: Year ___2003___ (12th grade):

1st Team All Berks County QB / 1st Team Lancaster-Lebanon QB
All Berks & Lancaster-Lebanon Offensive Back of the Year /
1st Team All State Pennsylvania QB / Parade All American /
U.S. Army All-American / District III All-Time Passing + TD Holder
147 comp / 249 att. / 59.0 pct. / 1743 yds / 19 TD's / 6 ints /

CHAPTER 13

Rashan Gary

As a freshman in high school, a young and wide-eyed Rashan Gary looked at his mother, Jennifer Shepherd, and told her he wanted to be the No. 1 ranked player in the country by the time he was finished with his high school career. Being a supportive mother, Shepherd told him that he would one day achieve that goal if he worked hard and lived the right way, and Gary indeed ended up as ESPN's No. 1 ranked prospect in the 2016 recruiting class.

His journey started as an eighth grader near Plainfield, New Jersey, where his athletic ability stood out even at an early age. His youth football coaches suggested to Gary and his mother that they sign him up for an upcoming big man camp at Rutgers University. There weren't many expectations from Gary or his mother since he was so young, and both were so new to the camp circuit and recruiting process.

He had always been a standout player, but that was against other athletes his own age. This camp would put the eighth grader against high schoolers vying for a scholarship from then-Rutgers head coach Kyle Flood. This would be a challenge he was yet to face, and neither he nor his mother knew what would be the outcome. "They did one-on-ones, and I noticed that Rashan did pretty well. Then the coaches started gathering around Rashan, so I couldn't see anymore," Shepherd said. "Rashan trotted over to me afterward and asked how he was doing. I said, 'I guess you're doing well.' But he said the bench press was up next and he had never bench pressed anything before."

Gary was nervous about how he would fare among bigger and stronger athletes, some of whom were three years older than he was. His mother told him to do the best he could and not to worry about the outcome—all while hiding her fear. Shepherd noticed some of the other prospects were able to lift the 175 pounds of weight a few times. Many squeezed out four repetitions, so she silently hoped her son would just make it to four as well. Gary got into position and lifted the bar 12 times in front of many surprised onlookers. After Gary finished, Flood introduced Gary to the rest of the campers and coaches as the youngest participant that day, and nearly everyone's mouth dropped. They figured it was a high school junior who just had put on a show. "I remember after the camp I was in the kitchen cooking, and Rashan was in his room. One of the Rutgers coaches called me and said, 'We'd like to offer Rashan a scholarship,'" Shepherd said. "I said, 'A scholarship to what?' He said, 'A scholarship to play football at Rutgers.' I yelled to Rashan to come here and I asked that the coach tell that to Rashan."

Gary and his mother were shocked that he now had a scholarship offer at a major university. They never thought the outcome of that camp would lead to coaches fawning over his potential and recruiting him at such a young age. The good news wouldn't stop for Gary as he jumped straight to varsity in ninth grade and started to show what he was capable of on the field. After his freshman season in 2013,

Shepherd wanted her son to compete against higher level competition to see how far along he was. Since the last camp he attended was such a success, she decided to sign him up for a few more.

In the spring and summer, Gary traveled to Temple, where then-coach Matt Rhule offered him a scholarship after his performance. The two then drove to Ohio State, where defensive line coach Mike Vrabel brought Gary over to meet head coach Urban Meyer. "Coach Meyer introduced himself to me and Rashan and he said, 'I want to give this kid a scholarship. He is going to be something else.' At the end of the camp, Urban Meyer offered Rashan a scholarship in the ninth grade," Shepherd said. "We went to UConn, and they offered him, and the final one was Penn State, and we met Larry Johnson. Even to this day, I love Larry Johnson. He's just a guy I could see Rashan aspiring to work with."

At the time Johnson was the defensive line coach for Penn State under head coach Bill O'Brien. Johnson connected immediately with Shepherd and Gary to the point that the Nittany Lions became the leader in the Gary recruiting derby. Both Gary and his mother felt very good about what the Nittany Lions had to offer as long as Johnson was there. "I got to have a great relationship with him because he's the one I'm going to spend the most time with," Gary said at the time. "I didn't know anything about Penn State, but throughout the camp, coach Larry Johnson just showed he was a nice guy. I loved it there. Coach Johnson I really liked."

By July of 2013, Gary was up to seven total offers from the likes of Ohio State, Penn State, Miami, Temple, UConn, and Rutgers. The process was still new to Shepherd and Gary, but bigger names and more recognizable coaches kept coming in to see what all the buzz was about. Heading into his sophomore season, Gary had started to become a household name for the potential he had shown at the camps he attended.

Gary's high school coach one day frantically called Shepherd at her place of employment. Talking fast and very excitedly, he left a voicemail for Shepherd to call him back. Shepherd was nervous because she never received calls at work and now wasn't able to reach Gary's coach. "I finally get him, and he says, 'You'll never guess what just happened.' All I wanted to know is that Rashan's okay, and he says Mario Cristobal came to the school and offered Rashan," Shepherd said. "I said, 'Who is Mario Cristobal? Right now, I'm getting upset because you're calling me at work all emotional and I'm thinking something is wrong with Rashan.'"

Cristobal was the offensive line coach at the University of Alabama and had come to Gary's high school to offer the sophomore. Shepherd had no idea who he was or what it ultimately meant in terms of recruiting or football. She instructed her son to get all of his info, and they could talk about it later. Now looking back, she realizes the gravity of what that scholarship offer meant and how important it was to have one of the top programs in the country targeting her son at such an early age.

Around this time, there was a coaching change that would shake up Gary's recruitment. Ohio State had hired Johnson away from Penn State in January of 2014. That move knocked the Nittany Lions out of the top spot and ultimately out of his recruitment, and Johnson taking the defensive line coaching position at Ohio State immediately moved the Buckeyes to the top of his board. Johnson meant that much to the family that they believed if the school was good enough for him, it was good enough for them. "In my head wherever Coach Johnson was going to be, that's where Rashan was going to go," Shepherd said. "I liked him that much."

After his sophomore season, more change would come as Gary's father decided he was going to relocate and wanted to take Rashan with him. Shepherd ultimately decided that Gary would stay with her, but she lived in Plainfield, New Jersey, and wasn't comfortable with the public school education and environment there. Gary's parents decided that since he had received so many scholarship offers and likely would not have to pay for his education in college they would use the money they had saved for his tuition to find a parochial school in the area for him to attend. After looking at various schools, they ultimately chose Paramus Catholic in Paramus, New Jersey.

Head coach Chris Partridge took Gary in and immediately introduced the family to one of his defensive line coaches, Steve Kanoc, to assist the family in their recruiting journey. Kanoc, a Paramus Catholic alum, immediately gained the trust of Gary and his mother. He ultimately became the main advisor during Gary's recruitment, attended nearly every visit, and helped organize his new pupil's process. "I was new at all this with recruiting, but I watched Partridge handle Jabrill Peppers' recruitment and I learned from him what was going on. Jen said, 'Do you want to go on some unofficial trips with us?' And I said, 'Yes,'" Kanoc said. "The funny part was now all these big college coaches are calling me because Jen is giving them my number. Jen would say, 'Do you mind talking to the coaches and setting up the trips?' So I would plan the trip and get it all organized."

Shepherd had given Kanoc's number to most of the coaches recruiting her son, but Johnson was one of the first to reach out to

Gary's new assistant coach. Kanoc immediately saw how significant Johnson would be in the process and how Gary would open up whenever he interacted with the Ohio State coach. Gary was very introverted and shy but would have a big smile on his face anytime he was around Johnson. There, though, was still a lot to learn about his potential new home with the Buckeyes that would require further investigating.

Kanoc had grown close with Gary and Shepherd, and after Gary went through his sophomore season in January of 2015, the University of Michigan hired away his high school head coach, Partridge. Gary had already dealt with quite a bit of change, but this was yet another piece of movement. It was a positive that he now knew someone at Michigan because the Wolverines had recently changed coaching staffs, adding Jim Harbaugh as the head coach.

It was a negative, though, that the most experienced coach in terms of recruiting at Paramus Catholic was now gone. It also posed an interesting question: because of Partridge's relationship with Gary as his high school coach, how would that impact his recruitment?

Many believed that the Wolverines were immediately his leader because of the addition of Partridge, but that was not the case. "Right from the beginning, the first thing I told them was: 'I'm going to show you the opportunity Michigan has, but I'm not going to use myself in this at all. I'm going to recruit you like I'm going to recruit any other person,'" Partridge said. "Obviously, as we went through the process, he was more comfortable at Michigan because I knew him, and I was able to show him the benefits of Michigan. There was an advantage. I'm not going to say there wasn't, but I really tried to stay out of the pushing, the selling."

By this time Gary had received offers from Florida State, USC, Tennessee, and was already gaining more and more interest. In April of 2015, Gary, Shepherd, and Kanoc set out on a tour of visits that included South Carolina, Georgia, and Clemson. Those weren't the first unofficial visits they had taken, but now with Gary about to finish his junior year in high school, everything was starting to get a little more serious.

The first trip the three went on was to South Carolina to meet Steve Spurrier. This visit was only a few months before Spurrier retired, and after spending only 15 minutes with Spurrier, Shepherd and Kanoc could tell that he was close to his way out. The biggest takeaway from the trip was that Gary realized he could play on that level after seeing who South Carolina had on the roster and how he stacked up.

During this time Ohio State was very much in the mix because of Johnson, Alabama was in the mix because the Tide had been a dream school for Gary growing up. Auburn and coach Gus Malzahn got into the mix after a visit. And Georgia, Ole Miss, and Clemson were other schools that Gary and Shepherd were really focused on. "Alabama, we were being recruited by Cristobal, and Rashan probably had the most involvement at Alabama with the assistant coaches. What turned Rashan and Jen off from Alabama was Nick Saban," Kanoc said. "Saban spent like eight minutes with us and he was the only head coach not to give her his cell phone number. He would never call from his phone. It was always from a school phone or his assistant's, and Jen didn't feel confident that they really wanted Rashan based off their interactions."

The next stops on the tour were supposed to be Michigan and then Ohio State—in that order. Partridge had a trick up his sleeve, however, and convinced Kanoc, Gary, and Shepherd to visit Ohio State first and Michigan second. "The main benefit that we received from all of that was that I went on Ohio State visits before with other players as a coach. They have this clear-cut agenda of how they run their visits," Partridge said. "I specifically remember throwing them a curveball where they were going to come to Michigan, then Ohio State, and I got them to switch it so they came to Ohio State and then Michigan, so we could back up the Ohio State visit, knowing exactly what they were going to do. The first big win in our recruitment for Rashan was getting them to switch that."

Though it was still early in their thought process, Johnson's presence at Ohio State was alluring to both Gary and his mother. They were more excited to visit Ohio State than Michigan as they prepared for the two visits. As it usually happened, Shepherd would look at her son and ask him if he wanted to sit in the academic meetings with her, he would roll his eyes, she would nod her head, and Gary would go with the coaches to hear the football-related pitch while his mother learned about the academics. While at Ohio State, that same scenario ensued, and Shepherd went to hear about what the Buckeyes would provide her son from an academic standpoint and how they would help him have success in the classroom.

The presentation did not go as she had hoped, and Shepherd readily admits that she was less than pleased with what she heard and saw while on the trip. "It was very generic. A lot of schools catered it to Rashan, and this one could've been anyone coming in with what they presented to her," Kanoc said. "They had two young women speaking to her and they couldn't answer her questions and they weren't good at answering them. I remember Larry Johnson going, 'I don't know why they let these two young ladies handle his academics on this recruiting trip,' because they blew the whole thing."

The presentation went so poorly that Shepherd credits that academic presentation for the reason why Ohio State began to fall out of favor with Gary. When she was looking for answers about tutors, assistance, and how Rashan would succeed, she didn't get many answers. "What I got was football, football, football, Joey Bosa, football. Even though I love Larry Johnson, we had to put what we felt was important for Rashan to have a full college experience," Shepherd said. "I'm a whole lot smarter now to know that a full experience doesn't happen, but at the time I didn't know. I liked Urban Meyer. I liked him, but I felt they kind of primarily focused on football."

Partridge's plan to switch the visits was starting to pay off, which was good because Gary and his mother were not all that excited to make the trip to Michigan prior to the visit. Kanoc had to convince the two that they should at least check out what Michigan had to offer. So Gary and Shepherd made their way to Ann Arbor to see what the Wolverines had to offer.

It was late June of 2015. The weather was favorable, and the Michigan campus was full of students and people buzzing around. From his one season coaching Gary, Partridge knew exactly what Gary and Shepherd were looking to hear and see on the visit. He also knew exactly where Ohio State's visit would be lacking and made sure that Michigan put everything in front of the No. 1 prospect. "They took us around the whole campus and they were going back to Schembechler Hall. I'm not a football person, so I don't want to go to Schembechler Hall. The campus was so beautiful. So I said, 'Let me out here, and I'll walk back,'" Shepherd said. "While I was walking, I went through the library, and there was maybe six or seven girls sitting in the quad. I asked them where the M Den store was and then asked them some questions about Michigan. They were so sweet. We ended up getting up, going to the M Den together, got ice cream, and we went to Walmart."

The visit was already off to a better start than Ohio State's, as another important factor in his recruitment was a level of comfort with the campus, the surrounding area, and what the whole school had to offer. Coach Jim Harbaugh took the three on a golf cart ride through campus, and since Harbaugh was still new himself, they were all seeing some of the campus for the first time together. Gary, Kanoc, and his mother were supposed to spend 10 minutes with counselor Greg Harden, who has been an instrumental part of the success of many former Michigan athletes, but ended up staying for nearly 45 minutes.

Then the academic presentation was set to take place. Partridge was ready to show them everything Michigan had to offer from the schooling side and pulled out all the stops. "We had the director of the entire business school meet with them. That was a big home run for us because Rhonda Todd, the director, is awesome. Rhonda directs the program that Rashan would have gone into, and then the director of the whole business school came down and toured them as well," Partridge said. "We had other academics as well, sports management, and then our whole academic support. We led the visit off with that, knowing how Ohio State presents their academics and what they do."

The plan worked as all three were blown away by what Michigan had shown them and presented to them. Coming away from the visit,

Shepherd felt as though a student-athlete couldn't fail at Michigan because of all the support provided to the athletes. Michigan focused so heavily on the academics because Partridge knew that it was truly important to them. Some recruits and parents say that they care about the education aspect, but they don't really mean it. Gary had about a 3.6 GPA for his entire high school career, proving he and his mother really meant it when they talked about academics.

The Michigan visit was a hit, and the three traveled to Georgia in July for a barbecue. Then they traveled to LSU to see what the Tigers had to offer. Once those visits were complete, Gary had a top five of Auburn, Clemson, Ohio State, Ole Miss, and Michigan. Alabama had dropped to six, and Georgia was still somewhat in the mix but behind the others. Gary's senior season was approaching, so the three figured out where he would be able to take official visits and what schools he would want to see. Kanoc mapped out the Paramus Catholic season and the potential dates for schools Gary wanted to visit.

Because they wanted to see the Iron Bowl between Alabama and Auburn, they decided to take an official visit to Auburn on November 28. They scheduled a visit to Ole Miss on November 21 and then told Partridge that Gary would take his official visit to Michigan on September 25 for the game against BYU. Partridge didn't want them to come in that early because he knew it would be a dog fight to the end for Gary, and they wanted to be able to close on him.

Partridge tried to convince them to move the visit to December, but Kanoc told him it was happening in September. Michigan had already gained momentum with the first visit earlier in the year, and despite the earliness of it, this official visit strengthened the

Wolverines' position on his list. Although Partridge thought that Gary coming up for a game against BYU would be a negative, it wound up being a positive. Because there weren't many other prospects visiting for the game, the coaches were able to spend more time with Gary and his mother to give them a personal feel. "From that visit I knew it would be Michigan and one other school for Rashan. Jen loved the fans, got to really meet everybody, and Rashan got to spend a lot of time with the players," Kanoc said. "You could see at the time that he just fit right in. The stadium, coming out of the tunnel—it all just felt like home for him."

On their first trip, Harbaugh took Gary and Kanoc to Pizza Bob's, a local restaurant in Ann Arbor, for milkshakes. That became a tradition for Gary and his high school coach, so the two once again got a milkshake at Pizza Bob's on this trip, and it started to sink in that Michigan was a place where Gary could feel at home. It was a great feeling, but they were still considering other schools. It wasn't enough for him to shut things down on the recruiting front.

They continued their trips, but various events started to drop schools from the list. They liked Ole Miss, but incidents that took place—like defensive lineman Robert Nkemdiche falling out of a window at a hotel—dropped the school further down the list. The Rebels coaches tried to negatively recruit against Michigan by knocking Harbaugh, which initially caused some doubt but ultimately worked in Michigan's favor because Gary wanted to see more of the positive sides of Ole Miss rather than hear about the negative side of an opposing program. "The thing with recruiting is you have to know what the other schools are doing," Partridge said. "With Rashan people assumed we were leading because I coached him, so we were getting attacked negatively more than a regular athlete who had five schools on his list. They did a good job of putting doubt in his mind about Jim and Michigan, but I knew he wasn't going to Ole Miss."

The three visited Auburn, and initially the Tigers had a very real shot with Gary. There was a lot to like about what Auburn had to offer, but a coaching change with defensive coordinator Will Muschamp hurt their chances. "What killed it for Auburn was Muschamp because he sat down with Jen at Paramus Catholic the day before he left Auburn and said he wasn't leaving. He said he has moved his kids nine times, and it was like two days later, the headline came out, saying he was the head coach at South Carolina," Kanoc said. "Jen went out and called him a liar. She wasn't happy about that, so it squashed everything with Auburn."

Michigan also went through a coaching change when defensive coordinator DJ Durkin left to take the head coaching job at Maryland. There was no conversation with Durkin about whether or not he was leaving, though, and very little scuttlebutt about the move happening beforehand. Besides, Partridge and defensive line coach Greg Mattison were the main coaches recruiting Gary. So that coaching departure didn't impact him as much as Muschamp leaving Auburn.

From his top five, Auburn and Ole Miss were out, Ohio State had fallen back, Georgia never pushed forward after head coach Mark Richt was let go, and the family felt as though Alabama wasn't serious about Gary. That left Michigan and Clemson, but a few schools were still trying to get in the mix, and Gary still wasn't sure where he would end up. USC was starting to get in the picture as Gary's senior season was now over. It looked as though the Trojans were gaining some momentum. They convinced Gary and his mother to take an official visit in January, leading up to Signing Day. "One of our best visits was to Los Angeles. Their recruiting guy at USC, he took us sightseeing, and me and Rashan were in awe of everything," Shepherd said. "We were on Rodeo Drive in Beverly Hills, I was like, 'Rashan, I like Los Angeles.'"

After that visit USC had moved into Gary's top group with Clemson and Michigan. The Trojans had placed themselves in the picture, but the distance from home and the cost to travel back to New Jersey from Los Angeles was in the back of his mind. He is close with his mother and sister, and being that far away was somewhat daunting.

It was the middle of January, though, so he still had a few weeks left until Signing Day in February to make his decision. Other schools and coaches tried to make last-minute pitches and tried to get back in the picture with in-home and in-school visits, but none of them worked. Ohio State brought in Greg Schiano as its new defensive coordinator, and, thinking that his ties to Rutgers and New Jersey would help, the Buckeyes tried to get back in the picture. "Schiano came up with Urban Meyer because they thought they'd have a shot with Schiano," Kanoc said. "I finally said to Larry that, 'Jen can't get over what happened on the unofficial,' so he told Urban they weren't going to be in his top two or three. I felt bad for Larry because he was definitely their No. 1 defensive line coach until they really got to know Greg Mattison at Michigan."

The month of January was starting to wind down, and Gary and Kanoc decided to take one more visit to Michigan. This unofficial visit would prove very helpful to Michigan's efforts since it had been a while since Gary was on campus in Ann Arbor. It was also right before he was scheduled to take his official visit to Clemson, so it gave Michigan an opportunity to see him in person before that trip. Kanoc brought Gary's cousin and his younger teammate, Drew Singleton, who would eventually also sign with Michigan, on the visit. Unexpectedly, the weather took a turn for the worse while they were in Ann Arbor, and a large snowstorm cancelled their flight back home, forcing them to stay in Ann Arbor two days longer than expected.

Gary was able to spend an extended amount of time with the Michigan players and on the campus, which ultimately brought him that much closer to the Wolverines. "That last visit did help us because we had Drew Singleton there on the visit, Jordan Fuller was there, who is doing great at Ohio State. Rashan fit in, so he enjoyed the visit," Partridge said. "When they got snowed in, the coaches can't talk to you, but you can hang out and do whatever you want. I think that comfort level just got better and better through that."

Gary eventually made his way home and was prepping to travel to Atlanta to accept the Maxwell Award as one of the top high school players in the country. Quite a few SEC coaches usually make their way to the award presentation. Although they are technically not allowed to talk to the recruits at the event, just being there is usually a way to get in front of the prospects at the event. Partridge found out that this took place and the day before the presentation he travelled to Atlanta to make sure he was also in attendance. He bought a suit at a local store in Atlanta and plopped himself down at a table with Saban and Malzahn and other SEC coaches. "Even though it's off limits, I knew these guys would try to hang out with them. I wasn't allowed to communicate with Rashan and his mom, so I just was there to support them," Partridge said. "I knew that it deflated those guys because I could see the wind drop out of their sail because I was there. And Rashan was going to Clemson right after that award, and I didn't want Clemson to have four days of communicating with him."

It was another plan that paid off because none of the other coaches spoke with Gary—at least publicly—at the event. Following that event Gary and his mother made their way to Clemson, and the trip started off in an unusual way. An anonymous person left a voicemail on the Paramus Catholic president's phone posing as a Clemson fan and mentioned the Ku Klux Klan. The voicemail said that Gary better be serious about his Clemson visit, but neither Gary nor Shepherd took the voicemail as threatening, and it didn't play a part in his school choice.

Kanoc was not on the visit with Gary and his mother, which was something that caused concern for Michigan. Gary's uncle lived very close to the Clemson campus, so there was family nearby, which also concerned the Michigan coaches. "The last visit was Clemson, and Clemson put on a full-court press. I thought it was Michigan before that visit, but I also thought there was a chance there was a Clemson hat coming out because of how that visit went," Kanoc said. "Brent Venables [Clemson's defensive coordinator] is probably one of the best coaches in college—period—and probably one of the nicest guys you'll meet. Recruiting-wise, he was very influential."

Because Gary was very quiet throughout the process, none of the coaches really knew if they had a real shot or not. Everything seemed up in the air. Once his visits were over, there were only a couple of days left until Signing Day, when Gary would announce his decision live on *SportsCenter*. Two days prior to the announcement, Gary and his mother went on a lockdown to figure out where he wanted to go and what school would win out.

Coaches called Kanoc to ask if he had heard anything, but Kanoc had promised the family that he would keep everything they talked about between them. That meant he didn't even reveal information to Partridge, his former head coach, because that would have betrayed the family's trust.

Before the Clemson visit—nearly two weeks before Signing Day—Gary and his mother told Kanoc that they believed he would choose Michigan. But the Clemson visit threw a wrench in that decision and made Gary think twice about which school would be the best. USC had been dropped because of the distance. So it was down to these two schools. Gary and his mother prayed during their two-day lockdown and had conversations about the pros and cons of each school. They came out of the couple of days silence with some clarity but still some uncertainty.

During the last minute that Partridge was allowed to contact the family, he made his last pitch as to what Michigan had to offer. "I sent Rashan a long message stating why I believe it's the right choice for him and then I let it be. I wasn't going to push it or be overbearing," Partridge said. "When you don't push a recruit and it's at the last hour, you get nervous about what the other schools are doing. *Are they pushing him? Are they saying really good stuff?* Later I found out that they were just sending him pictures of the dorm. So they weren't, but I just said something from the heart and left it alone."

Once Signing Day arrived, Gary was set to travel to Bristol, Connecticut, to announce his final decision on ESPN's broadcast. The nearly two-hour drive was quiet as Gary had grown nervous about the decision. He arrived on ESPN's campus with a blank stare and obvious concerns. He stayed quiet throughout the day, which was normal for him, but this was a different kind of quiet. "I told Rashan, 'You're going to have to go and pray. Don't feel rushed because you don't have to sign on Signing Day,'" Shepherd said. "'Just because we're here doesn't mean we have to commit.' He said, 'No, Mom, I'm going to do it today because I want it to be over with.' So we had two hats. We had a Clemson hat and a Michigan hat."

Gary went off on his own to gather his thoughts. When he rejoined his family and friends, he looked at his mother and said he was sure he knew where he was going. She asked him which school it was, and he answered Michigan. The family stepped on the set to broadcast his announcement live, and as the camera panned to Gary, he announced that the Wolverines were his choice and made it official. "I didn't tell Partridge a thing, and if you watch the commitment, you can see me in the back, texting Partridge about 20 seconds before Rashan announces," Kanoc said. "I said, 'I just want to let you know, Go Blue.' I didn't leak it to anybody. I didn't even tell my dad."

The weight had been lifted off of Gary's shoulders. While being interviewed about why he chose Michigan, Gary choked up and said he knew it was the right place for him. The decision didn't come easy, but now that it was over, Gary knew he had made the right choice. "It was very close," he said. "Those are schools that I love, and it was very hard to pick between them, but I feel like I did what was best for me. I was talking to the coaches the night before and I just had a feeling before I announced it."

That feeling has led to a successful Wolverines career. He played as a true freshman, recording 23 total tackles in his first season. During his sophomore season, Gary continued to improve and tallied 58 total tackles with five and a half sacks on the year. He has flourished in Ann Arbor, and everything he saw throughout the process has come to fruition. He was named an All-Big Ten selection, an Academic All-Big Ten winner, and was awarded the Richard Katcher award, which is presented to Michigan's most outstanding defensive lineman or outside linebacker.

CHAPTER 14

Aubrey Solomon

In Jim Harbaugh's short tenure as Michigan head coach, he has ruffled the feathers of his SEC foes through various recruiting tactics. His tour of satellite camps throughout the South caused the biggest reaction, but no one recruit stirred up as much commotion as defensive lineman Aubrey Solomon. Harbaugh and assistant coach Chris Partridge went into the state of Georgia—deep in the heart of SEC territory—and shocked everyone by signing the big defensive tackle. Every major program was after Solomon, and after a roller-coaster recruitment, Solomon unexpectedly found himself landing in Ann Arbor.

Michigan wasn't originally his first choice, though. Ole Miss and Mississippi State were the first schools to offer him, which they did all the way back in his freshman year of high school. The offers were surprising to him and his mother, Sabrina Caldwell, and despite offers from two SEC schools, neither thought that many more schools would jump into the fray at the time.

Because Solomon dealt with a knee injury his sophomore season, he didn't see many offers come in then. It wasn't until he took a visit to South Carolina that Solomon saw his recruitment really take off.

It's also when he and his mother both started to take the process a little more seriously. Caldwell had an older son play football at an NAIA school, but she never thought the recruiting process would take so many turns for her younger son. She wanted to make sure that any college had everything he needed.

Academics were very important to Caldwell, and she made sure that was known to every coach, and it started on the visit to South Carolina. The parents of the visiting recruits got some time to ask the coaches questions and hear the plan they had for their sons. "One parent said, 'When is my son going to see the field?' And I looked at him like, you're getting this all wrong. My first question was, 'When it comes to the mentor/mentee match, how do you identify who is the best mentor to best tutor my son, and do you do entrance inventory,'" Caldwell said. "Everybody got quiet and stared at me like I was diseased or something. The lady that was the director of the tutoring hall said, 'That is a great question,' and I said, 'Now that we established that, what is the answer?' She just stared at me, and I said, 'Okay, this is going to be a long day.'"

As Solomon described it, his mother would interrogate the hell out of the coaches and the programs. She wanted to make sure her son was making an important decision with all of the facts and that no coaches were just telling them what they wanted to hear. Because of that, Caldwell brought a notebook with her on visits and wrote down important things she heard on the visit from coaches and included the date and time the coaches said it. If a coach ever contradicted himself, Caldwell could go back to her notebook and remind the coach of what he had told them and when he said it.

The South Carolina visit helped shape how they needed to go about the process, as Caldwell's questions largely were not answered.

It also jumpstarted his recruitment, as offers started to steadily roll in from programs across the country in the spring and summer before his junior season. Solomon received offers from most of the SEC programs, including Georgia, Auburn, and Alabama, to go along with South Carolina. As Caldwell put it, offers seemed to fall from the sky for her son.

Once those offers started to roll in, the two knew that they needed to get his list narrowed down because Caldwell's cell phone was ringing off the hook with coaches from all over calling trying to get her on campus. Coaches quickly found out that she would be the key to landing Solomon. Much to his mother's chagrin, he tweeted that if a school wanted to know if he was serious about them, check if his mother is on the visit with him. If Solomon wasn't all that serious about a school, he would visit with his coaches and friends. If he was highly interested, then she would accompany him on that visit. Of course, coaches then targeted Caldwell to get her on campus for an unofficial visit.

As a working, single mother of five, Caldwell had an early bed time and made sure that her son told coaches that they were to respect her time and not call past 8:30 PM on any given night. Most followed the rule, but some broke it and saw very early on: when Caldwell said something, she was serious about it. "There were nights I was cussing out coaches because you call me at 8:30 PM, and you're asking for your ass to get chewed out. Nobody was off limits. A couple Alabama assistants got cussed out," Caldwell said. "An Alabama assistant called around 11:00 PM once, and I answered it, and said, 'Is this booty-calling hours because I know you're not the hell calling me after 8:00 PM.' Aubrey always told coaches: 'If you piss off my mom, you might as well take me off your board because I have to live with that woman.'"

Because so many schools were after him, Caldwell and Solomon decided they should cut his list down to 10 schools before his junior year to limit the phone calls and distractions. Their home mailbox would become so stuffed that their postal worker once had to make a second trip to their house with the overflow mail. The teams that made the cut were Alabama, Auburn, Clemson, Georgia, Michigan, North Carolina, Ohio State, Oregon, Penn State, and Tennessee. "At that time I really thought I would probably go to Alabama because Nick Saban is there. They're prestigious, and their players always get drafted," Solomon said. "I thought Alabama would be the choice because Bama's been dominating the SEC, so I'm going to Bama."

That thought came after quite a few unofficial visits that included Alabama, Auburn, Georgia, and North Carolina, among others. Solomon wasn't originally from Georgia, having been born in California, but he had been in the Peach State for nearly nine years at the time and was immersed in the southern football culture. The thought of playing in the SEC at a place like Alabama seemed appealing at the time, but Caldwell did not feel the same way. An unofficial visit to Alabama turned her away from the Crimson Tide. The two met with Saban, and as Caldwell puts it, Saban dominated most of the conversation. He spoke to Caldwell and Solomon for nearly 40 minutes and asked if they had any questions. Caldwell felt as though she wasn't given an opportunity to talk and emphasize what they were looking for, but Solomon still had interest in Alabama and wanted to pursue the school further.

Throughout the process Caldwell always respected Solomon's point of view and his interests because she knew he had to be happy with his decision. At the same time, she had hoped her son would include Stanford, USC, and Georgia Tech on his list because of the academics and what they provided their student-athletes. "We went to Georgia Tech for an unofficial visit. That's where I set the bar because they offer internships for football players," Caldwell said. "If they go to an institution that gets them a paid or unpaid internship, they are going to come out with the requisite skillset that they would be marketable and be able to find a job. Because if the NFL is not knocking on his door, I want my son to be in a position when he graduates with that degree [that] he actually has something tangible."

After that visit if a program lacked internships for its student-athletes, it was no longer in consideration. At the time Caldwell was unaware that Michigan provided internships to its student-athletes, and the program was still in the background for both Caldwell and Solomon.

Their lists were somewhat different, but it was only his junior year of high school. Solomon is a self-proclaimed mama's boy, so he expressed interest in staying close to home. Being from California, though, Caldwell was trying to push the West Coast schools to try to get him closer to family. Caldwell continued to accompany her son on his visits toward the end of his junior year and leading into the spring—until Solomon decided to visit Michigan on June 18, 2016.

Partridge had been the lead recruiter on Solomon and had only recently taken over Georgia as one of his main recruiting areas. A big part of Partridge's initial pitch to prospects in Georgia was to just take a visit to Michigan to see if they liked it. He didn't want his targets to have any preconceived notions about the North to get in the way of them at least seeing it for themselves. "Aubrey and his teammate, Otis Reese, had a coach who was from Michigan who was driving back home in the summer," Partridge said. "I talked to his coach, and he said, 'I'll put them in the car and drive them up.' It was so huge just to get them on campus."

It was huge because before the visit took place, Solomon didn't even want to take the trip to see Michigan. He didn't know that he held an offer from the Wolverines or much about the program other than the cold winter weather. "I wanted nothing to do with coming up to Michigan. I called my mom because she was on a trip in Louisiana," Solomon said. "I called her and said, 'I don't want to go. It's the last place I want to go.' She said, 'Just go and have a great experience.'"

Solomon listened to his mother and took the trip up to Ann Arbor with his coach and Reese, his younger teammate. Once they got to Michigan, Solomon had a less-than-impressed look on his face. The lack of enthusiasm was noted by Partridge to the point that the coach asked Solomon why he had that sour look on his face. Solomon told him that if he didn't have an offer from Michigan, he was unsure why he was even there in the first place, that it was a waste of everyone's time.

Partridge's eyes got wide, and his mouth dropped. He was shocked that Solomon didn't know that the Wolverines had offered him a scholarship nearly a year before. Realizing he had a scholarship offer changed Solomon's mentality and the entire tone of the visit. They continued touring the campus and athletic facilities and eventually met with Harbaugh. Solomon and Harbaugh hit it off almost immediately, which isn't too surprising as Solomon had admired Harbaugh from afar for quite some time.

Solomon was fond of Harbaugh during his time coaching the San Francisco 49ers and, once he left to take the Michigan head coaching job, Solomon looked at his older brother and said he would one day play for Harbaugh. Although it was flippantly at the time, that statement became prophetic. The visit was going so unexpectedly well that Solomon felt he was ready to end his recruitment and make his commitment. The only problem was that his mother was across the country in Louisiana, and she hadn't been to Michigan to see it herself and ask the questions she felt needed to be answered. "Otis committed before I did, and so while he was doing that, I went to the bathroom to call my mom because we were still in Coach Harbaugh's office. I said, 'Mom, everything we've been looking for is here. Everything,'" Solomon said. "My mom was pissed. She said, 'I know you're not going to commit.' I said, 'Mom, I gotta be here.' So she said, 'You can commit, but it has to be a subcommit.' I was like, 'I don't know what a subcommit is.' All I heard was commit so I'm doing it."

Solomon committed, and word got out publicly that the Georgia prospect would be heading north to the Big Ten. Solomon's high school head coach called to ask if it was a joke or if he had seriously committed to the Wolverines. No one, including Partridge and the Michigan coaches, expected that Solomon would commit on the visit, so calls and texts poured in to check to see if the news was real. Word eventually made its way back to his mother as well. She had initially wanted him to keep his commitment silent, which is what she meant by subcommitting, but her son didn't do that.

She called Solomon and asked him about the commitment, and he confirmed the news. Caldwell then asked to speak with Harbaugh, whom she had still never met, about her son's decision and what exactly had just happened. "Jim gets on the phone and goes, "Hey, Sabrina, how you doing?' I said, 'Yeah, I don't put sugar on shit. You got a minute?' And he starts laughing," Caldwell said. "I was pissed. He said, 'I like you. You've got spunk.' I said, 'Well, you know you're going to create a shitstorm for me back home because you're Big Ten, and we're in the SEC.' He said, 'Yup, yup, we're all up in the shit.' I said, 'All right, well, I'll talk to you later then,' and he said, 'All right, Sabrina, we're going to be best friends.'"

Partridge admits that he was surprised when Solomon committed on the visit because he could tell that both Caldwell and Solomon sought a well-thought-out process. But he also felt that the commitment wasn't an emotional decision made at the spur of the moment because the two had seemed to do so much homework on the programs. He felt as though Solomon's commitment was made for the right reasons, and having lured in the top-rated defensive lineman, the Michigan coaches seemed to have a major win in the state of Georgia. They just landed a prospect that every program was after and pulled him out of SEC country. Partridge, Harbaugh, and the rest of the coaches were obviously thrilled with the decision.

Caldwell, however, was less than thrilled. She felt betrayed that her son would go on a visit without her and make such a big decision. They had spent so much time together on the recruiting trail that Caldwell thought Solomon would have known to wait for her and that the two would sit down and talk through the decision before it happened. Solomon got home from the trip and was on cloud nine that he found the school he wanted to be at and that his recruitment was over. Little did he know that it would be just the beginning, and so much more was about to take place.

Caldwell expressed her disappointment to her son and told him she only gave him her blessing to commit because he was on the visit and she didn't know what else to say. Now Solomon realized he upset his mother and told her he would decommit if that's what she wanted. But Caldwell didn't want to make decisions for him in the recruiting process and told him that if Michigan was what he wanted, then he should stay committed but that she thought he acted too quickly. "Aubrey looks at me and says, 'Mom, you keep telling me that you gave me a toolbox to use and be my own man. So I picked that school based on the tools you gave me. Are you not confident in your tools?'" Caldwell said. "Well, I had to eat my words and I said, 'Okay, you know what? Then I stand behind you.' I had coaches calling me, saying he shouldn't have done that, but I said, 'I'm going to stand behind him because if I don't believe in the stuff I equipped him with as a young man, then there's something wrong with me.'"

They decided to stick with the commitment despite coaches from Auburn, Georgia, Ohio State, and others calling Caldwell to tell her that her son made the wrong choice and that he should decommit. She figured that if her son used all the questions she had been asking the coaches on their visits together and came away with that decision, then she would stand behind it.

Back in Ann Arbor, the coaches were celebrating their win, but Partridge knew that this wasn't the end. He knew that going into Georgia and pulling a player from the South was a big plus, but Solomon had not signed yet, and the real battle was only about to begin. Because Solomon was such a highly sought-after prospect, Partridge was ready for the negative recruiting and the other programs coming after the big defensive lineman even harder. "I took the mentality of now everybody's going to have the target against us," Partridge asked. "When you have the target on your back, it makes it so much harder because all the schools will use whatever they can against you."

Opposing coaches tried to pry Solomon away from Michigan, especially because they all knew that Caldwell wasn't on the visit. They didn't need to do much, though, because Caldwell was still upset with her son that he committed without her. While she said she was standing behind her son's decision, she still had some doubts since she neither saw it for herself nor met any of the coaches. The opposing coaches didn't have to wait long to get some help from Michigan either. In August of 2016 before his senior season, a recruiting assistant at Michigan sent Solomon and Caldwell a thank you card for attending a recruiting event that had just taken place in Ann Arbor. Unfortunately for the assistant, neither Solomon nor Caldwell were at the event. The cards thanked them for coming, said it was nice to meet them—and to add to the error—Solomon's name was even spelled wrong. Caldwell got a Grinch-like smirk and sat at home waiting for her son to see the mail.

Her son came home, and she handed him his mail, waiting to see his reaction. Now Solomon was upset, too. He was upset not only that they spelled his name wrong, but also that they sent the thank you card in the first place. "The thank you card made me feel like, *Dang, I'm not really important to this staff like they said I was.* It just built up because my mom was already not happy I committed, so I said I need to reevaluate the situation and decommit to take a couple steps back," Solomon said. "Coach Partridge was cool with it and said he was upset that I was decommitting but that they wanted what was best for me. He said they still had love for me and that they were still going to recruit me."

The opposing coaches received word that this happened and pounced. Reporters ran with the story almost immediately, and it spread quickly that Solomon was decommitting from the Wolverines.

He started to have doubts about everything Michigan had said and thought that maybe he just needed to stay closer to home to be near his mother and family. Solomon was ready to write off Michigan, but another phone call came in that was crucial to Michigan's standing after the mail snafu. It was Harbaugh, wanting to talk to his buddy, Caldwell. Harbaugh joked with Caldwell initially but then cut to the chase. He asked her to send a picture of the mail to make sure it was something sent by the Michigan coaches.

Once it was verified that Michigan had made the mistake, Harbaugh offered up his apology and told her his first act in righting the wrong was that she was to have direct contact with Harbaugh with any questions or concerns she had. He was going to get this rectified and he would be an integral part of her son's recruitment. That impressed Caldwell to the point that she was now telling her son that Michigan should not be out of the race. "I thought that was a class act. So Aubrey said, 'You didn't want me to be with them anyway,' and I said, 'I probably didn't help. But it takes somebody strong to say, hey, okay we messed up, but give us this opportunity to make this right,'" Caldwell said. "To call immediately when it happened, now I'm curious about this school. When I think about what my son could be as a man, you have to own up to mistakes—even if it's not yours—so I said, 'Give them a chance and don't write off Michigan.'"

Normally a decommitment would be a bad thing for a school, and it would be difficult to get back in the race. But in this situation, Michigan actually benefited from the decommitment and the mail mistake in a variety of ways. For one, the target was now off its back as some SEC schools felt that Michigan would drop down his list. Partridge said that it was almost a relief to have Alabama and Georgia start recruiting against each other instead of the two schools ganging up against Michigan. It allowed Harbaugh, Partridge, and Michigan to fly under the radar and recruit him without the negative pitches coming their way.

It also opened up Caldwell's eyes to how her son would be treated and the type of coaches he would be around in Ann Arbor. And when Solomon committed to Michigan, Caldwell took note of all the SEC fans on social media that had raked her son through the coals for leaving the SEC and heading to Michigan. She noted that the fans had been very negative toward her son when he committed, but now they wanted him to pick their favorite school. That turned her off toward some of the SEC schools because, as she told her son: "If the fans were like this now when he is a recruit, how will they treat him when he makes a mistake when he's a player?"

When his senior season arrived, Solomon took a step back and reevaluated what he really wanted and what schools would be in the mix for him. He decided to heed the advice of his mother and not write off Michigan. The Wolverines made his top four along with Alabama, Georgia, and USC, which had crept into the picture. Most of his top schools had remained a constant, but there was one school that was never truly in the picture because of the lack of communication. "Florida State dropped the ball because had they recruited my son the way they should have he would be at Florida State. My daughter went to FAMU, which is right by Florida State, and he wanted to be right by his sister," Caldwell said. "When we tried to call to do an unofficial visit, we either got the answering machine or no answer, so we couldn't get a hold of them. By then he was down to his top four, and Florida State tried to come to one of his games and said, 'Oh, Mrs. Solomon, how are you doing?' I haven't been Mrs.

Solomon for a long dang time, so I looked and saw the Florida State shirt, shook my head, and kept walking."

Solomon was mainly focused on his senior season and his high school team, so he asked the schools recruiting him to respect his space and give him some time to enjoy his final season. Most schools abided by that and limited the time they were in contact with him and his mother.

The communication with Caldwell remained open, however, and as Harbaugh had made himself more and more available to Caldwell with direct contact, she took note of it. Caldwell only had the cell phone numbers for two head coaches—Jim Harbaugh and Georgia's Kirby Smart—who were recruiting her son. "Some coaches sent their minions to contact me and then the coaches would get on the phone. Alabama was really notorious for this, 'Ms. Caldwell, Nick Saban wants to get you on the phone in an hour.' Well I'm busy in an hour," Caldwell said. "It's not personalized, and you want to personalize the experience. You don't want me to think that my son is a football mule, but when you send your minions to contact me and then get on the phone? No, I don't think so."

As that communication remained open, Caldwell was becoming more and more familiar with the coaches and the programs. As Solomon made his way through his final season, the two prepared to start his official visits. They initially planned to take all five official visits, but he narrowed his list down to four because he didn't want to waste any coach's time by taking a visit to a school he was less than interested in.

He also thought about taking an official visit to Georgia, but he and his mother had been there so much that they decided not to spend the extra visit. Besides, Caldwell had previously asked her usual questions and never felt as though they were answered properly. She figured if they failed to answer any of her questions on the previous visits, it wouldn't change now so they decided that Michigan, Alabama, and USC would get his three official visits.

In her communication with Harbaugh, he had noted that he wanted to make sure they answered every question she had. So if she wanted to send them her questions ahead of time, they would make sure they were prepared to answer them. That sparked an idea to even the playing field for everyone. Caldwell decided to create a questionnaire of 31 questions with space for responses that all three schools would receive ahead of their visit.

Georgia only filled out a questionnaire once the coaches found out they wouldn't be getting Solomon on an official visit. Then the staff told her they were preparing their answers. Caldwell also recalled that Alabama did not fill out the questionnaire but still received an official visit from her son. The first question on the list asked if her son could choose his own degree. And then the follow-ups: why or why not can he choose his own degree and who aids in ensuring it's a good fit? The second question asked if the football practices are predicated on the time of day or the type of degree being pursued. The questionnaire then asked what services exist when a student needs further help with their studies and how often players are required to seek out tutors.

The first 12 questions on the questionnaire dealt with education, which was what Caldwell was concerned about. "The Michigan visit was the first visit, and they set the bar high. The moment I got off the plane, Devin Bush picked us up and he handed me a folder that had responses to all my questions," Caldwell said. "That's when I knew that's where I wanted my son and I hadn't even opened the folder yet. He gave a folder to my son, so I had one, and my son had one, but when they gave me that folder, I knew they were serious about my son."

The visit could not have gone any better for Solomon or Caldwell. Others were present, but Harbaugh mentioned to Caldwell that they had fixed some of the issues that led to the coaches sending the thank you letter and spelling her son's name wrong. That they identified and fixed the issue impressed Caldwell because it demonstrated Harbaugh handled problems well. The coaches were prepared for this visit, and Partridge said he knew that football was going to have to be at the back end of the visit, but it still needed to be covered. They were also able to connect Solomon with Rashan Gary's mother, who was visiting her son at the same time. Gary was the No. 1 ranked prospect in the country and had been in Solomon's shoes just the year before. So Solomon was able to get the perspective of a mother, what they saw, and how Michigan had treated them even after the recruiting process.

The trip went as well as it could have, but the coaches still had to worry about the Alabama visit and the USC trip. Alabama's visit came only weeks after his Michigan trip, and the emotion of it all caused Solomon to make a quick statement about how he felt about the Tide. "After I took the Alabama visit, I was feeling really good and named Alabama my leader. My Michigan visit, I learned some new things I didn't know, but I was excited right after Alabama," Solomon said. "Then I thought about it a little more, and Alabama was a good school, but the academics at Michigan put Michigan back ahead. Then I went to USC, and everything changed. So after the USC visit, I went back and said it was between Michigan and USC because they had all of what we were looking for."

The Wolverines and USC were out in front, but Michigan had to weather one more storm in early January. While Solomon was out at the U.S. Army All-American Bowl, he was recorded by some fellow Georgia prospects on video saying, "Fuck Michigan." The video went viral, and many thought that it meant Michigan was out of the running. Not among the many that thought the Wolverines were out, however, were the Michigan coaches. Partridge and Harbaugh handled the mishap in the best way possible. This time, however, it was Solomon doing the apologizing to Michigan rather than the other way around. During his conversation with Partridge, the Michigan assistant coach told Solomon that he completely understood and that he, too, said "fuck" all the time. He understood but also reminded Solomon that the Georgia prospects he was around at the time of the video may not be the people with whom to surround himself.

Solomon explained to Partridge that a recruit asked him how he felt when Michigan got his name wrong on the thank you card and Solomon replied by cursing. He further detailed that it wasn't how he felt currently, but he owned the mistake and apologized. "That made me closer with the staff with them trying to help me clean up my mess. I talked to Coach Partridge and Coach Harbaugh, and they both told me the same thing," Solomon said. "'You're young, people make mistakes, but it's what you do after the mistake that matters.'"

The bond had grown closer, but since Michigan was the first official visit and USC got the last visit in January, there was still some work to be done. Since head coaches are allowed to have one in-home visit with each recruit leading up to Signing Day, Harbaugh, Partridge, and defensive coordinator Don Brown strategically decided what day Harbaugh would visit.

The USC visit happened on January 13, and Harbaugh and his crew went to see Solomon and Caldwell on January 16, which happened to fall on Martin Luther King Jr. day. That was no coincidence as the coaches knew Solomon would have the day off, allowing them to spend the whole day with the family. Harbaugh and the coaches got to Solomon's house early in the morning, and Harbaugh asked Caldwell what they wanted to do for the day. She suggested they go bowling, so they did. Once the group was done bowling, they suggested that they all ride go-carts. "Outside I was like, 'Yeah, let's do it.' But inside I was like, 'I can't fit in a go-cart.' So I said, 'Let's do laser tag instead. That seems more realistic,'" Solomon said. "And Coach Harbaugh is like, 'No, we have to do go-carts.' We get to the go-cart track, and my little sister wants to ride with Coach Harbaugh. Then they're all waiting for me to get in the go-cart, and it was a struggle. I barely fit."

Solomon recalled how competitive Harbaugh, Brown, and Partridge all were with the race. He had never seen a staff so competitive, especially with riding go-carts. He also couldn't recall any other head coach that would be in this situation, riding a go-cart with his younger sister. The group finished on the go-carts, ate, and then went back to the family's house and helped Solomon's younger sister with a school project, decorating a T-shirt for 100 days of school. "We got there around noon. And since we got there early, we knew we had the whole day. Georgia was supposed to get in that night at like 5:00 PM, and we ended up leaving at 8:00, so they were just sitting around waiting," Partridge said. "I'll never forget: the next day me and Don drove up to Atlanta. We're sitting there eating, and he gets an ESPN alert on his phone, and it's a picture of us riding go-carts. It was hysterical."

Coaches from Georgia and Alabama followed up Michigan's in-home visit, but none would compare with a full day of riding go-carts, food, and art projects. Michigan had all but sealed itself as the school of choice, but as Signing Day approached, Solomon and Caldwell needed to sit down and make sure they knew he was making the right choice. With USC and Michigan still sitting at the top, Caldwell listed qualities about all four schools but labeled each school as A, B, C, and D to leave out the name of the university. She sat her son down and had him look at each quality and statistic and asked him to pick the school he thought best fit what he was looking for—without any logo or name associated with it. "My son looked at all of them and said, 'A has this; B has this.' And he already had his list of specific criteria he wanted. Pretty much C and D didn't have most of what he wanted. So that left A and B," Caldwell said. "When he looked at it, he said, 'I want A.' Before I turned it over, he said, 'Is that USC?' I turned it over and said, 'No, baby, you're going to Michigan.'"

It was settled. Michigan and Solomon had endured a full recruitment with mistakes, apologies, and everything in between but wound up back together in the end. Michigan landed the highly sought-after lineman and fended off the SEC to bring him north. As it naturally happens, Solomon started to get nervous a few days before Signing Day. He wanted to make sure he made the right choice. And to calm her son down, Caldwell told him to think of a place that he would like to go, someplace nice. He said he would love to go to Miami, and Caldwell told him she would take him there over the summer.

Unfortunately for Solomon, he had that trip in mind while trying to calm himself down before making his announcement live on ESPN on Signing Day. As he pulled a Michigan hat up from underneath the table, Solomon announced that he was committing to the University of Miami. "I'm in the auditorium and I'm talking and I'm feeling pretty dang good. I'm going to wow this crowd. So I start talking and I say, 'I'm going to further my academic career at...' And I go down to pull up the hat, and everyone starts clapping. So I froze," Solomon said. "So I said the first M word that came to my head and I said Miami. The real messed up thing is Miami sent me an enrollment package about a week later with a brochure and I was like, *they really did this*."

Solomon signed with Michigan despite blurting out Miami during his announcement.

Because he is a self-proclaimed mama's boy, Solomon admitted that his first few months at Michigan were difficult. Being away from his mother was hard, and transitioning from high school to a college academic load—in addition to football practice and the expectations of the team—weighed on him. He got homesick and eventually asked that his mom come up to spend some time with him and talk to him about how he was feeling. Caldwell made the trip up to Ann Arbor during the season and spent four to five days with her son. She explained to him that the best thing he could do was get outside his comfort zone and put himself into situations that would allow him to grow.

She gave him a stack of family photos and told him she was always there for him—even if it wasn't there physically. She attended the Michigan State game, and despite the loss, Solomon had a big grin on his face when he saw his mother waiting for him after the game. That visit was just what he needed to realize that he would be okay and that he was on a road to success in Ann Arbor. "When I got to Michigan, it was the hardest thing I've ever done. You're no longer the best, you're no longer in the spotlight, and you have to play a role, so I played that role," Solomon said. "I told myself: No matter what, I'm going to have fun and contribute any way I can. Playing, it might take me time to get on the field. I thought I wasn't going to play, but the people around me on the team made that transition so much smoother."

He did play, though, and appeared in all 13 games for the Wolverines as a true freshman. He made his first career start against Rutgers on October 28 and continued to rise up the depth chart the further he got in the season. Solomon finished his first year with 16 total tackles and two tackles for a loss. But it was off the field where Caldwell and Solomon became comfortable with the decision he made to become a Wolverine.

Acknowledgments

First and foremost, I need to thank my wife, Laura. A lot of people say that without their spouse they wouldn't be where they are, but I can say unequivocally without my wife I would not be where I am today.

We have three beautiful children and I have a demanding job, so writing this book meant all of my free time was spent writing and talking to players and coaches. Throughout the entire process, and my entire career, she has rooted me on and motivated me to continue pushing forward. Not once has she ever complained about the time my job demands—even when I miss big life events or have to cancel on a concert on her birthday to travel. She has always stood by me and cheered for my success. I love you and don't know what I would do without you.

I wrote this book for a couple of reasons. My wife was one. The other was because of my children. Tommy, Emma, and Jack have been an inspiration to me to be a great dad and role model in hopes that they lead great lives. I wanted to show them that anything is possible, and through hard work and doing things the right way, you can do anything you want in this world.

I started my career on a completely different path and have put in a ton of work to get to where I am within the sports industry. I would be remiss not to mention Brian Cook at MGoBlog.com. Brian is a big reason why I am in this position because he was the only person to give me a chance when I first started writing. Even though I didn't have a portfolio or any writing samples, Brian allowed me to begin my career within his website, and I will always be grateful for that.

People always tell me it will be a great story to tell my kids when they get older that their dad works for ESPN, but the real story is the work I was willing to put in to achieve it. I hope they take as much pride in that later in life as I do now about that I had a dream and a goal and I put it to paper and then made it reality.

I wrote this book and got it published without an agent, which will one day be another great lesson for my kids: taking no for an answer is not an option if you know you have something great. My children keep me on my toes daily and motivate me to be great for them. I'd also like to thank my parents, Tom and Deanne, and the rest of my family for their support.

I have to thank Triumph Books for working with me on this book and offering me the opportunity to tell these great stories. Jeff Fedotin for taking a massive amount of time to edit through my mistakes and help create an awesome, well thought-out package of stories that help bring Michigan fans into the lives of their favorite players.

Whether he knows this or not, Bobby Morrison was a big inspiration for this book. Morrison was a part of the Michigan football program from 1987 to 2002. Coaching with Bo Schembechler, Gary Moeller, and Lloyd Carr, Morrison had a big impact on the Michigan football program and a big impact on me. I spent a considerable amount of time with Bobby, and he was always more than willing to help where it was needed. He originally told me the story of Tom Brady's recruitment and how it all came about, initially sparking the idea for this book. I don't believe I could have written this book without his help and I am grateful for his time that he gave me.

I want to make sure to thank all of the former Michigan football players and coaches who helped with this book as well. Not one ever asked for anything in return, and they were always willing to share stories or help reach a teammate or coach if it was needed. Mark Messner, Reggie McKenzie, Tripp Welborne, Jarrett Irons, Brian Griese, Rashan Gary, Jennifer Shepherd, Steve Kanoc, Aubrey Solomon and his family, Tim Biakabutuka, Jamie Morris, Braylon Edwards, Stan Edwards, the family of Tom Brady, Desmond and Rebkah Howard, Chad Henne, Cam Cameron, Billy Harris, George Mans, the Harbaugh family, J.T. Rogan, and everyone else that helped make this possible.

It was inspiring and humbling to hear some of the people so involved with Michigan's deep, rich history in football talk about how they were drawn to the University of Michigan. I am grateful that they let me into their world and gave me hours of their time to ensure I had the entire story.

I was impressed at the level of detail that some of the coaches and players remembered with their story, some of which happened so long ago. George Mans recruited McKenzie in 1967 and he remembered the same exact story as McKenzie. Mans remembered details that seemed impossible down to the name of the family doctor, Dr. Bernard Levin, who helped get Michigan interested in McKenzie. I asked Mans how it was possible that he could remember such details of a life event that happened so long ago. He told me that many of his players, McKenzie included, left a lasting mark on him in such a profound way that he couldn't possibly forget their story. Mans, and many of the players and coaches I spoke with, all echoed the sentiments and feelings they have toward the University of Michigan and the football program they were a part of.

Their time in Ann Arbor and experiences at Michigan were once in a lifetime and something they cherish and hold dear. They were eager to tell their stories, and it was clear that they all felt a little nostalgia remembering how it all began and where they started from. There is so much pride in what they were able to contribute to the football program, but maybe more importantly, how their time spent in Ann Arbor helped shape who they are today. Whether it was the coaches, their teammates, or family, there was always someone who helped to mold them into the men they are today. I am thankful that I was allowed into those stories and feelings and given a glimpse at that experience firsthand.

Thank you to everyone who helped make this book possible and thank you to all the readers and fans who have supported me along the way. You all are a big part of this journey and have been there to drive conversation and motivate me to keep moving forward.

Sources

Bentley Historical Library archives

Michigan record book

Schembechler, Bo and Bacon, John U. *Bo's Lasting Lessons: The Legendary Coach Teaches the Timeless Fundamentals of Leadership.* Grand Central Publishing, 2008.

Detroit Free Press

Los Angeles Times

Associated Press

The (Lexington, North Carolina) *Dispatch*

The New York Times

Sports Illustrated